STRANGER FROM ABROAD

◆ ◆ ◆

STRANGER FROM ABROAD

◆ ◆ ◆

Hannah Arendt, Martin Heidegger,
Friendship and Forgiveness

DANIEL MAIER-KATKIN

W. W. NORTON & COMPANY
NEW YORK   LONDON

Printed in the United States of America
First Edition

For information about special discounts for bulk purchases, please contact
W. W. Norton Special Sales at specialsales@wwnorton.com or 800-233-4830

Manufacturing by Courier Westford
Book design by Ellen Cipriano
Production manager: Anna Oler

Library of Congress Cataloging-in-Publication Data

Maier-Katkin, Daniel, 1945–
Stranger from abroad : Hannah Arendt, Martin Heidegger, friendship, and
forgiveness / Daniel Maier-Katkin.—1st ed.
p. cm.
Includes bibliographical references and index.
ISBN 978-0-393-06833-7 (hardcover)
1. Arendt, Hannah, 1906–1975—Friends and associates. 2. Heidegger, Martin,
1889–1976—Friends and associates. I. Title.
B945.A694M35 2010
320.5092—dc22
[B]

2009043992

W. W. Norton & Company, Inc.
500 Fifth Avenue, New York, N.Y. 10110
www.wwnorton.com

W. W. Norton & Company Ltd.
Castle House, 75/76 Wells Street, London W1T 3QT

1 2 3 4 5 6 7 8 9 0

To the memory of my parents,
who brought me into one world,
and to Birgit,
who showed me another

ACKNOWLEDGMENTS

I am grateful to my children, Andrew, Rebecca, Rosalia and Hannah, for their support and encouragement during long years when I must have seemed too often preoccupied with Hannah Arendt. Rebecca was among the most thorough and thoughtful of my readers and Hannah was always happy to discuss whatever I was working on, especially on our long morning drives to the Magnolia School. Other readers for whose helpful suggestions I am grateful include Maria Foscarinis, Nathan Stoltzfus, Elliott Currie, Bill Cloonan, Neil Jumonville, Martin Kavka, Karl Sabbagh, Mary Delina Wright, Peter Fleming, John Davis, Edward Katkin, Sylvia Katkin, and Caryn Pally. Sumner Twiss, my colleague at the Center for the Advancement of Human Rights, has been invaluable as a source of ideas and references.

Conversations with Jerome Kohn, when I was just beginning to think that the story of Hannah Arendt and Martin Heidegger had never been properly told, helped to shape my thinking. I am indebted to Bert Lockwood, editor of *Human Rights Quarterly*, and Christina Thompson, editor of the *Harvard Review*, who both saw the value of this project early on; without their decisions to publish early versions of the story the book might never have come to fruition. Dan O'Connell also saw the value of the project early on. His support and advice were immensely helpful to me.

My tough, challenging, and gifted editor, Alane Mason, taught me how to turn a story into a book and never stopped demanding additional detail, clearer thinking, and better, more precise, and more elegant use of language. I should add too how impressed I have been by the kindness and competence of the people who work with her at W. W. Norton.

I also want to acknowledge several friends, Bruce and Lisa Bullington, Ray and Nonnie Fleming, Frank Kron, Alex Wender, Teddy Tollet, Diop Kamau, and Lorenz Böllinger, from whom I have learned a great deal over many years about people and the diversity of cultures. Their influence on my way of thinking about human relationships is reflected between the lines and in the fundamental conception of the story I have tried to tell.

Then there is Birgit, my beloved life companion and guide to all things European and to scholarship in the humanities. Without Birgit there would never have been the germ of the idea that has culminated in *Stranger from Abroad* nor the will or skill to write it.

Much of what has been written in the past about the relationship between Arendt and Heidegger is the work of their detractors. Arendt was judgmental and controversial, and her youthful love affair and subsequent reconciliation with Heidegger have been used to throw some of her critical judgments into doubt. I have tried to tell their story differently, more accurately and with greater sensitivity to the complexity of their thinking and feelings. If I have not succeeded, the responsibility, despite all the help I have acknowledged here, is mine alone.

STRANGER FROM ABROAD

◆ ◆ ◆

I

◇◇◇◇
◆

TO SAY THAT A THING ENDURES, Hannah Arendt wrote to Martin Heidegger around the time of her sixtieth birthday, means that there is something in the end that is the same as it was in the beginning.[1] The "something" she had in mind was an aspect of their relationship—their love—that had changed but endured despite everything that happened between them and to Germans and Jews in the twentieth century.

As thinkers, both professionally and by temperament, Arendt and Heidegger were attentive to beginnings and ends. He celebrated the power and radiance of beginnings, but experienced them as distant and cooling explosions like creation itself or the Greek invention of philosophy. His thought was drawn to the brevity of each individual's existence and the infinite nothingness that surrounded it. Nevertheless, at the center of Heidegger's thought is the meaning of being, which every person must establish for him or herself.

Familiarity with ends came early for Hannah; her father and grandfather both died the year that she was seven. Fear of death cast shadows across her early life, but these faded or came under control as she matured, and her thought focused on natality: the recurrence of beginnings and the force of new beings and transformative ideas inserting themselves into the continuity of the world. Even at the conclusion of *The Origins of Totalitarianism*, her account of the cataclysmic collapse of European civilization in the first half of the twentieth century, there is an optimistic note about the potential to start anew: "Beginning is the supreme capacity of man," she wrote, then quoting St. Augustine—*Initium ut esset homo creatus est*—that a beginning be made, man was created. "This beginning," she concluded, "is guaranteed by each new birth; it is every man."[2]

It was central to her thought that beginnings, which are by definition unprecedented and which cannot be predicted, are the wellspring of human spontaneity and freedom. Equally central was pluralism: the observation that the world into which every individual is born is shared with others. The world is already in motion when we arrive, and it is only by joining the dance that we become ourselves.

Hannah's own beginning was an insertion into the world of Germans and Jews in Hanover in 1906, barely twenty-five years before the Nazi rise to power, at a time when there was not yet any harbinger of impending disaster. The circumstances of Jews in Germany were as good as they ever had been anywhere in the Diaspora. In the second half of the nineteenth century, enlightenment and emancipation had opened the gates to the ghetto, and ushered in an age of tolerance. While anti-Semitism and dislike and distrust of Jews persisted in some corners of society, legal barriers to full participation were abolished and German Jews had established themselves in the realms of commerce, banking, the arts, sciences, and learned professions. Conversions to Christianity and interfaith marriages were common, reflecting not only the desire of Jews to fit into the dominant culture, but also the openness with which they were received.

When Hannah was still very young, her family moved to Königsberg, where her parents had been born and where their parents were established, respected members of the community. Königsberg, the capital of East Prussia, was a remote, well-fortified, but nonetheless cosmopolitan Baltic seaport and university city that had been the capital of German enlightenment in the nineteenth century during the lifetime of Immanuel Kant. Forty years before her birth Königsberg would not have been a place (if indeed there had been any such place) where a young Jewish woman could have been educated in Latin, Greek, the classics, or philosophy. Forty years after her birth the city, cleansed of all its Jews, lay in ruins. Hannah's opportunities, like everyone else's, depended upon the accident of birth.

Königsberg, an ancient harbor town on the Baltic, its streets lined with narrow four-story timbered brick and stucco buildings under ornate Rococo roofs, had been a center of trade since the Hanseatic League and was still a vital residential and commercial quarter in Hannah's childhood. The old city, paved with wide cobblestone boulevards and commodious squares, extended inland from the hub of government and commerce surrounding a Gothic Teutonic castle. Further up the river Pregel, the modern city, where the Arendts lived, contained more spacious estates along canals and tributaries. Königsberg was of the water almost as much as it was of the land; and many buildings, including the ornate Moorish-style synagogue, had back entrances along a dock or quay, as in Venice or Amsterdam.

The city was always part of the boundary between east and

west in Europe. Territorial adjustments at the end of World War One left the city under German control but separated from the rest of the country by the Polish Corridor at Danzig. Hitler's initial military successes in the east restored contiguity, but after a fierce three-month campaign in 1945, Königsberg, largely destroyed, fell to the Red Army, was renamed Kaliningrad, and became part of the Soviet Union. In the previous two hundred years, however, Königsberg had faced firmly westward in its embrace of enlightenment and modernity. Like other German centers of trade along the northern seacoast, the city was electrified early, with trains, trams, and cultural resources including a university, libraries, schools, museums, bookstores, *Antiquarität,* theaters, music halls, restaurants, and *gemütliches Kafes*. Königsberg was not a great metropolis, but it was a city where for hundreds of years people with different languages and customs from adjoining and remoter countries lubricated the global commerce of their day, and where, as Kant observed, one could learn something about the world without traveling.

So far north, summer days are very long and pleasant, but only rarely warm or bright, and even then at the beaches one needs blankets and a *Strandkorb* (constructed of wicker, something halfway between a small tent and a park bench) for shelter against the cold wind and blowing sand. Winter days are short, the low sun refracted into blues and purples by snow-covered earth and gray or frozen water, the sky mostly dark and cold, with occasional brief episodes of clear, crisp sunshine. For much of the year Königsberg was an inviting place to be indoors, near a fire, talking to friends, or reading. Hannah particularly loved philosophy, poetry, literature, and classics: the Greeks and Romans (which she was reading in the original as a teenager); Königsberg's own local genius, Immanuel Kant; and also the ideas and rhythms of the great German writers of the late eighteenth and early nineteenth centuries—Lessing, Herder, Goethe, Schiller, Hölderlin, Brentano, Uhland, and Heine—and the poets of her own time and what was to her the recent past—Mörike, Spitzweg, Storm, Fontane, Keller, Nietzsche, George, Lasker-Schüler, von Hofmannsthal, Rilke. Their words found receptive lodging in Hannah's memory, and the writers themselves became the companions of a lifetime, even when Germany itself, as she had known it, was gone.[3] All her life she thought of friends as those with whom we can think and converse across the distance that the world places between us, which can be a matter of time as well as space; and love for her was a matter of simple gratitude for the being of others in their own place, where or whenever that might be. Her thinking about the world and about thinking itself was greatly influenced in subsequent years by Martin Heidegger, but the lifelong practice of regarding thinkers as friends and the habit of holding friends close were already established in childhood in Königsberg.

The city was a center of trade and tolerance, where enlightenment conceptions of universal human dignity and rights took hold early, and Jews in Königsberg were therefore more liberated and prosperous than Jews in most urban ghettos and rural shtetls across Europe. At the beginning of the twentieth century there were about 600,000 Jews in Germany, a little more than 1 percent of the population; the concentration of Jews in Königsberg was about twice that, 5,000 in a city of almost 200,000 people. The experience of Jews in Christian Europe varied profoundly from place to place and century to century. In 1906, when Hannah was born, Königsberg was a propitious place to be a Jew in the same way that the whole of the twentieth century was a propitious time to be a Jew in America.

◆ ◆ ◆

Before political emancipation in the nineteenth century the conditions of Jewish life throughout Europe had been medieval. The community of secular, intellectual German-Jewish citizens with equal rights—into which Hannah made her appearance through the accident of birth—sprang into existence in conjunction with revolutionary enlightenment conceptions of liberty, human rights, and citizenship that took hold on the Continent first in France and then under pressure from Napoleon as far east as the Hapsburg Empire and Prussia. Liberal conceptions of equal human dignity independent of nationality, class, or gender were embodied in the German intellectual tradition at the beginning of the nineteenth century by Goethe and Schiller; but most German states proceeded haltingly and unevenly with legal reforms, and many of Napoleon's progressive innovations on the treatment of minorities were rolled back after his defeat at Waterloo. Restrictions on Jewish participation in community life were restored, then fell away gradually as democratic ideals of the French and American revolutions developed in the modern European mind; finally the emancipation of Jews with full rights of citizenship became law in Prussia in 1850 and in all of Germany by 1871, only thirty-five years before Hannah was born.[4]

The de facto situation in cities like Hamburg, Berlin, and Königsberg had always been ahead of the curve; and the Jews in these cities were on the cutting edge in their embrace of Haskalah, the Jewish enlightenment which, under the guidance of Moses Mendelssohn in Berlin and the banner of emancipation waving across Europe, opened Jewish spiritual and intellectual activity to the emerging secular and scientific ideas of the West in the second half of the eighteenth century. The possibility of a relatively assimilated Jewish life had attracted earlier generations of Hannah's family to Königsberg. Her maternal grandfather, Jacob Cohen, arrived in 1851, escaping from conscription in the czar's army—which for Jews in those days was either a life sentence with a slim possibility of parole, or death. The Arendt side of the family had already been in Königsberg for almost a hundred years when Jacob Cohen arrived; her paternal grandfather, Max Arendt, was so established in the city that he was what the Germans call a *Beamter*—a public official, a member of the civil service with offices in City Hall.[5]

Emancipated, enlightened, and secular though they were, Hannah's parents and grandparents were nevertheless active in the Jewish community and the Reformed Jewish Synagogue, which was second in influence only behind Berlin in shaping modern Jewish alternative sensibilities to Orthodox observance of religious holidays, daily rituals, and dietary laws. Reformed Judaism, the major Jewish denomination in the United States, and the smaller Conservative and Reconstructionist movements, are all derivatives of the theology invented by enlightened, secular German Jews in the nineteenth century. Hannah's grandparents' generation was the first to embrace vernacular translations of the Pentateuch and Talmud and to incorporate German language and mores (such as men and women sitting together) into their liturgy and religious services. These accommodations to modernity made it possible for some German Jews to feel comfortably German and Jewish at the same time, as some American Jews, for example, feel both American and Jewish in their synagogues today. For many, however, including Hannah and her parents, participation in the various structures of Jewish life was primarily an act of ethnic affiliation rather than religious conviction.

This world of Germans and Jews in Königsberg into which she

made her appearance was a microcosm of the short-lived flowering of German-Jewish identity in the late nineteenth and early twentieth centuries, at the very time that Germany emerged as a unified nation, a world power, and a global leader in the arts and sciences. Emancipation gave Jews equal rights as citizens, including access not only to commerce and finance, but also to universities, learned professions, and all the institutions of German cultural production. German Jews, eager to participate in a receptive and attractive culture, set out to demonstrate their worth, make contributions, and experience the fruits of enlightenment and emancipation. Many rose to positions of prominence as physicians, lawyers, scientists, writers, philosophers, artists, politicians, activists, and businessmen. The Arendts and Cohens of Königsberg were representative of this flourishing community of educated, freethinking intellectuals. Hannah's father, Paul, was an engineer and her mother, Martha, a musician; both were socialists.

German Jewry seemed stable and secure at the beginning of the twentieth century. Years later Stefan Zweig[6] wondered about this illusion: He had been born in the same house in Vienna, built by his grandfather, in which his father had been born, and the family believed it was insured against any possible catastrophic loss. How differently things turned out! But German openness to Jews and the Jewish embrace of Germanic culture in the years surrounding Hannah's birth have parallels only in the Hellenic period, Moorish Spain, or contemporary America. Like Zweig in Vienna, Hannah felt secure and happy in the companionship of family, friends, and classmates in Königsberg.

After anti-Semitism exploded upon the German scene a few years later, it would never cease to amaze Hannah that such a trivial social question involving such a small group as the Jews could have become the flash point for the destruction of Europe and the whole of modernity. As a child, she knew that she was a Jew, and felt that dark brown eyes made her look a little different than other Königsberg children, although we may wonder what she meant by this since not all Germans are blond and blue-eyed. There may have been an anti-Semitic comment here or there, but anti-Semitism was not a serious problem in those years. Hannah and her mother had an agreement: anything that involved children, Hannah dealt with by herself; anything that involved teachers fell within the maternal domain. Martha Arendt was completely areligious. She had no feeling of faith and little interest in tradition or ritual. Nevertheless, Hannah told an interviewer years later that her mother "would have boxed my ears if I denied being Jewish or if I talked about baptism, which, you know, was very common in Germany in those days."[7]

If Hannah did not feel especially Jewish, neither did she feel German. Certainly she was a citizen of Germany, and very happy to be that, and German was her mother tongue and the language of the poetry and philosophy she loved best. Even after forty years of exile, statelessness and immigration, she liked to think that she still knew "half" of German poetry by heart, and in many situations these were the words that came to her first. She was keenly aware that the German language never committed any crimes; that it too was a victim, given the way the Nazis used and abused language.

Yet despite enlightenment, the emancipation of women and Jews, and her immersion in German culture and education, Hannah never felt that she had a place in the culture the way that every peasant girl in whatever province or region knows that she is part of the German, French, or whatever people. Much as she loved the German countryside with its rolling hills, stately trees, and fertile meadows along meandering streams, she never felt that all this beauty was part of her patrimony. In his wartime diaries Victor Klemperer[8] wrote that he always felt that he was German, and when he was hiding from the Nazis, he wondered where the other Germans had gone; but Hannah never felt that she was German in that way. Karl Jaspers was put off by this. "Of course, you are a German," he told her. "Of course I am not," she said, "you need only look at me to see that."[9] Years later, she wrote to Martin Heidegger that she had come to understand herself as, in the words of a famous line from Schiller, a "*Mädchen aus dem Fremde,*" a girl from afar. He wrote a poem for her about that, with a twist on Schiller, playing on the fact of her exile and transforming the "girl" into a "stranger from abroad."

Stranger, home of the solitary gaze . . .
outglowing all the fires' ashes,
igniting embers of charity.
Stranger from abroad, du,
may you live in beginning.

2

HANNAH'S WORLD BEGAN TO EXPAND BEYOND Königsberg by the time she was sixteen years old. The beginning of her life away from home was precipitated by a crisis at school. She had always been a good student, but resisted the stifling institutional tendencies and the regimen of school and was eventually expelled from *Gymnasium,* unjustly she felt, as retribution for having organized a student boycott of a rude teacher: an early manifestation of Hannah's lifelong habit of making judgments and acting on them.

Martha Arendt, ambivalent about her daughter's outspokenness, was nevertheless supportive and arranged for her to spend two terms studying in Berlin, where the family had friends. Hannah lived in a student residence and audited classes in Latin and Greek at the university, where she was introduced to theology by Romani Guardini, a vibrant Christian existentialist. By that time Hannah was reading Kierkegaard and Karl Jaspers. When she returned to Königsberg, it was for a period of concentrated preparation for the *Abitur* (university entrance) examination with a private tutor, her mother's friend Adolf Postelmann, the headmaster of the all-male *höhere Schule* in Königsberg. Hannah had a great deal on the line, knowing that if she failed it would be her responsibility and would be attributed by others to her rebellious personality. In the end, she passed the exam and moved on to university a year ahead of her classmates and a few days before turning eighteen. Then, a very little while later, she fell in love with her professor, Martin Heidegger, and he with her.

She was young for such a relationship but was not altogether innocent. It was, after all, the years of the Weimar Republic. Not only Jews had been emancipated, but also, at least to a degree, women. Hannah had already been involved in a romantic relationship by then, with Ernst Grumach, who was five years older than she, very dashing, a budding Greek philologist, and later a world expert on Aristotle; and certainly the year in Berlin had shown her something of the world. She was not part of the wild Weimar scene, certainly not the way Christopher Isherwood described it in his *Berlin Diaries* (and much less so the way he was burlesqued in the theatrical *Cabaret*); Hannah was too fastidious, and her taste, she explained to Heidegger a year later, "resisted the loud, extreme, extravagant and somehow desperate, shameless efforts of art, literature and culture to explore their own illusory existence." Knowing that she faced difficult and important examinations at the end of her year in Berlin, Hannah had studied diligently and spent time with friends reading and discussing philosophy, literature, and poetry in Greek, Latin, and German. Still, she was seventeen, relatively independent, and curious about her environment. Perhaps in the 1960s her own students at the progressive New School for Social Research on the fringe of New York's Greenwich Village had a similar experience: even the serious, hardworking ones, who turned away from the excesses of their environment, saw something of the world; and so did she, even before she met Martin Heidegger.

She knew enough of the world, including the world of philosophy, to know that she wanted to go to university at Marburg because Martin Heidegger was on the faculty there. She had heard from friends, including Ernst Grumach, who had taken classes with him, that from Heidegger one could learn to think. This was still several years before the publication of *Being and Time*, but Heidegger already enjoyed a reputation as a fresh mind and gifted teacher. Dressed in the dark hues of Black Forest style, with severe good looks, dark eyes, and black hair, he seemed like a magician,[1] and he could weave a spell. Sometimes in winter he arrived at his lectures with skis over one shoulder and snow on his boots. Then he would start to talk from the lectern, and his talk was not about philosophy, it was philosophy; it was a public demonstration of the art of thinking, the human capability that most intrigued and appealed to Hannah.

In November 1924, her first semester at Marburg, Hannah attended a series of lectures by Dr. Heidegger (he did not yet have what was in Germany the highly esteemed title of *Professor*) on the subject of Plato's *Sophist*. This short dialogue in the original Greek was the only reading assigned, although his lecture notes for the seminar, published some years later, are almost twenty times more extensive than the text on which they are based.[2] In other seminars students would have been expected to read half of all that Plato wrote and to immerse themselves in secondary literature, but Heidegger's students in the fall of 1924 were led by him to consider the meaning of almost every word and phrase in Greek. Thus, Plato became the substance of Hannah's first exercise in thinking with and against Heidegger. Heidegger's purpose was to demonstrate to his students that it was not Plato's thought that was decisive, but their own thinking arising from direct personal confrontation with the matters about which Plato thought. Heidegger taught that the only meaningful approach to philosophy begins with recognition that it is not the thought of great philosophers that matters but the fact of their thinking.

The *Sophist* is Plato's report of a dialogue conducted in the presence of Socrates but led by a courteous stranger from Elea, who employs a logical method of categorizing and dividing increasingly small clusters of like things until finally an indivisible singularity remains. The stranger reveals the Sophist as a self-aggrandizing dissembler, who trades in superficialities and persuasion rather than substance or truth, and tricks people through the artful juggling of words. What is present through its absence in the Platonic dialogue, Heidegger taught, is the definition of the antagonist of the Sophist, the philosopher, who seeks truth beneath the world of appearances.

Nevertheless, Heidegger thought that philosophy had gotten onto the wrong path with Plato. Neither Plato nor even Socrates was the father of philosophy; that honor belongs to Thales of Melitus, who famously fell into a well one night more than a century earlier while concentrating on the stars above. The Greeks before Socrates, Plato, and Aristotle had already invented philosophy, history, politics, higher mathematics, literature, and natural science. They achieved towering masterpieces of art and architecture, hypothesized the existence of atoms and the space-time continuum, and revealed the mathematical structure of music. All this in the dazzling first efforts of Western thought to explain the physical universe and the meaning of Being on the basis of perception, reason, and intuition without recourse to mysticism or theology. Since this beginning, Heidegger thought, everything had been in decline: the gradual fading of a great explosion of light and energy toward the equilibrium of nothingness. This fading, which we call "the intellectual tradition of the West," began, he taught, with Plato, who turned away from awe-filled contemplation of the actual existence of things toward an abstract metaphysics of ideas and ideal types, which are at best indirect, derivative, and secondary manifestations of Being.

Though Heidegger preferred the pre-Socratics Parmenides and Heraclitus, only fragments of their thought survive, while Plato's writing in profusion has been the starting point for millennia of thought. This is not just a matter of chance: the pre-Socratics, like Socrates himself, worked within the Greek oral tradition, while Plato pioneered written language for science and philosophy.[3] Needless to say, written texts have proven a more lasting medium for the preservation and transmission of culture than the epic verse with which the Greeks for hundreds of years recalled the knowledge, experiences, and beliefs of generations going back to Mycenae and Homer. Plato's lasting influence also benefited from his establishment of the school at Academe that became the prototypical social institution for logical inquiry and scientific method. In addition, his pre-Christian belief in eternal ideal types and the unity of the universe made him especially attractive eight hundred years later to St. Augustine, who sought to establish an intellectual basis for Christian thought.

Heidegger objected to all of this. Where Plato preferred the precision, freedom of form, and analytic mode of prose and dialectic, Heidegger thought that human experience and understanding both lie closer to the realm of feeling and mood that inheres in poetry (an idea with strong appeal to Arendt). He argued that Plato's conception of ideal forms (the abstract table, for example, against which all real objects are evaluated to determine whether they are tables) had carried philosophers away from awestruck appreciation of the existing world in favor of nonmaterial ideals that exist only in the mind. He preferred the pre-Socratics because their thought focused on actual existence. Emphasizing distance from the Church of his childhood, Heidegger argued that the decline of civilization from the earliest heights of pre-Socratic thought had been accelerated by Christianity, which distracted one from the essential fact of existence by directing attention to an afterlife.

Years later, on the occasion of a radio address in honor of Heidegger's eightieth birthday, Arendt spoke of him as having been from the beginning the hidden king of thinking.[4] It was with him that she began a lifetime of thinking, including a persistent line of thought about thinking itself, about what we are doing when we are thinking. Everyone thinks, but this is mostly the calculative thinking of making plans and figuring out how things work, whether crossing a street, feeding a family, or drafting blueprints for a skyscraper. Heidegger, following Plato, distinguished meditative thinking, which is not instrumental, but which has the potential to lead us toward an understanding of the significance or meaning of existence.

This sort of thinking is not just introspection, although it may include that, but—like memory—is among the mind's connections to the world of experience. Unlike the calculative thinking of everyday life that is the basis for survival in the world, meditative thinking requires withdrawal from the world (which paradoxically provides the substance without which there would be nothing to think about) into periods of quiet isolation. The thinker, like Rodin's statue, appears to be quietly at rest, but beneath appearances—in the actual life of the mind—there is no greater intensity. As Cato observed more than two thousand years ago, a thinking person is never "more active than when he does nothing, never less alone than when he is by himself." Plato associated this type of thinking with the spark of divinity in the human soul; and philosophers—being no less self-indulgent than anyone else—find this idea attractive.

The central characteristic of this type of thinking is the presence of a second internal voice to hear and test ideas: responding, revising, or rejecting. The second voice reacts to what the first proposes, if indeed the two can be told apart definitively. It is the two-in-one duality of the mind that makes it possible for the self to reflect on itself, to assess its ideas, even to judge itself. This internal dialogue enjoyed pride of place in Arendt's lifelong thinking about totalitarianism, crimes against humanity, and politics, by which Arendt meant the way people live together in a shared world. It was, in part, gratitude to Heidegger for having illuminated this path of thinking when she was his student that sustained her connection to him years later, even after his shameful infatuation with the Nazis.

For Heidegger nothing was more powerful than questions about the meaning of existence: Not simply why should you or I exist, but why should anything exist, why should there not be just nothing? What is the meaning of the nothingness by which Being is surrounded in the moments of its existence? The air around her brilliant professor seemed to crackle with ideas and questions; and like him, young Hannah was a creature who thrived in such air. She seems to have loved him from the very first day, and he seems to have been drawn to her immediately; twenty-five years later, after the Nazis and the destruction of total war, after his self-serving betrayal and disloyalty, Heidegger wrote a poem that recalls the excitement and dissipation of listlessness he experienced at the moment in November 1924 when he first saw Hannah in the seminar on Plato's *Sophist*: "If only she, from withdrawn grace, would fall towards me. . . ."

At the end of class one day at the beginning of February 1925, Heidegger approached the stylish young woman with stunning eyes who sat in the seminar room taking careful, thorough notes and asked her to come to see him in his office. The days are gray, wet, and cold in Marburg at that time of year, and the old buildings were chilly and damp. When she came to his office, Hannah was wearing a coat, buttoned to the collar and a hat with a large brim against the rain and cold. He asked about the lectures and about the philosophers she had been reading; she answered briefly in a soft voice, sometimes in Greek and Latin. She looked away demurely, but he took her in with his eyes and years later admitted to Hannah that he had retained the image of a shy girl quietly answering his questions all the rest of his life.

A few days later Hannah received a note from him that began "Dear Miss Arendt, I must come to see you this evening and speak to your heart."

> Everything should be simple and clear and pure between us. Only then will we be worthy of having been allowed to meet. You are my pupil and I your teacher, but that is only the occasion for what has happened to us.
>
> I will never be able to call you mine, but from now on you will belong in my life, and it shall grow with you. . . .
>
> "Be Happy!"—that is now my wish for you.
>
> Only when you are happy will you become a woman who can give happiness, and around whom all is happiness, security, repose, reverence, and gratitude to life.

From this moment on, he was Martin to her; and he promised that he would be loyal, and that she, "du, liebe Hannah," must also be true to herself. A week later he wrote to her that "love is rich beyond all other possible human experiences . . . because we become what we love and yet remain ourselves. . . . Love transforms gratitude into loyalty to our selves and unconditional faith in the other. . . . The other's presence suddenly breaks into our life—no soul can come to terms with that. A human fate gives itself over to another human fate, and the duty of pure love is to keep this giving alive as it was on the first day."

That is how their love began. We are most aware of existence and perhaps live it most intensely in intimate experiences with and of "the other," as the lover and the beloved; and this moment with Heidegger, even after other and greater love, never ceased to be the personification of passion in Hannah's memory and understanding of the world.[5]

What we know about the first months of their love affair comes mostly from Heidegger's letters to Arendt, which she saved. For whatever reasons, he did not save hers. The two saw each other often. They met on campus benches and took long walks, sometimes ending at Hannah's little attic room. There were meetings at Martin's office; sometimes lights turned on or off would signal whether he was alone. "The demonic struck me," he wrote to her after one such meeting, referring to the Greek *daemon*, a voice of divine wisdom: "the silent prayer of your beloved hands and your shining brow. . . . Nothing like it has ever happened to me." One night they were caught outside in a sudden rainstorm, and the next day Martin wrote: "You are even more beautiful and wonderful like this. I wish that we could wander together like this for nights on end." One Saturday night they sat apart but near each other at a concert, the awareness of their situation almost unbearable. The next morning Hannah received a note of "loving greeting" from Martin: "After the concert," he said, "I was so moved by being near you that I could not bear it any longer—and left, when I would much rather have wandered through the night with you, walking silently beside you . . . not asking what for and why but just being. Thank you—even if I can not and may not do so—for your love."

Hannah was captivated by the intensity of Heidegger's affection, was dazzled by his erudition and by the physicality of the relationship, with its aura of sexual excitement. She loved the way Martin talked, every word and phrase the perfect consort blending meaning and feeling with sound as if prose were poetry; perfect German, the language of Goethe and the voice of *Bildung und Geist*. Walking through a meadow one afternoon, they talked about the existentialist Max Scheler, who taught that love is the great principle of human association. One Sunday evening, the campus deserted, they met at Martin's office and talked until late about Thomas Mann's suspension of time in *The Magic Mountain*. They lived in the joy of those hours but were also aware that there was danger of being discovered which, whatever Martin's license at home, would have been a public embarrassment and burdensome to both of their reputations and careers.

It was never Arendt's intention to recite Heidegger's thought, but to think with and against him in what Karl Jaspers called the loving struggle of the mind. From the beginning she resisted Martin's emphasis on the finality of ends, countering it with her own awareness of the endlessness of new beginnings made possible only by the disappearance of the old; and this in time helped her to face and overcome childhood fears. In a long note about her innermost feelings, Arendt confessed that her ability to embrace existence was compromised by existential panic, awareness of being instantly generating fear of the impending, all-encompassing nothingness of death "stealing with the hidden uncanniness of a shadow across her path," accompanied by anxious wonder about "what makes up a life, what can constitute it." And with no deep sense that she knew "how to care for herself," or make something of her own life. Writing about herself in the third person, Arendt declared that she "had fallen prey to fear of existence itself . . . [and that] the sense of being hunted . . . ran through her as if she were dead flesh." She hoped somehow to establish meaning through "experiments and curiosity . . . until finally the long and eagerly awaited end takes her unawares, puts an arbitrary stop to her useless activity."

"There are shadows only where there is also sun," Martin wrote to her, "and sunshine, beloved Hannah, is the foundation of your soul, before which I am helpless—made helpless by your elementary joy and by your shy, resolute persistence." It was not only Martin's love that fortified Hannah's courage; it was also his thinking, which begins by not running away from the anxiety that arises when Being is confronted with the void and the groundlessness surrounding existence. Only by embracing the inevitability of nothingness can humanity appreciate the moment of existence and become capable of embracing its possibilities for love and freedom.

Heidegger approached life as a clearing in dark woods; one enters out of darkness and recedes into darkness. In ordinary life the fear of death is repressed; individuals seek distractions and forget their own Being in day-to-day concerns. Work, family, and politics, whatever else they are, are all distractions from Being in the present moment—with its concomitant awareness of the impending catastrophe awaiting each man. For Heidegger the existential challenge was to face the finality of death head-on, no backing away into spirituality. However much his subsequent behavior hurt her, it was with Martin that she first faced the awareness of existence without fear or illusions. After that, and despite everything else, she was always grateful to him for the lesson that it is necessary to approach life with firm determination to confront ultimate questions, and for his nonnegotiable position that serious human thought must dwell persistently on first and last things. For Heidegger this involved wonder about the Being of things and the meaning of life in a universe without a transcendent God, consisting only of moments of existence. Arendt, in contrast, reached back into the shared world of social life and politics into which people make their brief appearances through the accident of birth, which remains behind after their deaths, and which must be loved because there is no other.

3

◇◇◇◇
◆

THE EARTH IS OUR PLANET, BUT the world is a social construction. It fills the spaces between us and organizes interactions, much like the table around which dinner guests sit. Hannah Arendt and Martin Heidegger both made their appearances into a world in which it was possible for love to flourish across religious boundaries. In 1924 when the brilliant young Jewish woman with piercingly beautiful dark eyes had a love affair with the leading figure in continental philosophy, it did not seem on the surface as if the world of Germans and Jews was drawing near to a cataclysmic conclusion.

Hannah was just past eighteen when they fell in love; Martin Heidegger was thirty-five years old, married, and the father of two sons. She was taken by the beauty of his thought and language, and her desire for him was intensified by his for her. An adulterous relationship between an older professor and a young student is inherently suspect as seduction based on differences of status and power. Conversely, many admirers of Arendt's work are dismayed by her inability to see with clarity until some years later that Heidegger was a man of weak character and a "notorious liar,"[1] and/or about her insensitivity to the interests of his wife, Elfride. Yet, she was eighteen years old and head over heels in love. She did not see that Heidegger's behavior indicated a pattern of deceit, nor that she would soon be touched by it.

It was not so much that she did not consider Elfride worthy of Martin, or doubted that she provided him with a comfortable physical environment for his work, but she felt superior to Elfride, who she thought could not participate in Martin's deepest thought or be the companion in Being that he needed to overcome his alienation from the world. Between the two of them, Hannah and Martin, she felt that there was in contrast a full and fully appreciative embrace each of the other. From the outset Martin was clear that he would never leave Elfride, the children, and the respectability of his position, but Hannah was confident that the love between them deserved to be preserved and nurtured independently of any social convention or competing obligation. Even if she did not expect their love to last forever, neither could she deny it or feel in any way ashamed. It was naïve, however, not to see that a deceitful and adulterous husband might also be untrustworthy and undependable as a lover.

Besides being presumptuous and self-serving, Hannah's dismissal of Elfride was perhaps also naïve. Elfride was no genius; but she was intelligent, independent, and well educated for a woman of her generation. She had lived and studied in France and England, and had completed not only the rigorous training required to be a high school teacher, but also the *Abitur*, which meant that she was qualified to begin university study in economics. Indeed, like Hannah some years later, Elfride had fallen in love with Martin Heidegger while attending his lectures in philosophy at Freiburg.[2]

Elfride had a reputation as a hard woman, and was not very well liked, indeed was deeply resented in some circles.[3] Although she had some Jewish friends—whom she thought of as "exception Jews"—Elfride was openly anti-Semitic in the sense that she did not want German culture to be influenced by "alien" ideas and aesthetics. She was a traditionalist who loved to hike and climb on forest trails singing popular folk songs, exulting in the German countryside and way of being. Elfride's attraction to the Nazis was rooted in these attitudes and her distaste for the pluralism and disorder of the Weimar Republic.

There was a day when the Heidegger family and a group of advanced philosophy students went for a hike and a picnic lunch in the Black Forest. Although Hannah was not present, she heard that there had been an athletic competition and that Elfride was mightily impressed by Günther Stern, who stood on his head for a full five minutes and was clearly the best at all the sports. Günther was not only an outstanding athlete, but also a very fine musician, with additional talents in philosophy and literature both as a writer and critic. In any event, on the day of the picnic Elfride said to Günther that he was an exceptional specimen of humanity and that such a young man ought to be a member of the Nazi Party. She was shocked and looked away when he told her that he was Jewish and did not think the party would have a place for him.[4] No doubt this aspect of Elfride's character also explains why Hannah did not have much sympathy for her.

Heidegger's detractors (of whom there are many), looking for the roots of his later attraction to the Nazis, argue that he was always an anti-Semite.[5] But the evidence for this is very weak: he had been raised by devout parents in rural small-town poverty in the southern Black Forest not far from the borders with France, Switzerland, and Austria, where he was no doubt exposed to anti-Semitic attitudes. He was educated with scholarships at conservative Catholic schools in the region, and several of his teachers published anti-Semitic tracts in journals that lionized such prominent anti-Semitic figures as the seventeenth-century Augustinian monk Abraham a Sancta Clara and the contemporary mayor of Vienna, Karl Lueger. Victor Farias makes much of the young Heidegger's commitment to Catholicism, of his childhood aspiration to become a priest like his teachers, and of the fact that his first published essays appeared in the same journals in which his teachers published;[6] but there is no hint of anti-Semitism in any of his essays. Indeed, what seems clear is that as he became less dependent on the largesse of the Church, Heidegger's point of view and interests grew increasingly distant from those of his teachers, shifting first from theology to philosophy, and then from Catholic philosophy to the secular, pluralist (and to the Nazis, Jewish) phenomenology of Husserl and Jaspers. Elfride Petri, whom he married in 1917, was Protestant, and when their first son, Jörg, was born at the beginning of 1919, he announced his formal break from the Catholic confession of faith. The baby was baptized Protestant; and Heidegger, who did not change confessions, seems to have placed himself outside of the conventional morality of Christian tradition,[7] although this is by no means a straightforward matter. In a letter dated January 9, 1919, Heidegger informed his friend Engelbert Krebs, the professor of Catholic dogmatism at Freiburg University that while the system of Catholicism had become "problematic and unacceptable" to him, he was doing everything in his power "to further the spiritual life of man and work in the sight of God." As late as 1921, Heidegger is reported to have characterized himself to his student Karl Löwith as more of a Catholic theologian than a philosopher.[8] Hans-Georg Gadamer suggests that a deeply religious and fundamentally Christian element persisted in Heidegger's understanding of both Being and time, with their intimations of eternity.[9]

None of this suggests any more than that anti-Semitism was a familiar background noise to Heidegger, which he neither embraced nor confronted. His relationship with Hannah, friendship with many other Jews, and receptivity to Jewish students all through the 1920s suggest that when Heidegger joined the Nazi Party in 1933 it was not the Party's anti-Semitism that appealed to him, but something else in the Party program, or perhaps it was opportunism. Occasional anti-Semitic asides appear in the recently published correspondence between Martin and Elfride Heidegger, but as even the most hostile and thorough of Heidegger's critics have not been able to find more than two or three other examples in all of Heidegger's voluminous correspondence and publications over a long life, these remarks seem more like a duplicitous concession to Elfride's anti-Semitism than an indicator of deeply held personal values. The more fundamental fact revealed in the letters between husband and wife is that their relationship was deeply troubled.

Heidegger enjoyed the respectability of family life, but there was from early on a certain distance between the newlyweds. In the months after their marriage he established the lifelong habit of traveling away from home to pursue his research, writing, and other interests. In 1918, through much of which Elfride was pregnant, Martin was mostly away from home with military duties. Jörg was born in January 1919, and over the following year the new father was away from home several times on various research projects, sometimes for extended periods. Elfride found comfort in the arms of her childhood friend, now a physician, Dr. Friedel Caesar, and became pregnant with his child. Hannah never knew any of this; none of it became public until after she and Martin had both been dead for three decades.

Heidegger seems not to have been disturbed by Elfride's extramarital pregnancy; perhaps, being freethinkers, they had agreed in principal upon an open marriage. He wrote to her that he understood her love for Friedel. In the end, they concealed this indiscretion from the world, continuing as husband and wife, holding the child, Hermann Heidegger, out to the world as their second son, with Friedel as godfather. Thus they remained, or seemed to remain, within the community of traditional values, and to avoid the stigma of adultery in her case and of having been a cuckold in his. After this, however, Martin, seems to have felt a degree of freedom in relation to his marital obligations; which after all is not so uncommon among men and perhaps only marginally less so among women. Nevertheless, Martin's lifelong silence about all this reveals a depth of commitment to Elfride that cannot be overlooked, neither in terms of her importance to him nor in terms of his relationship with Hannah.

Within the marital relationship there may have been a tilt in the balance of power. Elfride, the more cosmopolitan of the two and the daughter of a more prosperous and influential family than Martin's, was now occupied with two children and hardly in a position to question her scholarly husband's need for privacy and quiet, or his occasional affairs with other women; but she could insist on discretion. Two years after Hermann's birth, Elfride arranged to receive her share of a family inheritance early. She used the money to buy land and build a small *Hütte* (cabin) of her own design accessible only by footpath alongside a creek on the side of a hill overlooking a long valley and the tiny farming village of Todtnauberg; and she made a gift of this place to Martin as a retreat for quiet and work. Perhaps this marks the end of a stormy period in their marriage and the beginning of a new stability. Whatever happened between them in the months before and after the birth of their second child, it must be observed, to Heidegger's credit, that he took the boy as his own and his relationships with both sons seem always to have been loving and cooperative. Hermann, for his part, was a loyal son who regarded Martin as his father even after learning the truth in adolescence from his mother. He strove all his life as a historian and later as literary executor to preserve and protect his father's work and reputation.

What are the effects of living with a secret concealed so deeply in the privacy of the marital bedroom? In time, the memory may be almost completely suppressed; concealed but present nonetheless in other relationships because one party knows something relevant that the other does not. That Heidegger was already deceitful at the very beginning of their relationship (and perhaps all through his life) became clear to Hannah in time; but she concluded that the fact that a man lies about facts does not mean that the evidence one has about his feelings is necessarily unreliable.[10]

4

BY THE SUMMER OF 1925, MARTIN was more or less gone. He was immersed in his work and family at their Black Forest mountain hut at Todtnauberg. Hannah was at home in Königsberg, alienated and detached in the bosom of her family; touched by extraordinary love, but unable to possess the beloved or speak of her love, let alone assert a place for it in the shared world of public life.

At summer's end Hannah did not return to Marburg, but went instead to Freiburg to spend a semester studying with Martin's mentor, Edmund Husserl, who always treated Martin with care and concern as if he were a son. Freiburg is a wonderful ancient city, much more beautiful, cosmopolitan, and stimulating than Marburg, which is little more than a provincial university town, but Hannah felt sad and alone, longing for Martin, who grew increasingly distant, neither visiting nor writing very often. On January 9, 1926, she came to see him, complaining that she felt forgotten, and to say that she had decided not to return to Marburg, but to study with Karl Jaspers at Heidelberg.

The following day Martin wrote an apologetic letter conceding that he had forgotten her, but

> not from indifference, not because external circumstance intruded between us, but because I had to forget and will forget you whenever I withdraw into the final stages of my work. This is not a matter of hours or days, but a process that develops over weeks and months and then subsides. And this "withdrawal" from everything human and breaking off of all connections is, with regard to creative work, the most magnificent human experience . . . [but] with regard to concrete situations, it is the most repugnant thing one can encounter. One's heart is ripped from one's body.

Did Hannah, even then, suffering with hidden longings, desires, and frustrations recognize deceit in the service of cooling ardor?

Overall, her time in Marburg and Freiburg had involved intense isolation and estrangement from others caused by her hidden love. She made few new friends during that time, and old friendships suffered neglect. The circumstance of concealment meant that every conversation with Martin had the closeness of a secret known by two people only, and every other conversation was a sort of half-truth because of what was not said. During the semester in Freiburg, Hannah was especially lonely, not only because Martin became increasingly distant, but also because she felt isolated socially and intellectually. Husserl was approaching seventy; and the circle around him was not characterized by youthful enthusiasm. Heidegger recognized that Husserl was no longer moving forward and that his productivity had come to an end.[1] Even in his prime, Husserl's phenomenology, which aimed at creating a science of consciousness, had taken its inspiration from mathematics and the natural sciences, which had less appeal to Hannah than Heidegger's existential interest in poetry, literature, and art as inspirations for philosophy.

When she told Martin that she would not return to Marburg, but planned to study at Heidelberg with his friend Karl Jaspers, he did not suggest that she reconsider, but encouraged her instead to have the strength to go away to be free, to grow, and to avoid the danger of being known as Heidegger's acolyte. Perhaps her decision, he wrote, would have a bracing effect on him, clearing the air: "If it has a good effect, it can only be because it calls for sacrifice from both of us. . . . May each of us be a match for the other's existence, that is for the freedom of faith and for the inner necessity of an unalloyed trust—that will preserve our love." Whether this was genuine or only Heidegger sweet-talking himself out of an illicit relationship once the blush was off the rose, he was right that it was better for Hannah to go. Jaspers became her most important teacher and over the course of a lifetime her most respected friend. But the break from Heidegger was far from clean.

They wrote to each other and there were secret meetings. Sometimes when Martin was traveling, they would meet at a train station in a small town en route to his destination and spend the night in a hotel. Once, she interrupted a vacation with friends to run off with him for a night;[2] but these rendezvous became less and less frequent. His letters (like others, it turns out, that he wrote to Elfride when he was away from home) contained assurances of abiding love and longing, and he was always apologizing for his absence with excuses of ill health, obligations, meetings, work, and family obligations. Even after Hannah began to understand that he was a liar who said whatever was necessary to manage a moment, she always believed that Martin loved her more than he ever loved anyone else.[3]

The word "love" appears only once in all five hundred pages of *Being and Time*. Heidegger's thought proceeded by asking questions: "What is existence?" "What is time?" "What is a thing?" "What is a work of art: Is it only the canvas and oils, or does something less tangible also exist there?" But he never questioned the meaning or existence of love. He was so captured by death, which carries us out of this world, that he failed to notice that it is love which connects us to it. Karl Jaspers, who was still at the time Heidegger's great friend and who admired his genius, nevertheless noted that because love was absent from *Being and Time*, the book's style was unlovable.[4]

In Heidelberg, Hannah immediately became part of the group of intellectuals that revolved around the Jaspers household, which (as Randall Jarrell said years later about her own home with Heinrich Blücher) was a sort of "dual monarchy" presided over by the philosopher and his wife Gertrud, who was Jewish. As part of the Jaspers circle, Hannah once again had friends. Hans Jonas was one, and he brought her into renewed contact with Kurt Blumenfeld, who was by then the president of the German Zionist Federation, through whom she gradually became involved over the next few years with what was then called "the Jewish question." Blumenfeld was a powerful personality: like Jaspers, deeply intellectual, intimate with German poetry and thought, a man of strong and very decent convictions, active in the world, and full of life and playfulness. Jaspers and Blumenfeld were each only five or six years older than Heidegger, but Hannah loved those two with the sort of regard and affection that an adult child might have for a deserving, thoughtful father.

Among Hannah's many other friends in Heidelberg, there were also two or three with whom she had romantic relationships, but her secret love and desire for Martin interjected a certain distance. Karl and Gertrud Jaspers strongly approved of her affair with Benno Georg Leopold von Wiese und Kaiserwald, who was tall, thin, fair-haired, refined, aristocratic, brilliant, and although only a few years older than Hannah, was already professorial and a respected figure in the field of literary history. Hannah and von Wiese were together for two years, but in the end he claimed to need a wife more dedicated to domesticity. Perhaps he was also unwilling to stray from his roots by taking a Jewish wife, or recognized, though it was never articulated, that her love was directed elsewhere. In later years he, like Heidegger, was also compromised by early enthusiasm for the Nazis.

Hannah, still suffering in silence, having been touched by love both as transcendent attachment and as desire, unable to possess the beloved or even to talk about him except to one or two of her oldest friends from Königsberg, made love the central theme of her scholarship and thought for the next few years. In 1927 she began work on her dissertation, *Love and Saint Augustine*, under Jaspers' supervision. She had little contact with Martin, but he was familiar with her work and progress through Jaspers and as a member of her faculty committee, and he wrote letters in support of her various applications for research funding. They saw each other only from time to time, though Hannah craved those encounters and lived in anticipation. Martin wrote to her early in April of 1928 (around the same time that the romance with Benno von Wiese was ending) to say that he had been invited to assume the chair in philosophy at Freiburg made available by Husserl's retirement. This solidified his position as a leading figure in philosophy, and the simultaneous publication of *Being and Time* made him famous. He and Hannah met a few days later, and Martin made it clear that because of the visibility of his new position he would not be coming to see her again. A few days after that she wrote to him, obviously suffering but accepting the condition of separation he had imposed:

> I have been anxious the last few days, suddenly overcome by an almost bafflingly urgent fear. . . . I love you as I did on the first day—you know that, and I have always known it. . . . The path you showed me is longer and more difficult than I thought. It requires a long life in its entirety. . . . I would lose my right to live if I lost my love for you, but I would lose this love and its *reality* if I shirked the responsibility [to be constant] it forces on me.

She concluded with the last lines of the forty-third of Elizabeth Barrett Browning's *Sonnets from the Portuguese* (which begins "How do I love thee, let me count the ways"): "And if God Choose, I shall but love thee better after death."

After this, her dissertation was the only link between them. It was not only that Martin was a member of the committee, nor that the work drew on his method of phenomenological inquiry (as well as Jaspers's compatible *Existenz* philosophy), but also with Augustine she was on ground Heidegger had covered; with love as her theme Arendt was thinking against Heidegger, but was still with him in the thinking.

The dissertation was completed in 1929. It did not receive a score of 1, the best possible, but 2-A, just below. Jaspers thought it wandered in places and that not all ideas were equally well developed, but liked it enough to have it published in the philosophical series he edited.[5] By and large, critics did not like the book; they thought there were gaping holes in the discussion of Augustine's theology and of their own modest hermeneutical contributions. Perhaps it seemed odd to them that a young Jewess, unschooled in Christian faith, should take on Augustine; but there was really nothing strange about it: one cannot master German philosophy and remain unfamiliar with Christian thought. Even Hans Jonas, who chose to study philosophy at the University of Berlin so that he could simultaneously take classes at the Academy of Jewish Studies, wrote a book about St. Augustine and the Pauline problem of freedom. The critics, stuck in the fading light of classical and humanist philosophical traditions (just as Husserl, Heidegger, and Jaspers were initiating the new existential tradition), failed to comprehend that there was no place for theology in Arendt's dissertation because she was not interested in Augustine the Bishop, but in Augustine the thinker, who in his own time, like Jaspers and Heidegger in the twentieth century, was attuned to the Greek awareness of Being.

Augustine understood that transcendent love and worldly love are both driven by appetites; that love itself is a craving for the object that gives rise to it. Love is a kind of motion, and all motion is toward something. What we are drawn to in love always seems good and beautiful; otherwise we would not seek it for its own sake. Arendt often said that, for her, every thought had something to do with personal experience, that every thought was a glance backward, an afterthought, a reflection on earlier matters or events. Any reader of Augustine's *Confessions* will know that this was true for him too. Hannah read Augustine in the freshness of her own experience of love as unsatisfied appetite.

Desire's burning quality, Augustine recognized, is craving, which constantly anticipates, and can only be stilled by, the presence of the desired object. Happiness springs into existence when the gap between lover and beloved has been closed; then desire yields to satisfaction and calm quietude. Love is each human being's possibility of gaining happiness. Once we have the object of our desire, however, we begin to feel threatened by the possibility of its loss. Fear of loss corresponds to the desire to have. The great paradox is that since all things of the world are temporary, love threatens to leave us in a perpetual state of fear and mourning.

Heidegger and Augustine agree: since the being of individuals and things on earth is inevitably temporary, love that seeks anything safe on earth is constantly frustrated. Love turns away from things and people, becoming finally only the desire to be free from fear. If man most craves freedom from fear, he will turn away from love of worldly things that can only be lost, and will embrace the eternal Being that exists outside of past, present, and future, the Being from which we come and toward which we are propelled, each at the still point of a turning universe.

In Heidegger's thought this leads away from the socially constructed world of humanity, and other men become the "they" whose gossip distracts from awestruck appreciation of Being in the face of nothingness. Augustine seems at first to take a similar position eschewing *cupiditas*—the love that clings to things of the world; but the place of Being in Heidegger's thought is occupied by the Supreme Being in Augustine, and this turns him to *caritas*, which seeks and loves the eternal. Augustine advises Christians to crave and cherish eternal life with the same appetite with which temporal life is cherished. Then, he says, the stricture to love one's neighbor will arise not as an obligation, but from craving and love for God. It is not that we earn God's love by loving our neighbor; rather if we love God with burning desire to possess and be possessed by the beloved, we will naturally be drawn back to the world that is God's creation, and will see God and God's love in every person. For Augustine, love carries man beyond the realm of fear and time (which is otherwise always running out) into a transcendent union in which each present moment is experienced in the presence of the timeless eternal.

To observe that Augustine's love of Being brings man back into the world, while Heidegger's gaze at the nothingness drives man away from the world, was for Hannah a sort of loving rebuke to Martin. It was also, perhaps, a way of overcoming loss and grief.

5

IN JANUARY 1929, STILL IN A state of emotional turmoil over Martin Heidegger, Hannah attended a masquerade ball at the Museum of Ethnology in Berlin. It was a fund-raising event on behalf of a small left-wing magazine. In keeping with the ethnological theme, she came to the party dressed as an Arab harem girl and was escorted home at the end of the evening by Günther Stern, whom she had not seen since 1925. Within a month they were living together, and that September, just weeks ahead of the stock market crash that precipitated international economic and political disaster, they were married in a small civil ceremony attended by their parents and two friends who acted as witnesses. In later years Stern achieved a degree of prominence as a writer, philosopher, and antinuclear activist under the name Günther Anders. He took this name after a Berlin editor complained that he had too many writers named Stern on his staff, and asked if he couldn't call himself something different (*anders*). "Alright," came the response, "call me Anders."[1]

Stern was the son of prominent Jewish intellectuals, child psychologists whose book based on observations of their own children was widely popular in Germany in the early part of the twentieth century. In him they succeeded in producing a cultured, kind, intelligent person, accomplished on piano and violin, and as Elfride Heidegger had noticed, a good athlete. Despite all this, Martin, with whom Günther had studied in Marburg, did not consider him first-rate;[2] and in the end neither did Hannah. Years later she advised a student that it is a mistake to marry a man because you admire his parents. Perhaps the bigger mistake was to marry at all when she was still in love with another.

In the days just ahead of the wedding Hannah was still writing to Martin. With Günther, she told him, she had found a haven from her restlessness and a sense of belonging; though we may wonder about this as she begged Martin not to forget her and told him that the continuity of love between the two of them was still the most meaningful thing in her life:

> *Do not forget how much and how deeply I know that our love has become the blessing of my life. This knowledge cannot be shaken, not even today. . . . I often hear things about you, but always with the peculiar reserve and indirectness that is simply a part of speaking the famous name—that is something I can hardly recognize. And I would indeed so like to know—almost tormentingly so, how you are doing, what you are working on, and how Freiburg is treating you. I kiss your brows and eyes.*
>
> *—Your Hannah.*

Martin, whether out of curiosity, jealousy, or desire to see Hannah in a situation that could not be construed as compromising, visited the newlyweds in Frankfurt a few days after the wedding. After coffee, when he and Günther left together to catch the same train, Hannah made her way secretly to the station to have a last glimpse of Martin. Seeing Günther with him, where she felt she ought to have been, the past came rushing back. She remembered a time as a little girl when her mother played a game with her, pretending not to recognize her. She was terrified and kept crying: "I am your child, I am your Hannah." That, she wrote to Martin is how she felt looking at him and knowing that he could not see her as the train was about to leave and there was nothing left for her "but to let it happen, and wait, wait, wait."

Life with Günther was pleasant enough, at least at first. The two of them worked together on several projects; he helped with the final proofreading of her manuscript on *Love and Saint Augustine*, and they published a book review together and an article on Rilke's *Duino Elegies*. They moved to Frankfurt, away from Berlin (which was more a place for singles than young married couples), and Günther began working on his postdoctoral *Habilitation* at the famous School for Social Research. His topic was the philosophy of music, and his faculty committee included Max Horkheimer, Max Wertheimer, Karl Mannheim, Paul Tillich, and Theodor W. Adorno. The last, who was born Theodor Ludwig Wiesengrund, Hannah viewed as a contemptible man because he adopted his mother's maiden name in an effort to deny his Jewish father and pass as Italian. Years later she suspected that he would even have cooperated with the Nazis if they would have had him.[3] In the end, Adorno kept Günther from completing his academic work because he found it insufficiently Marxist.

At about this same time, even before *Love and Saint Augustine* was published, Hannah had begun to think about her own *Habilitation*, the second book without which one cannot be appointed to a permanent academic position in Germany. A dissertation marks the end of one's studies; the *Habilitation* is one's emergence as a scholar. With letters of support from Martin Heidegger and Karl Jaspers, she received a grant from the Notgemeinschaft der deutschen Wissenschaft to undertake a phenomenological study of German Romanticism. Hannah's attention soon focused on a single person, Rahel Varnhagen, a literary figure of the late eighteenth and early nineteenth centuries, part of the first generation of emancipated Jews, in whose time enlightenment opened the gates of the ghetto and granted rights of citizenship to its residents, making possible the emergence of Jews into German culture.

Anne Mendelssohn, Hannah's closest friend and confidante since early adolescence—who knew about Hannah's relationship with Martin and understood her unhappiness—had purchased the complete correspondence of Rahel Varnhagen in several dusty leather-bound volumes from a bankrupt bookseller, and gave them to her. In those old pages between decaying covers, she told Hannah, she would find a kindred spirit, an unspoiled, unconventional, intelligent woman, interested in people, passionate and vulnerable. Anne was right, and was in some ways replaced for a time by Rahel as Hannah's closest friend.[4] It did not matter that there were more than a hundred years between them: love is regard for another from whatever distance the world puts between us.

With Rahel, Hannah shared the sense of self as a *"Mädchen aus der Fremde,"* that is, as a person who did not fit comfortably into the world of Germans and Jews into which she was born; and in her longing for Martin Heidegger, Hannah also felt close to Rahel's unfulfilled love for the elegant but ultimately superficial Count Karl von Finckenstein, and her later heartbreak with the dashing Spanish diplomat Don Raphael d'Urquijo, about whom Rahel had written:

> This man, this creature wielded the greatest magic over me, still wields it. I . . . gave him my whole heart. And once the heart is given, only love and worthiness can give it back; otherwise it is gone from you. . . . It is as though he still had something of mine which I must have again, and as if his love could still delight and cure me. . . . In short, so long as I cannot love someone more intensely, the part of myself necessary for happiness remains in his power.[5]

The most fundamental fact of Rahel's life, Arendt wrote, was that she was never able to have the most elementary and alluring simple joy of natural existence—life with the man she desired. Perhaps it was because she experienced this same condition so intensely herself that Arendt could dare to write in the preface that she had undertaken to narrate the story of Rahel's life as Rahel herself might have told it.

The phenomenological method that Arendt learned from Heidegger and Jaspers recognizes the importance of feelings in human experience. The truth of history cannot be known through reason alone, because the experience of each passing moment of existence involves feelings and moods, which are more accessible to our understanding through mechanisms of emotion than through pure reason. It was not only Rahel's experience of unrequited love, but also her ambivalent experience of herself as a Jew, that required Arendt's fine attunement to feeling.

Rahel was part of the first generation of emancipated German Jews, a bygone world that Arendt was making her intellectual home at the very time that her own experience was being transformed by the right-wing challenge to enlightenment ideals of human equality. The "Jewish question," which is to say the question of what place if any there might be for Jews in European life, the question that came to such a tragic resolution in Arendt's generation, was fresh and promising in Rahel's. So too was its obverse: could Europe embrace a pluralistic conception of citizenship in which all people shared? There had been Jews in Germany at least since the time of Charlemagne, but with the exception of a few merchants, scholars, and courtiers, they lived in ghettoized obscurity and poverty in urban centers like Frankfurt, or peasant lives in shtetls further east as Prussia expanded into Slavic territories with sizable Jewish minorities. Before Rahel's generation these Jews, though present, had not been part of the fabric of European life. As itinerants, peddlers, and bankers, they served as conduits and intermediaries in international trade and finance. These enterprises were perfectly suited to the dispersion of the Jewish Diaspora with its network of settlements extending from Persia and Egypt through the center of Europe, north to the Baltic and westward to the Atlantic. But the Jews were everywhere a marginal people, never part of the nation; aliens whose presence was tolerated, but only under the most severe conditions of apartheid—in crowded, polluted urban neighborhoods where gates were locked at night to keep them in, or isolated in rural settlements. There was no question about their station in society.

The conditions of Jewish life in western Europe remained medieval until the end of the eighteenth century and well into the nineteenth in the east,[6] well into Rahel's lifetime. Even in law, the Jews retained corporate identity when other guilds and classes of the old dispensation were already yielding to the new individualism. Talmudic Orthodoxy and Kabalistic obscurantism still focused Jewish intellect on otherworldly concerns. Hierarchical, repressive, and corrupt systems of Jewish community governance by wealthy elites mirrored the institutions of monarchical Christian Europe in which they were embedded, and which were about to crumble before enlightenment's revolutionary conceptions of liberty, human rights, and citizenship.

Emancipation of the Jews in the Age of Reason was a logical extension of the enlightenment conception of universal human dignity. This ideal was not extended (beyond the sentimental conceptions of "noble savage" and "white man's burden") to Africans or indigenous first peoples; but the Jews were nearby, not too numerous, within the biblical tradition, and they played a desirable role in expanding economic development and international commerce. The idea that despite their backwardness the Jews could be enlightened and made part of the nation took hold first in France and America, and then under pressure from Napoleon as far east as the Hapsburg Empire and Prussia, where a few relatively cosmopolitan cities were receptive. Rahel's era is the prehistory of the Arendts and Cohens of Königsberg and of the largely assimilated, secular, intellectual German-Jewish tradition that constituted the world into which Hannah was born.

Rahel was an autodidact, because her father did not value the education of women. She may have had some private lessons in reading and writing from a tutor and help from her brothers or friends, but German would at first have been a foreign language to her; Yiddish was the language of her home and of the Berlin ghetto. Rahel's spelling and handwriting remained terrible all of her life; yet through reading and correspondence she became proficient in German and French, well versed in the ideals and Romantic sensibilities of enlightenment, and achieved prominence in Berlin's literary salons, which were experiments in the French ideal of *Liberté, Egalité, Fraternité.*

In the 1790s and the first few years of the next century, one of the nine salons run by women in Berlin was in Rahel's comfortable and spacious garret apartment. There guests of different social classes enjoyed private conversations and moments of intimacy, mingling freely and forming liaisons outside of the conventional rules of etiquette. If not hotbeds of free love, the salons in Berlin were at least potentially places of assignation. All in all, there were only about 100 individuals who attended these salons, less than one-tenth of 1 percent of the population of the city; but like the Beats in America 150 years later, they were influential beyond their numbers.

On any given day half the people in attendance were likely to be nobles, both men and women, mostly well educated, all Christian. Some were published authors or accomplished musicians, but even they were mostly dilettantes, overindulged members of the landed nobility at the very time the group was entering a period of downward mobility in an increasingly mercantile world. Another third of the guests on any given day were likely from the bourgeoisie (*Bürgertum*) ranging from diplomats, high civil servants, military, scientific, and educational leaders to teachers, pastors, and master artisans. Like the nobility, these guests were also Christian, but there were few women among them. The *Bürgertum*, even when prosperous and powerful, seem not to have valued the education of wives and daughters. The remaining *salonnières* were Jews, and almost all of them were women. It was their presence, less as educated women than as representatives of an outcast pariah people, that gave substance to the enlightenment ideal of a community of equal citizens. To attend a salon and be casual, friendly, even intimate with people of different classes and castes was the avant-garde experience of the age.[7]

Regular visitors at Rahel's attic room on Jägerstrasse included the naturalist and explorer Alexander von Humboldt and his brother, the philosopher, linguist, and politician Wilhelm von Humboldt; such prominent authors as Friedrich Schlegel, Friedrich Schleiermacher, and Ludwig Tieck; and Prince Louis Ferdinand of Prussia with his Jewish mistress, Pauline Wiesel. In this environment, in which class and origins seemed to mean nothing, romances across distances became possible. Rahel had a series of friendships and love affairs with aristocrats of various origins including the Swedish Ambassador Karl Gustave von Brinckmann, Friedrich von Gentz (a career diplomat who played an important role in the Vienna Congress of 1815), and most significantly with Count Karl von Finckenstein of Prussia, to whom she was engaged for four years but who seems finally not to have had either the desire or the strength of character to alienate himself from his family or its traditions by marrying a Jewess.

Marriage into one of the great families of Prussia, to a nobleman enamored of her charm and personality, would have been a perfect Romantic exit from life in the ghetto into the glittering world of enlightenment Europe. For women, sexual liaisons and marriages were among the few doors open. For Rahel it was not only a way out of the ghetto, but also out of what she experienced as the greatest pain in her life, the stigma of being a Jew. In her love affairs with Count von Finckenstein and the Spanish adventurer d'Urquijo, and in her later marriage to Karl August Varnhagen von Ense, Rahel had hoped to transcend Jewish identity and establish herself in good society. This, she found, even after she converted, was unavailable to her because in "good society" she remained a Jew. For many years she took this to be the great misfortune of her life. In her last years, however, especially in her friendship with the poet Heinrich Heine, Rahel began to appreciate her position of marginality. This is reflected in her deathbed declaration recorded by her husband, with which Arendt's's book begins:

> What a history! A fugitive from Egypt and Palestine, here I am and find help, love, fostering in you people. With real rapture I think of these origins of mine and this whole nexus of destiny, through which the oldest memories of the human race stand side by side with the latest developments. The greatest distances in time and space are bridged. The thing which all my life seemed to me the greatest shame, which was the misery and misfortune of my life—having been born a Jewess—this I should on no account now wish to have missed.

Rahel's experience at the beginning of the German enlightenment made clear to Arendt that while Jews had been invited into citizenship as equal human beings, there had never been a place for them in "good" society and that "pariah" is the natural state of a Jew in the Diaspora; if not necessarily despised, at least always marginalized. Enlightenment did not bring an end to this: the emancipated Jew (however accomplished, even Einstein) was less a part of the nation than the lowliest peasant, whose place was never in question. In response to this insight, Hannah made the judgment that the proper course among a pariah people (whether one is religious or not) is to accept pariah status with dignity, participating in the larger culture to the extent possible, while accepting what one is and asserting solidarity with other marginalized people, working on behalf of justice and a radical improvement in the conditions of all oppressed people.

6

◇◇◇◇
◆

THE POSITION OF JEWS IN SOCIETY had changed profoundly between Varnhagen's time at the beginning of the nineteenth century and Arendt's at the beginning of the twentieth: Jews, lapsed Jews, and former Jews prospered for decades as beneficiaries of enlightenment impulses toward human rights and unprecedented access to German culture. In this environment many Jews achieved celebrity in the arts, sciences, and even in politics. A third of all the Nobel prizes won by Germans had been awarded to Jews.[1] Albert Einstein, the director of the Max Planck Institute, was Berlin's most famous genius. Sigmund Freud and Theodor Herzl were among Vienna's leading intellectuals. Kurt Tucholsky, Stefan Zweig, Franz Werfel, Anna Seghers, and Franz Kafka were among the leading literary figures in the German-speaking world. Max Reinhardt and Kurt Weill were at the forefront of German theater. Dozens of Jews had been elected to the Reichstag, and some served as cabinet ministers; many more were prominent in commerce and the learned professions. Still, at the very time that Hannah was writing *Rahel Varnhagen: The Life of a Jewish Woman of the Romantic Era*, political instability deriving from catastrophic economic conditions and the rise of right-wing extremism were portents that the explosion of German-Jewish culture and creativity that had begun in Rahel's generation was drawing to an end.

The effect this had on Arendt was to intensify her interest in the meaning of Jewish identity in the modern world. In her youth and the early years of the Weimar Republic, Hannah had been interested above all in German philosophy and the history of Western civilization. However, writing about Rahel's experience at the beginning of German-Jewish emancipation while observing the looming end of enlightenment in her own immersed her in the Jewish question. Her identity as a Jew arose not out of religious conviction or desire for affiliation, but from an embrace of the role of self-conscious pariah. That the Jews were becoming more than ever a hated and despised minority strengthened Arendt's ties.

Though she experienced herself as a stranger, a girl from afar, an alien in the world into which she had made her appearance, Hannah, unlike Rahel, was content to have been born a Jew: there is such a thing, she said on numerous occasions, as being grateful that everything is as it is.[2] This does not imply that she thought we live in the best of all possible worlds, but only a judgment that gratitude is the appropriate response to the simple fact of existence, even in the face of evil, injustice, and the certainty of death.

During the five-year golden era of the Weimar Republic, between the end of postwar inflation and the beginning of the Great Depression, roughly the time between Hannah's first encounter with Heidegger and the publication of *Love and Saint Augustine,* the Weimar Republic seemed to have promise for the future. Parliamentary democracy (with all its glitches and inefficiencies) was taking hold. A period of economic and political stability seemed to be dawning, and although the extreme political parties, especially the right-wing parties, remained a threat, they were in a state of disarray. The crowds greeting Adolf Hitler's speeches after the Beer Hall Putsch and his release from prison were smaller than they had been before, and in the Reichstag election of May 20, 1928, the Nazis received only 2.6 percent of the vote.[3] Still, Arendt recognized danger in the sophistication of the Nazi organization and the enthusiasm and commitment to the Führer myth among the growing ranks of the Party.[4]

By 1929, when she was beginning to think about Rahel, polarization and violence were threats to German democracy. Large gains were made by left-wing parties including the communists; street fights between rightists and leftists were increasingly common and brutal. The number of political assassinations perpetrated by right-wing extremists over the preceding decade was in the hundreds, perhaps approaching a thousand, including prominent Jews—early on, Rosa Luxemburg, and later the German foreign secretary, Walter Rathenau. This does not mean that things had to go the way they did; there was nothing inevitable about the Third Reich. It was, however, already clear to Arendt by this time that as a Jew one had enemies and that "if one is attacked as a Jew, one must defend oneself as a Jew, not as a German, not as a world-citizen, not as an upholder of the Rights of Man, or whatever."[5] She understood that it would have been meaningless under the circumstances of Nazi Germany to respond "I am a man," as Nathan the Wise did in Lessing's play when he was called a Jew, because it was precisely shared humanity that the Nazis denied. She did not worry that defending herself as a Jew was a rejection of solidarity with other oppressed people, because she was fighting not just for the rights and well-being of the group to which she belonged, but for pluralism, which allows all groups to coexist.

In the years leading up to 1933 when Arendt was writing about Rahel's experience at the beginning of the German-Jewish symbiosis, she had a growing awareness of the potential for a tragic end. No one had any premonition of the impending physical annihilation of European Jewry (because what was done was at the time unimaginable); but Arendt already sensed that German-Jewish culture, with its astonishing wealth of talent and productivity in the century after Rahel's death, would not survive the intense attack to which it was about to be subjected by right-wing extremists in the name of racial purity.[6]

Observing Rahel's experience, Arendt came to recognize that from the beginning enlightenment had presented Jews with the choice of accepting their status as pariahs or becoming parvenus. She appropriated this distinction from Bernard Lazare,[7] a late-nineteenth-century journalist and conscious pariah, who, eschewing not only the high society of his native France, but also the wealthy elite among his own people, preferred a mobilization of ordinary people against all of the enemies and oppressors of the poor. The parvenu, like Rahel, at least in her younger life, wants only a comfortable place at the table. The pariah locates himself outside of good society in the pursuit of justice. Having once recognized this distinction, Arendt placed herself squarely with Lazare in the belief that the Jewish people could not solve their problems by escaping into good society or separating themselves from the oppression of others.

The parvenu seeks a personal solution to the social problem by denying that one is a Jew and "passing" in polite society. Wanting not justice, but only one's own happiness and well-being, the parvenu seizes the opportunity to join the mainstream, abandoning Jewish identity and rushing to break the solidarity that might connect him or her to all oppressed people. Conversion did not mean one had to take religious dogma seriously; Rahel's friend Heinrich Heine, whose writing infused with Jewish themes delighted German readers, made clear that his conversion to Christianity was a matter of convenience having more to do with access to cultural production and publishers than matters of faith.[8] Some Jews seem to have felt that if they could not entirely escape what Rahel experienced as the shame of Jewish birth in one's own lifetime, that conversation and intermarriage might at least free their children of the burden of difference. But the parvenu is confronted by a society that will not let the Jew, not even the baptized Jew, escape the stigma that Arendt recognized as "imposed by others and therefore as inescapable through one's own efforts as a hump on the back, or a clubfoot."[9] Furthermore, Arendt observed, the person who really wants to assimilate cannot pick and choose among the elements to which she is willing to assimilate.

> In a society on the whole hostile to the Jews—and that situation obtained in all countries in which Jews live, down to the twentieth century—it is possible to assimilate only by assimilating to anti-Semitism also. . . . And if one really assimilates, taking all the consequences of denial of one's own origin and cutting oneself off from those who have not or have not yet done it, one becomes a scoundrel.[10]

Arendt's own commitment to embrace her identity as a Jew and as a pariah incorporated a deep ambivalence about Zionism.

Many of her friends were Zionists, but Hannah did not join the movement. She held the Zionists in high regard as the only Jews who accepted pariah status as the basis for political and communal action but disapproved of their impulse to withdraw into a culture of their own.[11] She also resented the politics of Jewish leadership, which, having always feared the anti-Semitism of the mob, preferred to play ball with anyone in power rather than forging alliances with other people at the bottom. She rejected the underlying (sometimes unspoken) postulate of the Zionist call for a homeland as antagonistic to pluralism in so far as it proposed a benign ethnic cleansing: tired of being unwelcome guests, often hated and persecuted in Europe, the Zionists advocated removal of the Jewish population to a historic homeland on another continent. Arendt could not accept Zionism's implicit rejection of the idea that different peoples could prosper together in multicultural societies. She was content in the Diaspora and had no desire to emigrate to Palestine. What Arendt wanted was to be allowed by all sides to be what she was, a product of European enlightenment and Jewish heritage; She never believed in separating identity (which is admittedly complex and not unitary) into parts.[12] The judgment Arendt made was that Jews should not look only for a solution to their own problems, but rather that they should show solidarity with all oppressed people to look for solutions that would promote justice everywhere.

7

◇◇◇◇
◆

IT IS ONLY AFTER THE FACT that we can recognize the years between 1929 and 1933 as the end of the short-lived Weimar Republic. The Germans living through the period knew it was a time of turmoil, but the denouement was not clear until the day Hitler seized power, and for many not even then, although Arendt seems to have had some premonition of the impending horrific end of the world she had known. Heidegger, rising to the zenith of his prominence during these years, may already have been drifting toward the Nazis (certainly Elfride was); at the very least, we can say that there were already connections between his thought, which was revolutionary within its own intellectual domain, and the much cruder ideology Nazis espoused.

The publication of *Being and Time* had been a historic event in European philosophy and cleared the way for Heidegger to accede to the professorship at the University of Freiburg vacated by Edmund Husserl's retirement—with Husserl's enthusiastic support. Heidegger, Husserl wrote, "is without doubt the most important figure among the rising generation of philosophers . . .

predestined to be a philosopher of great stature, a leader far beyond the confusions and frailties of the present age."[1]

Heidegger wrote to his friend Karl Jaspers, the leading philosopher in the generation between Husserl and Heidegger, that the great challenge at Freiburg would be to determine "whether anything of philosophy is left there or whether it has all turned into learnedness."[2] Years later Arendt wrote that Heidegger recognized before anyone else that philosophy was almost dead: it had been formulated into schools of thought and compartmentalized into disciplines such as logic, ethics, and epistemology, and was not so much taught as "finished off by abysmal boredom." Heidegger did not participate in the "endless chatter *about* philosophy," rehearsing the teachings of others. Instead, distinguishing "between an object of scholarship [knowing what Plato thought] and a matter of thought [thinking for yourself about the issues that concerned Plato],"[3] he set out to create an original philosophy of his own. He read all the earlier thinkers, and he read them, Arendt said, better than anyone ever had, and perhaps better than anyone ever will again. His intention was not merely to comprehend or absorb the lessons taught by others, but to interrogate the masters, to think with and against them. It was this "rebellious quality" in Heidegger's work that appealed to Jaspers, who wrote to Heidegger after a weekend visit in December 1929 that, listening to him expound this new conception of metaphysics, he "felt free as though in pure air in this incessant transcending."

What was the philosophical background against which Heidegger's thought stood out so sharply? The triumph of science in the preceding centuries—the heliocentric challenge to Church dogma that placed the Earth at the center of the Universe, the Darwinian alternative to Genesis's account of creation, the ascent of industrialized technology, and at the beginning of the twentieth century Einstein's reconceptualization of the material universe—had elevated reason above faith in Western culture. In comparison to the method and results of the sciences, philosophy, the queen of reason, had begun to appear vague and antiquated. Questions about the meaning of experience faded in the face of the scientific effort to establish the dynamics of experience. The various sciences broke away from philosophy, which had for centuries been their home; and all that seemed to be left behind was metaphysics.

In antiquity, Andronicus of Rhodes, the editor of Aristotle's work, placed the chapters on "first philosophy," dealing with questions about things that transcend what is physical or natural, immediately after (*meta*) the chapters on physics, which deal with matter and the forces to which it is subject in the material world. Over time, scholars came to think of metaphysics as meaning more than the location of these chapters in a book. Metaphysics came to signify the capacity of the mind to penetrate beyond the physical realm into an extended universe of intangibles filled with questions about the existence of God, the soul, what we are doing when we are thinking, or whether we can be certain that the world as it appears to us is the same as the world as it actually exists.

In the long run, metaphysical inquiry into what cannot be known empirically or through reason alone began to seem sterile. Descartes, the seventeenth-century father of modern philosophy, set out to prove the existence of innate ideas and such higher truths as God through a method of radical doubt throwing into question the existence of the entire physical world: might not all be a dream, mirage, or similar hallucination? In the end, he hit upon the existence of the mind as the one certainty: *cogito ergo sum*—I think therefore I am—and reconstructed the world from this starting point. (Though we may note, with Nietzsche, that the existence of thought does not prove the existence of a thinker. This too might be only a mirage produced by vagrant, wandering, homeless thought, alone in the Universe.[4])

In the next century Bishop Berkeley and David Hume went beyond Descartes' skepticism. Berkeley challenged the existence of the material world outright: Everything we perceive is brought into us by our senses, but the mountains, trees, and structures that we perceive cannot possibly have actual existence within us. The phenomena that we think of as "real" are creations of the mind, and there is no reason to think that the external universe of objects corresponds with our perceptions of it. Such certainty as humans can have exists only in the realm of ideas, such, for example, as the idea of God.

Hume, an atheist, set out to replace such "airy" metaphysics with a rigid empiricism. He doubted everything that could not be confirmed from experience, not only God and the soul, but even such commonplace assumptions of science as causality. All we really know from experience is that one thing follows another, the rising of the sun and the brightening of the sky, for example, but we cannot, according to Hume, ever go beyond our experience to say with certainty that the one causes the other, or that it might not be different tomorrow. Our conviction about the future remains a supposition. Causality is not an objective truth of the real world, but an instrument of the mind that struggles to make sense of experience.

Hume's writing awoke the slightly younger Immanuel Kant from "dogmatic slumbers,"[5] and set him upon the task of restoring metaphysics from Hume's devastating skepticism. At the outset Kant simply takes the existence of things as given but accepts that this does not mean that our perceptions of them are accurate. What we see exists only in the mind's eye, light impinging on the retina, producing neurological action that is interpreted as a mountain, tree, or building. The answer that Kant proposes to the classic question of philosophy—how can we know with any degree of certainty what relationship internal subjective experience bears to external objective "reality?"—is that what we call "real" is a synthesis of object and subject. The material world exists but impinges on us as a confused jumble of sensations until our subjectivity (the thinking mind) gives them form by imposing order. Space and time, for example, are not "objects" in the external world, but subjective strategies through which consciousness imposes order on the universe. Thus the mind itself and the relationship of subject and object rather than an unseen spiritual world became the themes of Kant's new metaphysics.

Kant opened two doors for succeeding generations of philosophers: one is highly analytical, inquiring into the structures of the mind that categorize perception on the basis of abstractions about quantity, quality, relationships, and modes of being, thus constructing the world we know. This approach to Kant lights the way toward such modern sciences as linguistics and neurobiology. The other door, perversely, led to German idealism and back toward the old metaphysics of a world beyond the world of experience through what Karl Jaspers described as a "confused and disastrous transformation of reason into spirit."[6] This path led from Kant to Hegel, who imagined a world spirit guiding all of history in the direction of Western civilization at its pinnacle. Hegel's phenomenology of history captured the imaginations of the most prominent German thinkers of subsequent generations, who tacitly dropped or expressly rejected Kant's central positions, replacing reason with intuition. Karl Jaspers wrote that these philosophers cast off Kant's humility and dared to think the thoughts of God.[7] Then, rather suddenly in the second half of the nineteenth century, German idealism collapsed. The sciences captured the intellectual imagination, the prestige of philosophy declined, and "from what remained of the philosophical spirit, the cry arose: Back to Kant."[8]

By the beginning of the twentieth century, however, this "neo-Kantianism" had also grown stale. Learned professors wrote erudite tomes on the meaning of a phrase in Kant's *Critiques*, or argued over whether Kant's proof of this or that point was accurate. Originality and excitement seemed to be gone in philosophy. Husserl's phenomenology pointed in a new direction, trying, in essence, to make philosophy more scientific. Husserl overcame the ancient problem of understanding the relationship between the perceived world and the "real" world by "bracketing" the question of reality. Whether the seen tree, the tree as object of consciousness, is the "real" tree does not matter; it is in any event the "real object of consciousness," and the stream of consciousness could itself become the focus of scientific study.[9] For Husserl, the real world of human experience was the world of phenomena within the mind rather than the external noumena that give rise to it.

This was the background against which Heidegger made his appearance. Of course, there were already inventive philosophers in the nineteenth century thinking outside of the mainstream—Kierkegaard and Nietzsche, for example, by whom Heidegger was influenced. These two became increasingly important over time, but neither was well known or widely read in their own lifetimes or in the early years of the twentieth century. So

Heidegger, Husserl's most brilliant student, who was youthful, dynamic, and charismatic, seemed a breath of fresh air to his students; and after the mechanized, industrial destruction of the World War, when it was no longer possible to think of science, technology, and modernity as unambiguous harbingers of progress and improvement of the human condition,[10] fresh air was sorely needed.

Shortly after taking up his professorship at Freiburg, Heidegger wrote to Elisabeth Blochmann, a distinguished professor of pedagogy and a (half-Jewish) childhood friend of Elfride's (with whom we now know Elfride thought Heidegger was having a love affair, although it appears to have been unconsummated)[11] complaining that the hullabaloo being made over his person and work interfered with scholarly productivity. Nevertheless, despite the distractions and diversions that followed upon his celebrity, Heidegger's first years in his chair at Freiburg were very productive. His lectures on "The Fundamental Concepts of Metaphysics: World—Finitude—Solitude," were considered something of a sensation, not only by Jaspers, but also among young people interested in philosophy. These lectures aimed to disquiet students with the idea that philosophy is not "comfort and assurance," but rather "the turbulence into which man is spun," an "attack" on self-assurance bringing us into the "perilous neighborhood of supreme uncertainty," a dangerous enterprise with no goal other than to drive us into "fruitful questioning." Philosophy, Heidegger argued, is born out of boredom, the mood that arises when *Dasein,* the "being" of man, encounters the emptiness of life, the moments in which time will not pass, or passes without meaning.

To be bored is to be in the presence of the nothingness that always surrounds Being, but by which we are mostly diverted by the things and concerns of the world. Anxiety arises out of boredom, which is a fundamental awareness of finitude and solitude, the feeling of being left behind by the world. It is this awareness of nothingness, Heidegger taught, that opens the possibility of asking questions about Being. The job of the philosopher is to exploit the terror that arises from awareness of Being in the face of nothingness in order to drive men to a sense of wonder and amazement that there should be anything instead of just nothing. Thus philosophy overcomes boredom through thinking and the search for meaning.

The life-inducing terror of which Heidegger spoke was not political; even the Great War of 1914–1918, he noted, had not awakened humanity from its stupor. It was a philosophical awakening that would be needed to restore men to the meaning of Being. Heidegger offered a new (he claimed the rediscovered original) definition of the word "metaphysics" to refer not to some mystical world beyond the realm of physical experience and sensation, but to an intellectual revolution, a "peculiar turnaround in the face of everyday thinking and inquiry." If Heidegger did not dethrone "man" from the center of philosophy, where Kant placed him, he turned attention in the direction of "Being," which calls and reveals itself only to man.

Among students, who felt without fully comprehending why, that philosophy had become an idle game of erudition, a rumor circulated that Heidegger had broken the thread of tradition and was discovering the past anew. Plato, Kant, and the generations of philosophers and their ideas were not just talked about; instead, Heidegger brought them into a dialogue across the generations so that there was nothing antique anymore in philosophy. Suddenly the great ideas and questions stood revealed in all their contemporary relevance: not as received wisdom but as problems worthy of thought. Years later, when Heidegger was eighty, Hannah told an audience that all this might sound familiar to them because now so many philosophers work this way, but that before Heidegger, no one did.[12]

Between March 17 and April 6, 1929, just months after he had ascended to the professorship at Freiburg, Heidegger participated in a seminar and debate with Ernst Cassirer, a leading neo-Kantian, at Davos in the Swiss canton Graubünden, which then (as now) was a center of rest, recuperation, winter sport, and summer play for the elite of Europe. Access to high culture and the life of the mind has always been part of the Davos experience. The confrontation between Heidegger and Cassirer in those icy heights was the intellectual event of the year, very much resembling the great imaginary debate of Thomas Mann's *Magic Mountain* between the humanist Settembrini, an unrepentant child of enlightenment (represented by Cassirer), and the Jesuit Naphta (represented by Heidegger), who wants to rouse people from the humanist "bed of idleness."

Cassirer, an Olympian figure, tall and elegant, had just been elected *Rektor* of the University of Hamburg, the first Jew to hold such a position. His philosophical work on symbolic forms derived from Kant's understanding of reality as arising from the relationship between subject and object; his goal was to unite scientific and nonscientific ways of thinking in a unified philosophical vision. Politically, Cassirer was progressive and an outspoken supporter of Weimar democracy.

Many of those present for the debate at Davos had right-wing inclinations and were unsympathetic to Cassirer's liberalism. Parliamentary democracy did not have deep roots in Germany; it had been imposed by the Allies at the end of the World War when the kaiser fled to Holland, and there was widespread sentiment among Germans that democratic institutions were inefficient and incapable of responding to serious economic and social problems. Heidegger, whose politics were not yet publicly formulated, was no democrat. He was an anti-Communist, liked good order, and was drawn to German "ways of being," often thought to contain a degree of authoritarianism. Readers of *Being and Time* already knew that as a philosopher Heidegger longed for a radical break with the traditions of Western culture in order to reestablish the original, "pure" way of thinking that had emerged among the ancient Greeks. This disdain for the recent past and present moment, combined with longing for old ways, endeared Heidegger to the Nazis and soon-to-be Nazis who made up a good portion of the audience.

Lectures and debates at Davos were scheduled for evenings, and Heidegger spent his days with his friend Kurt Riezler (a distinguished diplomat, philosopher at Frankfurt University, political liberal, and anti-Nazi, who when the chips were down left Germany for exile in America) on "magnificent" cross-country excursions, turning up late for dinner "with beautiful weariness, full of sun and mountain freedom, the whole élan of the long downhill runs still in our bodies."[13] Cassirer and other guests at Davos came to dinner in elegant evening clothes; Heidegger stood out by joining them still wearing his ski outfit. Mrs. Cassirer, who sat next to Heidegger at meals, found his attire unfashionable and described him as an "unimposing little man, shy as a peasant boy who had been pushed through the portals of a mansion. . . . His black hair and those piercing dark eyes at once reminded me of some journeyman from Austria, or Bavaria, an impression only strengthened by his manner of speech."[14]

She and her husband had been warned that Heidegger was a difficult man with anti-Semitic inclinations (in light of his many associations with Jews we can only wonder whether this allegation is post factum) who rejected all social conventions. It was rumored, she wrote in her memoir, that his goal was "if possible to annihilate" her husband's philosophy; but eyewitnesses reported that the debate took place in a wonderful collegial spirit.[15] Nevertheless, the intellectual differences were clearly drawn and positions sharply defended.

Cassirer, the liberal democrat, proclaiming his cultural idealism, maintained that Heidegger's focus on man's finite existence in the face of nothingness ignores the transcendence of culture, and of eternal truths arising in moral experience, mathematics, and natural science. Man is born into a culture that shapes him, and that culture, which is an expression of the human spirit, continues after the individual has gone. While culture may not be infinite in the same traditional metaphysical sense as God, it nonetheless transcends and orders the lives of individuals, and signifies, Cassirer argued, that *Dasein*, the being of man, is not just "the mere self-preserving functions of a finite being."

Heidegger responded that man's efforts to avoid awareness of the impending nothingness, escape the terror of death, and find the illusion of security through diversions all incline him to grow too comfortable in the culture he has created and become frozen into at the price of loss of freedom. By trying to save man from the confrontation with his finiteness, Heidegger argued, Cassirer had mistaken the function of philosophy, which is not to liberate man from anxiety, but rather to deliver him back into his original homelessness in the universe. Then man can embark on a new flight into culture (without which he cannot live); but now with new clarity and freedom that can only arise from recognition of the true position of Being in relation to the void that surrounds it.

Cassirer thought that Heidegger was hostile to all received traditions for no other reason than that they are received; he worried that civilization is a delicate structure that might not withstand the storm winds of Heidegger's radical disdain. For Heidegger the necessity to step outside of culture in order to be free was a matter of philosophical rather than political conviction, but it brought him into the ambit of Nazi thought that would soon explode upon the German cultural scene.

The Nazis did not have a philosophy so much as an ideology. Philosophy is about questions; the Nazis came to power with answers. They misread Nietzsche, thinking of themselves as the supermen whose rise he had predicted, interpreting his call for resolute toughness as a justification for brutality. They misread Hegel and Darwin and concluded that all of history could be understood as a competition among the races of men to dominate the world.

Despite a tortured argument by Emmanuel Faye, full of innuendo about hidden meanings of Heidegger's words and assertions of guilt by association,[15] there is no credible evidence for the argument that Heidegger was already a Nazi in 1929. It is nevertheless indisputable that there were already points of contact between his thought and emerging Nazi doctrine: Certainly he shared in the almost universal belief in the cultural superiority of European civilization in the imperial age, without which totalitarianism would not have been possible. He was also a nationalist in the sense that he had special regard for German language, philosophy, science, and spirit. He believed in a special kinship between German *Geist* and the pre-Socratic Greek spirit that had brought forth Western civilization in the initial awe-struck creative awareness of Being, and also that after centuries of decline the last best opportunity to redeem the West was for Germanic culture to restore the power and clarity of the ancient Greek beginning in a new renaissance.

In addition to his fantasies about German destiny, Heidegger's thought also intersected with Nazi propaganda on the authenticity of rural life, especially at his beloved rustic cottage at Todtnauberg in the Black Forest. He believed that the character of the people there had been shaped over centuries by the hard granite and rugged beauty of the natural environment. This is resonant with Nazi claims about the superiority of German blood and soil (*Blut und Boden*), except that the Nazis meant race and homeland, and race was too materialist for Heidegger's metaphysical preferences; he located the destiny of the German people in their experience of Being—in which others could share—rather than in their genes. Still, Heidegger's antipathy for modern technology and his sympathy for pastoral values evoke primitive German folkishness and the longing for a rebirth of authenticity and originality. The Nazis, who extolled the countryside and the ordinary clod of German soil (but rushed to bury them beneath highways and armaments factories), played on these sentiments, but really valued modernization, militarism, and conquest.

Like all Germans of the period, including German Jews who were by-and-large intensely patriotic before the Nazi takeover, Heidegger was resentful of the attribution of national guilt for the First World War and the imposition of reparations imposed by the Allies at Versailles after the Armistice, which had not been an unconditional surrender but was treated as if it had been. To the extent that he thought of politics at all, Heidegger was put off by the petty foolishness of parliamentary democracy in the face of the real crises of the day: inflation, depression, and the threat of global communism (which had a substantial foothold in industrialized cities and terrified all propertied Germans down to the peasant class). This constellation of attitudes intersected Nazi sentiments, but these ideas and feelings were already widespread in Germany when the Nazis were only getting 2.6 percent of the vote in national elections. Not only that, but the same general malaise, the sense of civilization in decline, was widespread in Europe after the First World War, with troubling implications about progress and the alienation brought about by modernity. T. S. Eliot, for example, who also had right-wing tendencies, was one among many English-speaking intellectuals who shared these sentiments.

With historical perspective one can see that there was a definite orientation of thought through which Heidegger eventually fell—and not merely accidentally—into proximity with National Socialism. Grandiosity, arrogance, pride, provincialism, and ambition would contribute to his slide.

8

◇◇◇◇
◆

FOR ARENDT EVERYTHING BECAME MORE URGENT when Hitler became chancellor in January 1933. The Reichstag was set afire on February 27, and Hitler assumed emergency powers the next day. Gestapo raids and roundups began, and dissidents started to disappear. The Gestapo confiscated an address book from Bertolt Brecht; and Günther Stern, afraid that they would use it to conduct a sweep of leftists in Berlin, fled to Paris. Arendt stayed behind, knowing that she would eventually have to flee, but "feeling responsible," wanting to be "not simply a bystander," hoping to "help" in some way.

In the spring of 1933, Kurt Blumenfeld asked Arendt to help with the research for his presentation at the 18th International Zionist Congress being held that summer in Prague at which he would demonstrate that a tragedy of unprecedented proportions was being organized in Germany. She began making visits to the Prussian State Library to collect materials that would show the extent of anti-Semitism not only in official Nazi circles, but also in private clubs, business associations, and professional societies; the sorts of things that were unlikely to be reported in the German or international press. (There was not much reporting on this after the war either, when Germans and their new allies on both sides of the east-west divide found it easier to blame a small gang of Nazi thugs than to assess what had happened to an entire culture.)

Her research involved risk because the Nazi *Reichstaat* had already passed a law that criminalized criticism of the state as "malicious gossip" and "horror propaganda." But Hannah agreed with Blumenfeld that she was the right person for the job because she had no official association with the Zionist movement, was therefore less likely to be suspected, and even if arrested, was not privy to sensitive information that could put the movement in jeopardy.[1]

Arendt's activities at the library were detected; even at this early date there were ordinary people in positions such as that of librarian who were eager to cooperate with the regime. She was arrested and held in the police presidium at Alexanderplatz for eight days. Years later she characterized the young officer who arrested her as a "charming fellow . . . with an open decent face," who had recently been promoted to the political department of the state police, and was uncertain about his new responsibilities. Arendt played innocent, smiled coquettishly, and told him tall tales about her research and what she had been doing in the library, completely concealing the Zionist connection. He was chivalrous, did not yet know what it meant to be a police officer in Nazi Germany, and kept saying: "I got you in here; I'm going to get you out," which he did. But this experience made it clear that it was important for her to leave the country as quickly as possible.[2]

Hannah and her mother made their way by train without travel documents through the dense Erzgebirge forest (where the wooden nutcrackers are made). They crossed into Czechoslovakia by night. There was a house literally on the border that one could enter in Germany and exit into Bohemia. Martha Arendt returned to Königsberg, which suggests that they did not yet fully appreciate the magnitude of the impending disaster. It was not until five years later, after the Kristallnacht, when things were much clearer but the doors not yet slammed shut, that Martha Arendt made her way out again on her own. After that she and Hannah survived the war together.

Hannah arrived in Paris in the fall of 1933 and rejoined her husband. They presented themselves to the world as a married couple, helped each other financially and with moral support, and had friends in common; but right from the beginning Hannah thought it was time to dissolve the marriage. Stern felt otherwise, and she chose not to walk out on him. He was depressed, working on a novel in German—a parody of the Nazi state—that practically no one in France could read and which could not have been published in Germany. He—who had always been a rising star—felt diminished by the way world history had blocked his opportunities and ambitions, and this made him self-absorbed and introspective at the very time she needed engagement with and on behalf of others. His defeated state made it difficult for Hannah to live with Günther and also made it difficult for her to abandon him. They were still together in 1936 when Hannah wrote to Heinrich Blücher (whom she married three years later and who became her life companion) about her situation with Günther:

> I wanted to dissolve my marriage three years ago—for reasons which I will perhaps tell you someday. My only option, I felt, was passive resistance, termination of all matrimonial

> duties. It seemed to me that that was my right; but nothing else. Separation would have been the most natural outcome for the other party. Which the other party, however, never thought necessary to opt for.[3]

Despite the difficulty of her personal situation, Hannah found Paris beautiful and exciting from the moment she arrived: both French and cosmopolitan, alive with music, art, and every intellectual activity. But even in Paris, exile is a condition full of hardships and deprivations, beginning with one's native language, culture, and livelihood. The Sterns, like most stateless refugees, were reduced to modest circumstances, mostly single rooms in run-down hotels with insufficient space or amenities to entertain guests or undertake systematic intellectual work. To be at home under such conditions in Paris might be ideal for young lovers; but for Hannah home was not refuge so much as epicenter of her resistance to intimacy. She managed to avoid being at home with her husband not only by working long hours in a succession of administrative and social work positions, but also by organizing their time together around the circle of friends in which they traveled.

There were bustling communities of exiles and émigrés in Paris in the 1930s adding to the city's international élan: Jews and leftists from Germany and to a lesser extent Poland and Russia, but also Francophone Africans and American expatriate artists, writers, and musicians, including African-Americans who were received more cordially by whites in Paris than in New Orleans, Chicago, or New York.[4] There was so much jazz in Paris that French musicians clamored for government protection of nightclub jobs to protect both their economic interest and the honor of French culture. Arendt's circle was largely émigrés and Jews.

The friends with whom she and Günther Stern met regularly in coffeehouses, bistros, and other public spaces were philosophers, political theorists, art historians, or literary figures, and all were influenced by the work of Arendt's teachers, Husserl, Jaspers, and Heidegger.

Circles of friends were continuing features of Hannah's life from the earliest days in Königsberg to the last days in New York. That space of love, which is wholly or largely occupied in some lives by children, was occupied, for Hannah, by friendships. In Paris the political philosopher Raymond Aron and the philosopher of science Alexandre Koyré (one French, the other a Francophile Russian, both Jews) were prominent among the friends with whom the Sterns met regularly. Both had studied in Germany. In their conversation and intellectual and political lives, both maintained that historical developments such as the rise of National Socialism involve discontinuities and irrationality in a fundamentally absurd world. Like Arendt, both embraced the necessity of personal responsibility to establish one's own freedom through action.

Koyré, anticipating Sartre, argued that man's existence is nothing other than an *ensemble* of acts done and left undone. To Dostoevsky's famous assertion that if God does not exist then all is permitted, Koyré responded that all is permitted and therefore each man must choose how to live. In a world without God each man is responsible for what he makes of himself; this is what it means to be free. He advocated for a philosophy of history (including the history of science) as a series of dramatic—even cataclysmic—disruptions and discontinuities; not steady evolution or progress, but suddenly something new growing on the ruins of what had been established, which too will run its course and disappear, making room for something different and unpredictable.[5] This explained the rise of fascism, Koyré argued, not, as the Nazis claimed, a fulfillment of destiny and directionality in history. We do not know how Arendt responded to Koryé in conversation, but his influence is clear in her subsequent writing, beginning with *The Origins of Totalitarianism.*

Aron added to this discourse the idea that intellectuals have trouble seeing through claims of historical inevitability because they cling to utopian illusions. As religion is the opium of the masses, he argued, ideology is the opium of the intellectuals; thus leftist ideologues defended the historical necessity of Stalin's liquidation of Kulaks with the same ease that Nazis justified racial warfare. Aron was among the first to see—when antifascists could hardly imagine it—that Stalin was no better than Hitler.[6] Arendt was sympathetic to Aron's anti-Stalinism; and his early recognition of fundamental similarities in the new political systems that had emerged in the twentieth century influenced the development of her thinking about totalitarianism in the years ahead.

When France fell, Koyré and Aron both fled with de Gaulle: Aron to England, where he was editor in chief of the main resistance publication, *La France libre.* Koyré, who was almost sixty years old, was posted to the École Libre des Hautes Études, which operated for a few years as a center of Free French scholarship at the New School for Social Research in New York, and from this base served as a cultural representative of the Gaullist movement in the United States.

Walter Benjamin, a distant cousin of Stern's, was also part of the circle of friends through which Arendt maintained distance in her marriage and continued her own intellectual development in a brilliant informal seminar playing out in the cafés of Paris. In Benjamin, Arendt saw a mixture of "merit, great gifts, clumsiness, and misfortune."[7] She loved both the character of his thinking and the beauty of his language, and recognized him as a polymath genius, an erudite literary stylist who dabbled in philosophy, history, theology, textual interpretation, and literary and cultural criticism, producing minor masterpieces wherever he went.

Benjamin's thought embodied contradictions: He was attracted to Marxism because of its messianic identification with the oppressed and its promise of justice, and for similar reasons was equally attracted to Jewish mysticism and ancient traditions. He was constitutionally unable to abandon the past, which Marxist thought requires in its pursuit of a utopian future. Benjamin was by disposition a collector, not only of books, paintings, toys, and miniatures, but also of observations, quotations and ideas. He approached the past as a vast and growing pile of broken fragments of earlier and other experience, which he wanted to collect, catalogue, and organize in the hope of resurrecting dead moments of past existence in a present moment of insight and understanding.[8]

Benjamin's major (but never completed) Arcades project in the 1930s involved more than 15,000 handwritten index cards filled with phrases copied from old newspapers, magazines, and advertisements laboriously cross-indexed on topics including Paris neighborhoods and the leading intellectuals associated with them: boulevards, street battles, conspiracies, social movements, literary life, prostitution, idleness, the stock exchange, economic institutions, transportation, schools, labor arrangements, details of technology and construction, lighting design, artistic techniques, and so on. From these fragmentary "shards" of thought he intended to create a montage of quotations torn from the historical period to represent in its full dynamic complexity what had been alive in the streets and commercial centers of Paris in the late 1800s. That, Benjamin believed, was when Western civilization began its destructive detour down the road of commodity capitalism; he was, after all, a Marxist. In the computer age, efforts have already begun to realize Benjamin's project with a network of overlapping links technomagically capturing the experience of public life of an earlier time preserved in the collection of obscure fragments recorded on Benjamin's index cards, through which one can move in any direction without an overlay of historiography.[9]

Arendt saw the genius in Benjamin's conception and method. She approved of the way his thinking permitted contradictions in present understanding of the past and future, and she was drawn to his poetic language and mastery of many subjects. His thinking would always interest her. Years later, after Benjamin's death by his own hand in 1940 when clumsiness and misfortune blocked his escape from Nazi-occupied France, she played a major role in preserving and disseminating his then little-known but now-famous writings. She compared Benjamin's passion to that of a pearl diver who hopes to find and collect new crystallized forms and shapes arising in the depths of human experience from the decay and dissolution of what had once been living material. Noting his posthumous fame, for which she was partially responsible, Arendt quoted Cicero: "How different everything would have been if they had been victorious in life who have won victory in death."[10]

Another influence on Arendt in the circle of friends with whom she shared her life with Günther Stern in Paris was Kurt Blumenfeld, a continuing presence and point of stability in her transformed world; and Blumenfeld brought with him connections to international Jewish politics. In Paris, Arendt came closest to embracing the Zionist criticism of assimilation. Other German-Jewish émigrés tried to reassure themselves that they could become French: having been good Germans in Germany, they would also be good Frenchmen in France. But Arendt insisted they were nothing but Jews. In an essay entitled "We Refugees," she joked about a "Mr. Cohn" who had always been a 150 percent German, a German superpatriot:

> In 1933 Mr. Cohn found refuge in Prague and very quickly became a convinced Czech patriot—as true and loyal a Czech patriot as he had been a German one. Time went on . . . and the Czech government under Nazi pressure began to expel its Jewish refugees, disregarding the fact that they felt so strongly as prospective Czech citizens. Our Mr. Cohn then went to Vienna; to adjust oneself there a definite Austrian patriotism was required. The German invasion forced Mr. Cohn out of that country. He arrived in Paris at a bad moment and never did receive a regular residence permit. Having already acquired a great skill in wishful thinking, he refused to take mere administrative measures seriously, convinced that he would spend his future life in France. . . . As long as Mr. Cohn can't make up his mind to be what he actually is, a Jew, nobody can foretell all the mad changes he will still have to go through.[11]

Although this reads like a thoroughly Zionist critique of assimilation, Arendt continued to feel separated from the Zionists because she did not think the Jewish people should withdraw into themselves, isolated, fearing the hostility of the rest of the world, struggling to preserve the racial identity of a chosen people. The Jews, she thought, should not retreat to some embattled ancient homeland, but rather assert an equal place for themselves and for all pariah people in Europe and in the world. One does not avoid becoming a parvenu by withdrawing into a Jewish enclave, but by making one's own way across social boundaries, refusing to conform to social expectations.

It was not only the circle of friends and the ideas and concerns they brought with them, but also the demands of work—always centered on the crisis of European Jewry—that served as a buffer for Hannah in her relationship with Günther Stern. She worked very long hours: first as a secretary in a Zionist organization, then for a while as an assistant to Baroness Germaine de Rothschild, overseeing contributions to Jewish charities and monitoring expenditures. The baroness did a lot of serious work, but she also liked grand gestures, and so from time to time she would fill her car with sweets and toys to visit orphaned and refugee children, thinking they might feel they had been touched by something extraordinary. Whether this was meaningful or helpful in the situation is hard to say, but Hannah as well as the baroness loved to hold the children and see them smile.

The baroness and her assistant got along well, but Hannah was not well disposed to the rest of her illustrious family. The Rothschilds were the guiding force behind the Consistoire de Paris, the major philanthropic enterprise supported by rich French Jews; indeed, members of the Rothschild family were presidents of the organization every year between 1858 and 1948. They, and other Jewish leaders, including the banker Moïse de Camondo, Louis-

Lucien Klotz, the minister of finance during World War One, and Léon Blum, the prime minister of the Republic between 1936 and 1938, were hostile to immigrants, fearing that those from the East would provoke anti-Semitism with their Old World dress and manners, and that left-wing German-Jewish politics would inflame right-wing anti-Semitism in France. These prominent Jews were tireless advocates of behind-the-scenes diplomacy that could only be conducted by them, even though this strategy had by then been shown to be hopelessly inadequate in the rest of Europe. The Consistoire opposed everything that Arendt supported: a boycott on German goods, efforts to publicize what was happening in Germany, and any sort of solidarity with other oppressed people. The Consistoire did not even send delegates to the World Jewish Congress, so unconcerned were they with solidarity among Jews.[12] Arendt believed these elites exemplified the arrogance and self-interest that undermined unified resistance among the Jewish people and left them without allies. She did not blame them for what the Nazis did, but always viewed them as misguided, their judgment disastrous.

After a while Arendt left the employ of the baroness and took up a social-work position for Youth Aliyah, preparing destitute Jewish children for emigration to Palestine. They had to be clothed and fed, and it was necessary to get travel documents for them and to deal with their distraught parents. In order to accomplish any of this the staff was continuously involved in raising money.[13] In what spare time there was, Arendt continued writing the Rahel Varnhagen book with its themes of sadness, loneliness, and unrequited love. Finally, Stern, recognizing that Arendt found his depression hard to bear, capitulated to a separation and, sensing the danger of their situation perhaps more fully than she, immigrated to the United States with his parents.[14]

Years later Arendt explained to her students that it was a mistake to think that German Jews were shocked and disheartened in 1933 when Hitler came to power; naturally, she said, Hitler's rise was very bad, but the Jews already knew that the Nazis were their enemies, and that a large number of the German people supported the Nazis. That could not have been a surprise in 1933. What was shocking, she said after the war, was that "our friends" got in line with the regime: "The problem, the personal problem, was not what the enemies of the Jewish people did, but the way our friends turned on us in their eagerness to be part of the new Germany." The first wave of *Gleichschaltung* (getting in line with Nazism) among Germans at all levels of society (like the librarian in Berlin who informed on her to the authorities) was relatively voluntary, not yet under the pressure of terror that came later; nonetheless, Arendt and other Jews were aware of an empty space forming as their friends and even lovers turned away. In an interview on German television in the 1960s, Arendt recalled that, while she lived in an intellectual milieu, she also knew ordinary working people, and that it was the intellectuals who were most enthusiastic about cooperating with the regime: "I never forgot that," she said, "and when I left Germany I was dominated by the idea: Never again! I shall never again get involved in any kind of intellectual business. I want nothing to do with that lot."[15]

9

◇◇◇◇
◆

IN THE WINTER OF 1932, JUST months before Arendt began her long period of exile and statelessness, she wrote to Heidegger saying that there were rumors circulating that he was becoming a Nazi and an anti-Semite. He wrote back a brutal letter claiming that the rumors were slanders:

> I am on sabbatical this semester and announced well in advance that I wanted to be left alone and would not be accepting projects. The man who comes anyway and urgently wants to write a dissertation is a Jew. The man who comes to see me every month to report on a large work in progress is also a Jew. The man who sent me a substantial text for an urgent reading a few weeks ago is a Jew. The two fellows whom I helped get accepted in the last three semesters are Jews. The man who, with my help, got a stipend to go to Rome is a Jew. Whoever wants to call this "raging anti-Semitism" is welcome to do so. Beyond that, I am now just as much an anti-Semite in University issues as I was ten years ago in Marburg. . . . To say absolutely nothing about my per-

sonal relationships with many Jews. And above all it cannot touch my relationship to you.

At the very time that he was writing this letter, Heidegger was collaborating in secret with Nazi professors and sympathizers to destabilize the elected rector at Freiburg, Wilhelm von Möllendorf, a Social Democrat who refused among other things to fire all Jewish faculty. The student body was overwhelmingly National Socialist and clamored for the university to be brought into conformity with the regime. Behind the scenes Heidegger put himself forward as a candidate for rector, promising that he would join the party, restore good order, and enforce the Jewish Proclamation.[1] If not an anti-Semite, he was certainly an opportunist.

The permeable world of Germans and Jews that came into existence in Rahel Varnhagen's time and into which Martin Heidegger and Hannah Arendt made their own separate appearances in the late nineteenth and early twentieth centuries came to a violent end in the Third Reich. But how did it happen that the same Germans who studied with Jews, visited Jewish doctors and lawyers, whose children played with and sometimes fell in love with Jewish children, supported to the bitter end the regime that gave the world Dachau, Mauthausen, Treblinka, Buchenwald, Terezin, and Auschwitz? We understand what happened to the Jews; the brutal details of their victimization are clear enough. But what happened to the Germans—how did they become perpetrators? This question occupied Arendt for the last thirty years of her life; and her understanding of what happened to the nation was connected to the understanding she developed over time about what happened to Heidegger.

There is very little evidence in the years before 1933 to suggest any racial hostility on Heidegger's part; but there is some. His former student Max Müller reports that Heidegger once pointed out to him with a degree of annoyance that "originally only two Jewish physicians had worked in the department of internal medicine at the University, and that eventually only two non-Jews were to be found in the department.[2] There is also a letter dated October 2, 1929, to Viktor Schwörer, the prominent Nazi sympathizer who headed the philanthropic organization Hardship Committee for German Science, in which Heidegger argues for a scholarship for Eduard Baumgarten, an Aryan student, on the basis that nothing less was at stake "than the urgent awareness that we stand before a choice: once again to provide our German spiritual and intellectual life with genuine German manpower and educators, or to deliver it over definitively . . . to increasing jewification in both a broad and a narrow sense."[3] Heidegger could have been pulling out all the stops in telling Schworer what he wanted to hear in order to get his student the scholarship, but these comments certainly suggest that Heidegger resented, or to some degree felt threatened by, Jewish success and that he was familiar and comfortable with the language of anti-Semitism. Standing on their own, however, these comments are hardly proof of racial hatred; especially not when balanced against his extensive friendships and professional relationships with Jews.

Is it possible that Heidegger viewed Gertrud Jaspers, Elisabeth Blochmann, Hannah, the many Jewish students to whom he awarded doctoral degrees, and his Jewish colleagues throughout the academy all as "exception Jews," and that he held the rest of the community in disdain? Karl Jaspers, who had strong anti-Nazi credentials and clear sympathy for Jewish culture and traditions, asked about this after the war, replied that Heidegger was certainly not an anti-Semite in the 1920s. Perhaps, Jaspers wrote to the botanist Friedrich Oehlkers, who inquired on behalf of the denazification committee at Freiburg University, Heidegger did not always exercise discretion, but crude racial anti-Semitism went against his "conscience and taste."[4] In the same vein Rüdiger Safranski's thorough and balanced biography of Heidegger notes that he was insensitive to the suffering of many of his Jewish friends and colleagues, but that Heidegger was not anti-Semitic "in the sense of the ideological lunacy of Nazism."[5]

Yet in April and May of 1933, just as Arendt was beginning to help Kurt Blumenfeld on the project that got her arrested and signaled that it was time to leave Germany, Martin Heidegger made a public display of joining the Nazi Party and was made *Rektor* of the University of Freiburg. There were pictures of him in the newspapers: Heidegger, the leading German philosopher, with a Hitler-style mustache, wearing a brown tunic with a high collar and a Nazi Party pin with eagle, globe, and swastika. It might have been laughable in a Charlie Chaplin sort of way were it not for his international prominence as an intellectual. At this point it becomes more difficult to make an assessment of Heidegger's true moral position. He opposed a junior faculty appointment for Eduard Baumgarten, the same student for whom he sought a scholarship in 1929, on the grounds that he was too closely aligned with "the Jew [Eduard] Fraenkel," one of Germany's leading classicists, and that he was too closely associated with "the Heidelberg circle of liberal-democratic intellectuals around Max Weber," which included Karl Jaspers. Yet the person he hired instead was a Jew, Werner Brock. A few months later, on July 12, 1933, Heidegger wrote to the Ministry of Education seeking an exemption from the general expulsion of Jews from the University for Eduard Fraenkel, whom he characterized as a "Jew of exemplary character . . . whose extraordinary scientific standing was beyond doubt." It is impossible to resolve these contradictions here, but these letters do nevertheless confirm that during this period he was willing to harness the language of anti-Semitism to his goals and purposes.

Most significantly, as *Rektor,* Heidegger signed all of the letters dismissing Jewish faculty at the University of Freiburg, including the letter to his friend, mentor, steadfast champion, and enthusiastic supporter, the world-famous emeritus professor of philosophy, Edmund Husserl, a baptized Austrian Jew, professing Lutheran, and German patriot whose enthusiastic support over the years prepared the path for Martin's elevation to his chair in philosophy. Husserl loved Martin like a son, and had taken him into his family. "Nobody," he had written to Martin on the publication of *Being and Time,* "has more faith in you than I, and no one knows better than I the depth of the talent conferred upon you at birth." After the war, Hannah wrote to Karl Jaspers that if the letter dismissing Husserl and all the other Jewish professors at the university had been "signed by anyone else, Husserl would have been indifferent and could have risen above it; but as it came over Heidegger's signature it almost killed him. When I first learned of this I thought to myself that Martin was a potential murderer."

Heidegger's enthusiasm for the Nazis was in any case rooted in abstractions far removed from their real-world impact on his Jewish friends (and the actual existence he claimed to prize so highly). He interpreted the National Socialist revolution as a collective breakout from Plato's cave, a dramatic moment in the history of "Being." In Heidegger's philosophy, civilization had been in a state of decline since the time of the awestruck Greeks to whom Being had first revealed itself; humanity had drifted away from authentic existence, becoming absorbed in gossip, the distractions of the "they" among whom we all live, and the diversions of everyday life. The revolutionary moment erupting upon the scene carried within it the seeds of a new and authentic German reality. Philosophy, Heidegger told countless audiences, must not speak "about" conditions and events, but "out of" them; it must be part of the new revolutionary reality. He had always maintained that "mood" determines our Being-in-the-world; now he took the revolutionary mood as his starting point and wove himself into his own dream of the history of Being. Rüdiger Safranski characterizes Heidegger's moves on the political stage as "those of a philosophical dreamer. . . . It would have been different if he had hurled himself into the political adventure without a philosophical justification . . . but he had a philosophical reason for Hitler, he introduced philosophical motives, and constructed an entire imaginary philosophical stage for the historical happening. Philosophy had to be 'in control' of its time. . . ."[6]

In his public statements Heidegger rhapsodized over the spirit and power of the *Volk*, rooted in soil and blood, their granite will like the mountains of the German countryside, their hearts nourished by German sunshine. He applauded the glory and greatness of the new beginning, praised Nazi heroes, and declared that in the new Reich the university would take on the task of bringing into reality a new, selfless, hard race of young men and women reflecting the strengths and the will of the new Reich and its chancellor, Adolph Hitler, who "alone," he said, "is the present and future German reality and its law." He called upon students to make sacrifices, to undertake labor service and military service on behalf of the Reich, often ending his speeches with: "Heil Hitler," or "To the man of unprecedented will, to our Führer Adolf Hitler—a threefold Sieg Heil!"[7]

As *Rektor*, Heidegger abolished the Faculty Senate and instituted a dictatorial system of governance based on the newly established Führer principle. He wrote letters that effectively destroyed the academic careers of dissident graduate students and young faculty members. He went so far as to recommend that the famous chemist Hermann Staudinger (who won the Nobel Prize in 1953, and who was not a Jew or even a Social Democrat) be removed from his position as professor because of his pacifist and antinationalist inclinations in World War One. The Ministry of Culture concurred in this judgment, but the higher authorities "afraid of worldwide repercussions" allowed Staudinger to retain his position.[8]

The last time Martin Heidegger and Karl Jaspers saw each other, in June 1933 at Jaspers's home in Heidelberg, they argued. Jaspers asked how a man as coarse as Hitler could govern Germany, and Martin answered: "Culture is of no importance, just look at his marvelous hands."[9] Hitler's propagandists had a close-up photograph in widespread circulation of the Führer's hands, held in the air in front of and slightly above his head, palms facing outward, the thumbs and forefingers forming a triangle with the other fingers outstretched, over a caption that read: "The Führer's hands organize his speech."[10] Heidegger, who respected craftmanship and the work of hands, somehow found meaning or promise in that.

Gertrud Jaspers survived the Nazis only because the Jewish wives of German men, especially distinguished German men, if their husbands did not desert them, were the last group of German Jews targeted for destruction by a regime that always took a path of least resistance toward its goals.[11] Jaspers was one of those few men who stood with their wives, and his character, fortitude, and clarity of thought helped to keep them both alive. The final time that Heidegger visited their home, in 1933, Gertrud Jaspers spoke directly to him about the hospitality he had accepted in her house over many years, and about how awful and frightening she found the Nazis with whom he had associated himself. Jaspers lamented that Gertrud cried when reading the newspaper, and Martin, oblivious to the moment or unwilling to face it, said: "Sometimes crying helps to make you feel better." Then he left, never saying good-bye.[12]

Despite the foolish grandiosity in Heidegger's embrace of National Socialism, the actual impact of his actions cannot be underestimated: his intellectual stature helped to legitimize the Nazi seizure of power at a time when many ordinary Germans were still wondering whether the Nazis had the sophistication and intelligence to govern Germany. It was no small thing that Martin Heidegger had confidence in them.

Walter Eucken, distinguished as a liberal economist (and also as the son of the philosopher Rudolf Eucken, winner of the Nobel Prize for Literature in 1908), was a participant in the German Resistance movement in Freiburg as part of the circle around the Lutheran pastor and theologian Dietrich Bonhoeffer[13] (whom the Nazis imprisoned and eventually hanged). Eucken believed that Heidegger saw himself as the natural philosophical and intellectual leader of the Reich, and as the only truly great thinker since Heraclitus. Certainly, Heidegger aspired to a historic role as the foremost figure in the regeneration of the West. He aimed to shape and define National Socialism and philosophy for the coming millennium. But he could not compete with Hitler's long-time associate and Nazi Party ideologue, Alfred Rosenberg, whose "philosophy" revolved around the ideas that God had not created individuals but separate races, that only the race has a soul, that Aryan culture is based on a higher innate moral sensibility and more energetic will to power, and that the higher races must rule over and not interbreed with the lower races in order to preserve their superior physical and spiritual heredity.[14] (Rosenberg was eventually convicted of war crimes by the Allies and was hanged at Nuremburg.)

Heidegger's embrace of the Nazis stands among innumerable other acts of accommodation by leading citizens that effectively gave the country over to totalitarianism. Many educated, influential Germans rationalized cooperation with Hitler, believing that the responsibilities of power would temper Nazi extremism. They anticipated that military leaders, businessmen, and intellectuals, such as themselves, all much smarter and better educated than Hitler and his cronies, would moderate and direct the regime.[15] Optimism and opportunism formed a basis for *entente*.

In the summer of 1933, Heidegger was under consideration for the prestigious chair in philosophy at the University of Berlin and leadership of the Prussian Academy of University Lecturers. By then, however, he had enemies within the Party, particularly the Marburg philosopher Ernst Jaensch and Ernst Krieck, a schoolmaster and early Nazi supporter whom the Party had rewarded with a faculty position at the University of Heidelberg. They wrote to the Prussian Ministry of Science and to Reichsleiter Alfred Rosenberg saying that Heidegger's appointment would be "catastrophic," as he was a man who had propped up the old system on all issues of ideology, and had in turn been supported by the old system and especially its Jewish cliques, with whom he shared a passion for hair-splitting Talmudic distinctions. Jaensch called Heidegger a "scatterbrain," "eccentric crank," and "quintessential decadent archetypal representative of the age of decay," and declared that "men who are perfectly rational, intelligent and loyal to the new state argue among themselves as to which side of the dividing line between sanity and mental illness he is on." It was puzzling, Jaensch concluded, that Heidegger had joined the movement at all; perhaps the explanation lay in the fact that "Heidegger always wanted to be a revolutionary, always wanted to be the head of things," whatever the cause, and furthermore was always driven by the "almost boundless self-importance of Frau Heidegger." When our revolution is won, Jaensch warned, Heidegger will start working toward the next one.

Heidegger traveled to Berlin hoping to see the Führer and establish a personal relationship, but he did not even gain access to the highest levels of the appropriate ministries. Returning to Freiburg, and by then aware of growing resistance to his leadership among party stalwarts, he withdrew from consideration for the position in Berlin and delivered a radio lecture broadcast in the region surrounding Freiburg entitled "Why We Remain in the Provinces" as a cover for the fact that he had come to the realization that he had no future within the Nazi movement. In his cabin at Todtnauberg, Heidegger claimed, he worked in proximity to rural life, whereas the urbanite is cut off from that font of strength and fundamental understanding of the world. He described a meeting with a local seventy-five-year-old farmer, who mentions that he has read in the newspapers that "the professor" has been called to Berlin and, putting his "trusty and concerned hand" on Heidegger's shoulder, looks to the mountains of the Black Forest and shakes his head.[16] Thirty years later, in *The Jargon of Authenticity*, Theodor Adorno, who had by then returned from exile to his position at the School for Social Research in Frankfurt, attacked Heidegger's general use of language as vulgar balderdash, referring to this kitschy scene in particular as a washed-out cliché drawing on the "sixth-hand symbolism of the old farmer" designed to replace the need for thought.[17]

In April 1934, Heidegger resigned as *Rektor* at Freiburg. He later claimed that he stepped down because the minister of education ordered him to replace the deans of the law and medical schools with party members whom he considered unqualified, but more likely it was the consequence of his realization that the Nazis viewed him as a polite and deferential tool, not as a national leader to whom they would want to entrust the intellectual mission of the German nation.[18]

Total domination, Hannah Arendt wrote some years later, does not allow for free initiative in any field of life, or for any activity that is not entirely predictable. It was, she thought, a sign of Heidegger's naïveté that he ever thought the Nazis would have a place of leadership for a man who thought independently and whose thought was too complicated for them to understand. "Totalitarianism in power invariably replaces all first-rate talents, regardless of their sympathies, with crackpots and fools whose lack of intelligence and creativity is the best guarantee of their loyalty."[19]

That the whole Nazi escapade was only one year in Heidegger's life does not minimize its seriousness. In his postwar construction of reality, resigning from the rectorate was the moment at which Heidegger entered inner emigration;[20] but in the 1930s he still believed in the potential greatness and glory of National Socialism. On a visit to Rome in the summer of 1936, Heidegger, still wearing a swastika pin on his jacket, told his former student Karl Löwith, who was in exile there, that National Socialism was the right course for Germany, if one could "hold out long enough."[21] Heidegger had not abandoned his *völkische* ideology, his commitment to German rebirth, nor even his confidence in Hitler's leadership,[22] but the Party had too little regard for his intellectual leadership and could not be counted on to lead in the right direction. In his own mind it was still possible for him to feel even more National Socialist than the Nazis, without believing that either nationalism or socialism was intrinsically connected to biological racist theory.

This all took place years before the Kristallnacht, when Jewish property all across Germany was wantonly vandalized and destroyed, and long before Auschwitz, at a time when Hitler seemed to most Germans to be emerging as the final and best hope against economic depression, political stalemate, national disorder, and the communist menace. At that time, many international political figures and journalists were still enthusiastic about Hitler, turning a willingly blind eye to the smashing of the Constitution, the elimination of civil liberties, the persecution of political enemies, and the disenfranchisement of Jews. Hitler's economic and diplomatic successes were so great that had he been assassinated or even died in an automobile accident as late as 1937 or 1938 he would have been lionized by followers throughout the world. If Heidegger did not see the full horror before it materialized, few did; but certainly he saw that mindless intolerance, brutality, and repression had become a way of life in Germany. Why did he never utter a word of resistance? He may have grown fearful after the purge of June 30 through July 2, 1934, the infamous Night of the Long Knives, when Hitler ordered the Gestapo to execute the leadership of the Sturmabteilung (SA), the Nazi paramilitary organization that had swept him into power, accusing them of treason and warning that certain death would be the lot of all enemies of the state.[23] These dramatic events, combined with awareness of the concentration camps, which were first built for German dissidents, and only later for Jews, generated anxiety about standing too conspicuously outside of Nazi led mass conformity. Perhaps especially so for one, like Heidegger, who had conspicuously joined in.

In 1947, Karl Jaspers noted that many intellectuals who initially sought leading positions in the Nazi regime became resentful when they were shunted aside, but nevertheless continued to be positive about Hitler until about 1942 when Germany's military reversals sent them into opposition ranks; then after the war these same Germans claimed that they had suffered under the Nazis. Almost certainly Jaspers was thinking of Heidegger when he wrote that "[w]hoever took part in the race mania, whoever had delusions of a revival based on fraud, whoever winked at the crimes then already committed . . . must renew himself morally. Whether and how he can do it is up to him alone, and scarcely open to any outside scrutiny."[24]

In 1934, Arendt was in exile, and Heidegger, having seen his ambitions destroyed, was in the wilderness at home. The estrangement between them was complete. Hannah may have thought of Heidegger from time to time in sadness or in anger, and as the years passed he may perhaps have wondered if she was still alive, but there was no longer any relationship between them.

10

IN PARIS, WALTER BENJAMIN AND BERTOLT BRECHT became friends. Years later Arendt wrote that one was the greatest living German poet and the other the most gifted critic of the age, and that both knew this;[1] but Brecht had great success in his own time while Benjamin's genius, like Kafka's, was recognized by only a few cognoscenti until years after his death. The friendship between Brecht and Benjamin brought two circles into contact, and it was in that confluence that Hannah met and fell in love with Heinrich Blücher in the spring of 1936. Blücher was strong, smart, handsome—in the sort of way that movie stars are handsome—and more than that a good man in a storm. He was excitable and full of enthusiasms, but still the type who can keep his head when all about are losing theirs. If you were on a lifeboat in a storm in shark-infested water, Blücher would be the companion you would want to have. Tempest-tossed in a dangerous world, Hannah felt safe and secure with Blücher. It would be hard to imagine a steadier or more courageous man, or one more different than Martin Heidegger.

With Blücher, Hannah's world began anew in Paris. Because

of who they were, it was still a world of Germans and Jews (a world that had ceased to exist in Germany but was kept alive in France) but it was new because after years of loneliness and disappointment Hannah discovered that love was still a possibility. Blücher was a working-class German leftist in exile; representative of the class of political enemies for whom the Nazis originally invented Dachau. As a young man at the end of the First World War, he was a Spartacist—a militant revolutionary who fell into the ambit of the newly formed German Communist Party. He studied Marx and Engels and was effective, even gifted, as an orator and as a street fighter, but grew disenchanted with communism as the movement became increasingly dominated by Russian influences after Karl Liebknecht and Rosa Luxemburg, the leaders of the German Communist Party, were murdered (with the tacit approval of Friedrich Ebert, the Social Democratic president of Germany) by right-wing killing squads. After that, Blücher maintained dissident leftist political connections but was increasingly preoccupied with theater, together with his friend and collaborator, the popular songwriter, filmmaker, social critic, and entertainer, Robert Gilbert, through whom he came to know Brecht.[2] Before the Nazi seizure of power, Blücher's life and work had revolved around the countercultural arts and film centers of Weimar Berlin; the very scene that National Socialism abhorred as decadent.

When she and Blücher met, Hannah felt not ready for a new love. She had been living a celibate life for so long that she worried that she had to some extent stopped feeling like a woman, but Blücher would have none of that. "I am aware of what you are as a woman," he wrote to her, "and of what you will be; let me be the judge of these things, for what can you know about them." In the first moment it seemed a little strange to her, even "crazed" to be falling in love with a German: "Everything," Hannah wrote to Heinrich, "speaks against it. What is this 'everything'—apart from prejudices and difficulties and petty fears—except that we might not have a world in common?" But Hannah's independent judgment prevailed, valuing love above the conventionality of the "they" who might not understand such a relationship. A few weeks after they met, Hannah was attending a Zionist conference in Geneva and wrote to Heinrich from there: "Dearest, I think I love you. I mean it. And slowly, very slowly, I am beginning to see that no reasons should stand in the way of love. If only I didn't have such damned good reasons."

"You think you love me," he wrote back, "then I believe you, and I've never believed another woman before. Many have told me that they loved me—but I never believed a single one of them. *You* I believe; if you would only tell me. Put away your doubt and tormented words, better to have my kisses on your lips. If you think you love me, may I be so tender as to say that I long for you?" Comparing himself to the golem, the protective rough-hewn mythical monster made of clay by Rabbi Loew of Prague in the Middle Ages, he wrote:

> With your kisses you have placed into the mouth of the golem a note on which is written: "My darling, I love you!" And now he is singing and jumping all over the place—even if with heavy tongue and bumbling feet. . . . But later he found a very disturbing note between his teeth, which seemed particularly urgent, which particularly concerned him because he owes his existence to Jewish legend. Written on the note is: "Think of the Jews, you rascal! You've snatched away their best woman without thinking of them!

Blücher signed this letter "Your husband," and for all intents and purposes they were husband and wife after that, even though it took several years before they were each able to secure a divorce. Whatever lingering feelings she might have had for Martin Heidegger, and however these may have influenced her thinking and behavior toward him years later, Hannah always loved Heinrich Blücher and the life they made together in the face of catastrophic world history.

If Blücher was not a genius like Heidegger, he was nonetheless a man of substantial learning and intellect who achieved this without the benefits of formal education. An autodidact, he was an authority on art history, the history of ideas, and of philosophy, diplomatic and military affairs, and politics,[3] and he had a more than passing familiarity with poetry and theater. Arendt and Blücher were open and candid with one another and completely shared values about politics and people. She admired his strength, courage, and sound judgment, and felt confident about his love. Even as a child, Hannah wrote in a letter addressed to Heinrich as her "dear, beloved, one-and-only dearest," she had always known

> I can only truly exist in love. And that is why I was so frightened that I might simply get lost. And so I made myself independent. And about the love of others who branded me as coldhearted, I always thought: if you only knew how dangerous love would be for me. Then when I met you, suddenly I was no longer afraid. . . . It still seems incredible to me that I managed to get both things, the "love of my life" and a oneness with myself. And yet, I only got the one thing when I got the other. But finally I also know what happiness is.

Hannah trusted Heinrich's character and his sound common sense as much as she distrusted Heidegger—and trust was the foundation of happiness in her life. The most wonderful thing about her life with Blücher, she wrote to him after twenty years of marriage, was how marvelous each thought the other to be.

In September 1939, Blücher and all male German immigrants in Paris were deemed potential dangers to French security and were interred in camps in the provinces. It was only a few weeks until the authorities determined that Blücher was not a threat and released him, but Arendt was frightened, and became a bit indignant when she received a letter from him saying that for the past few nights he had been sleeping on a nice meadow under the stars thinking about her. She wrote back complaining that this was no time for small talk and sweet nothings, that she needed to know how he was and what was happening to him; and she told him that she was ashamed to be sleeping in a comfortable bed. In a series of letters over the next few days, he wrote back:

> My sweet, there's no reason for you to get all upset. I'm not chatty because there's no place for chattiness in wartime. Above all, one shouldn't make too much of a fuss about oneself. As you can imagine, there are quite a few people here who think of nothing but their own personal destiny—and in response I have gone a little to the other extreme. . . . My sweet, you should not be "ashamed" of sleeping between sheets. Just for that reason I am happier between my blankets. I love you with all my heart. . . . My beauty, what a gift of happiness it is to have this feeling, and to know that it will last a

> whole lifetime and will not change except to grow stronger. You know, you know. . . .
>
> I have patience, and I kiss you . . . [and] in the depths of my being there is a staying power that has its roots in my love for you, which is everywhere, in all my being and all my life. One of the main reasons for my love: our points of view in regard to the big things in life are always the same. There's no difference between us. This is how it is and this is how it will stay. My darling, my sweet love, I am happy when I think you are mine. And I think a lot.

Blücher brought not only love and loyalty into Arendt's life, but also tranquility, stability, and security in a dark time. They were married in a civil service in Paris on January 16, 1940. At the beginning of May, with war imminent, the *gouverneur général* of Paris, fearing a fifth column, ordered that all Germans except the old, the young, and mothers of children report as enemy aliens to internment camps, the men at Stadion Buffalo and the women at the Vélodrome d'Hiver. "Contemporary history," Hannah observed, "has created a new kind of human beings—the kind that are put into concentration camps by their foes and in internment camps by their friends."[4] She was one of more than 2,000 women from Paris transferred to the camp at Gurs in the southwest of France; there were also Jewish women from other parts of France at Gurs as well as members of the antifascist International Brigade and refugees from fascist Spain, almost 6,500 people in all.

The German attack came on May 10, and on June 25—with the British Expeditionary Force encircled at the Ardennes and barely rescued from destruction at Dunkirk, the Maginot line outflanked, and the French army defeated—France capitulated.

In the ensuing few days of confusion, before order was reestablished under the collaborationist Vichy Republic, a small number of women escaped from the camp that Arendt rightly predicted would soon be turned over to the Germans. Slipping away in the transitional chaos meant walking away with little more than a toothbrush. Most of the women at Gurs did not have the strength or courage to attempt it, or perhaps they lacked Arendt's clarity about the Nazis; those who stayed, whether Jews or leftists, were later deported to Auschwitz.[5]

In the chaos following the fall of France, Hannah made her way two hundred miles, much of the journey on foot, finding such rides as she could since there was no organized system of transportation,[6] to Montauban, a meeting point for escapees from the camps, where the socialist mayor was known to be sheltering people in abandoned buildings as an expression of opposition to the Vichy government. Day after day, she wandered the streets looking for Heinrich, hoping for a chance encounter with someone who might have news of him, and then one day they found each other on the street. Blücher had escaped from a forced march when it was strafed by German planes; everyone scattered, including the guards, and he kept going, headed straight for Montauban, thinking she might be there. Together again, even in that disaster, Arendt felt content. They stayed for four or five months with friends from Paris, the Cohn-Bendits (whose youngest son, Daniel, earned a degree of notoriety twenty-five years later as a radical student leader known as Danny the Red, and after that as a distinguished public intellectual, leader of the Green Party in Germany, and member of the European Parliament). Hannah and Henirich got about very little; he used the time to study Kant, she read Proust and Clausewitz. Even under these conditions of hardship and danger, their love gave both courage to bear the present and face the future; it fortified them against angst and defeatism, sustaining awareness that life may have purpose and meaning.

Between August and December 1940, at a time when there were 300,000 names on a waiting list, the United States issued 238 emergency visas; thanks to efforts made in America by Günther Stern's family and Arendt's associates at Youth Aliyah, she, Heinrich, and her mother were among the fortunate few. In January 1941 the Vichy government briefly relaxed its exit permit policy, and they made their way to Lisbon; three months later they set sail for New York with tickets provided by a Jewish relief organization. At that point Hannah was both a continent and a world removed from Martin Heidegger.

II

DURING THE YEARS OF ARENDT'S EXILE in France, Heidegger was increasingly isolated at home. In 1935 he wrote to Jaspers lamenting that he was having difficulty resuming the philosophical work he had set aside in 1933, because he was contending with "two great thorns in my flesh—the struggle with the faith of my birth, and the failure of the rectorship." He fell into increasing disfavor with the Nazis. In 1936 he was placed under surveillance by the German secret service, and while publication of new editions of *Being and Time* continued until 1941 (with the omission of the original dedication to Husserl) new editions of *Kant and the Problem of Metaphysics* were not authorized. Publication of his article "Plato's Doctrine of Truth" was permitted, but journal editors were instructed not to review the piece or mention Heidegger's name, because he refused to obey Nazi Party language rules that had replaced the word "humanism," which has a global connotation, with the phrase "Indo-Germanic intellectual history," which was thought to elevate the Aryan race.[1] Nevertheless, Heidegger continued to think of himself as a National Socialist and remained a dues-paying member of the Nazi Party. He felt, however, that the movement to restore Germany and salvage Western civilization had been betrayed by Nazi officials who did not understand its revolutionary potential as well as he did. When Heidegger left the Catholic Church in 1919, it was not with the feeling that he was more Catholic than the Church, but after he left his position as *Rektor* he continued to feel that he understood "the inward truth and greatness of National Socialism" better than the party.

A few years after the war, he announced in the famous "Letter on Humanism" that he had made a turn that refined and perfected his earlier philosophy,[2] and he dated this change in his thinking to a series of lectures on Nietzsche in the years between 1936 and 1940.[3] Heidegger's 1,100-page treatise *Nietzsche*, derived from those lectures, was not published until 1961; when she read it, Arendt concluded that there had been a significant change in perspective at a point between the first and second volumes. In the penultimate chapter of Arendt's last book, volume two of *The Life of the Mind*, published posthumously in 1978, she offered the judgment that Heidegger had come to see the will to rule and dominate as a kind of original sin, of which he found himself guilty during his association with the Nazi movement. She concluded that he had turned against the "self-assertion of man" which he proclaimed with bellicose pomp and enthusiasm in his public comments while serving as the Nazi *Rektor* of Freiburg University in 1933.[4]

Heidegger's turn was not a rejection of the thinking explicated in *Being and Time*, but an adjustment within it, a reversal in emphasis but not an abandonment of earlier principle. After the Nietzsche lectures Heidegger no longer looked upon *Being and Time* as seminal, or even as a completed work, but as the preparation for his later, more mature, understanding. Man is at the center of *Being and Time*. Heidegger began his approach to Being (the existence of all things) with the being of man (*das sein des Menschen*) which he analyzes under the name *Dasein*. While the term ordinarily means presence (or more literally "being-there"), Heidegger uses it to signify the distinctly human search for meaning. *Dasein* exists only in time, but not the time of chronometers measured in minutes, hours, days, or even years; rather the *nunc stans*, the always-moving standing now at the juncture of past and future. Only man is present in time in this way, always behind himself in memory thinking about what has been, and always extended ahead of himself struggling through the human will to shape the world. Only man is aware of Being and of the nothingness that surrounds it, and only man can ask such questions as "What is man?"

In the Nietzsche lectures, Heidegger turns away from his emphasis on the being of man and toward the centrality of Being itself, which resides behind all things in being, and which desires (or at least has potential) to reveal itself to man, who alone in creation is aware of Being's existence. Being is the quality of "*isness*" that all things share; not only material things from the smallest atomic particle to the universe itself, but even thoughts and feelings enter into existence and take on the quality of Being. What, for example, is the being of love, or of exile, or of a work of art? Is a painting by Van Gogh just oils and canvas?[5]

Without man, Being would never become manifest; it depends upon man, who alone offers it an abode, which is language, through which thought is made possible; but Being (like God) is concealed behind the being of things, as the forest is concealed by its own trees. Heidegger's insight was that Being cannot be known through the will to know; but only through a "letting go" that allows things to be. In his years in the wilderness, Heidegger had come to see thinking and willing not just as two separate faculties of the mind, but as oppositional. In this, Arendt, years later, detected an apology (or as close to an apology as Martin could come) for the will to power that had found expression in his embrace of the Nazis. Man's thinking about the meaning of existence does not arise from self-assertion, creativity, or spontaneity, but from obedient response to the call of Being.[6] These thoughts, with their intimations of Buddhist resignation and Christian vocation, suggest that Hans-Georg Gadamer is correct in asserting that Heidegger never wandered far from the religious impulses of his Catholic youth.[7]

An immediate consequence of Heidegger's turn toward the being of Being is the decentralization of man, and especially of man's will, which is always essentially a will to power, seeking domination and control of the world. Being, which is eternal, withdraws from the onslaught of the will and hides behind the being of things. Science and technology represent man's will to shape and control the world, and are therefore in opposition to the quiet attitude of letting go that allows the world to reveal (unconceal) itself in poetic contemplation. For Heidegger, study of what stars or microbes are distracts us from quiet contemplation of the ultimate meaning of the fact that they are. Things come into being out of nothing and disappear again into nothing, but Being, which paradoxically includes even the being of nothingness, is eternal.

Emphasis on *techne* rather than *poesis*, according to Heidegger, has driven Western civilization along the wrong path since the time of Plato: modern man ceased to be the steward of the natural world and sought instead to be its god. Thus, Heidegger seems to locate the origins of Germany's unfortunate enthusiasm for the Third Reich in Western civilization's impulse to master the world through technology rather than anything in the German philosophical or intellectual tradition. Arendt, who was sympathetic to the critique of modernity, quipped that by beginning with Plato, Heidegger at least came closer to a modern-day explanation than the many Germans who blamed the Third Reich on Adam and Eve's expulsion from the Garden of Eden.[8]

12

◇◇◇◇
◆

THE JEWISH MUSEUM BERLIN, LOCATED JUST a mile or so from the Holocaust Memorial on Hannah-Arendt-Strasse, is one of the city's architectural masterpieces. From the air, the dull zinc-coated building looks like a Star of David that has been broken apart at one corner with the raw edges stretched away from the central vortex to become terminal points of a long irregular line. Inside, the exhibits are organized along three axes. There is no direct access into the building; visitors enter along the central and longest axis, the Axis of Continuity, which begins in an older adjacent building and guides them through exhibits of artifacts extending from the earliest days of Berlin's Jewish community to contemporary Jewish life in the city. Two other axes start in the new building, bisecting each other and the Axis of Continuity. The Axis of the Holocaust becomes narrower and darker with displays that testify to the magnitude of death and suffering, and then ends at the Holocaust Tower, a tall, dark, cavernous empty space. Along the Axis of Emigration the walls are slightly slanted, closing in as the visitor moves further along the uneven and gradually ascending floor. At the end there is a heavy door that opens onto sunlight and the Garden of Exile, a place of disequilibrium where forty-nine irregular rectangular concrete pillars rise askew out of a square plot of uneven stony ground, steeply graded to discombobulate visitors, giving them a sense of the instability and disorientation experienced by people like Hannah who were driven out of Germany into new and alien cultures. Fragrant oleaster grows overhead, atop the pillars, symbolizing hope.

The fate of exiles, if they were not recaptured by the Nazis in places like Holland and France, is less terrifying to contemplate than the fate of those who were worked to death or gassed in camps and whose bodies went up in smoke, or of those who witnessed such horrors and survived to remember or repress their experience. Yet the suffering of exile ought not to be minimized in telling the story of German Jews. Exile inevitably involved deprivation, starting with the deprivation of rights of citizenship, one's mother tongue, and of everything that is familiar about home, of most if not all of one's personal wealth and the means of making a living. All of this was part of Arendt's experience in France, where there was also mounting fear as the Nazis extended their control and influence, proceeding from one diplomatic and military triumph to another.

Yet before the very end, when storm troopers marched into Paris, exile in France had some quality of adventure for Arendt. She was engaged in resistance and heroic efforts to send children to the relative safety of Palestine; and she was still embedded in European civilization as part of an exile community in which there were many people who shared her values and experiences, including familiarity with continental philosophy and the German language. Furthermore, her French was good, so Arendt was not deprived of the gift of easy communication. And from

1936 on, Heinrich Blücher, who fit in so well in Paris society that Hannah never stopped referring to him affectionately as "Monsieur," brought the excitement and happiness of love into her life. It is possible, especially in youth, to find pleasure in one's life even as world history is turning toward disaster.

Exile in America, at least at first, was a more difficult proposition. Hannah, Heinrich, and Hannah's mother, Martha Arendt Beerwald (who had remarried in 1920, but whose second husband, Martin Beerwald, refused to leave Königsberg), were penniless, dependent on support from refugee aid groups, and since none of them spoke even rudimentary English, they had very limited prospects. The first thing Hannah set about doing in a systematic way was learning English. She made arrangements through a refugee group to live with a family in the country in Massachusetts for a month in the summer of 1941 in order to be thrown into American culture and language.[1] Within a year her English was good enough that she could be a part-time lecturer in European history at Brooklyn College. She did not look for social work and administrative positions of the type that had occupied her in Paris, but returned to making a living by teaching and writing. This was what Arendt knew best how to do; and of the three of them she was the one with the most immediate prospects of finding work. As a Jewish refugee with Zionist connections and academic credentials, she had opportunities that were not available to Heinrich as a non-English speaking German leftist exile without any advanced degree.

Blücher worked for a while shoveling chemicals in a New Jersey factory, and then as a research assistant for the Committee for National Morale, an organization whose goal was at first to encourage America to enter the war, and then after Pearl Harbor to stoke antifascist sentiment. Martha Arendt, who lived in a single furnished room adjoining their two, resented Heinrich for not being the principal wage earner and let this be known. Blücher suffered with his failure to find meaningful work and was stung by his mother-in-law's rebuke that her daughter had made a bad marriage, even as he dismissed Martha Arendt as bourgeois. Hannah was both deeply committed to her mother's well-being and to Blücher, on whom she relied as an intellectual partner and loving companion; these tensions (still unresolved when Martha Arendt died in 1948) contributed to darkness of mood and the pain of exile.

In time, Hannah and Heinrich grew to love America, which she described to Jaspers as a real republic, where there is "a strong feeling among many people that one cannot live without freedom." She and Blücher were grateful from the beginning for the safety and opportunity provided, but life in New York in the winter of 1941 confronted them with customs and mores far more unfamiliar than *la vie* in France, and they found the materialism of American mass culture somewhat distasteful. They were torn out of every familiar routine and confronted with the disquieting experience suggested by the disorienting architecture of the Garden of Exile in Berlin's Jewish Museum.

Arendt found ways to remain closely connected to events in Europe. Almost from the beginning she wrote a biweekly column in the German-language newspaper *Aufbau*, which circulated among German-speaking refugees all over the world principally as a forum for German-Jewish émigré intellectuals. Her attention focused on two issues that were from this point on central to her life's work: what the Jews ought to do; and how to understand what had happened to the Germans.

Her first article published in the United States, written in German, was entitled "The Jewish Army—the Beginning of a Jewish

Politics?" This was not a popular idea among American Jews, who feared that support for a Jewish army could be construed as unpatriotic, nor in Britain, where the government suspected that a Jewish army might eventually turn its guns on Palestinian Arabs or on the British army in Palestine. Nevertheless, Hannah argued that the Jewish people needed a military wing for reasons of identity as well as defense. A Jewish army would demonstrate that the Jews knew Hitler had declared war on them as a people and would allow them to take their place as a people among the peoples engaged in combat against fascism. The Jewish people, she wrote, would not benefit from Hitler's defeat if they did not contribute to it: "Freedom is not a prize for suffering endured."[2] This was a continuing theme for Arendt; a few months later an article in *Aufbau* warned that "who does not participate in the war effort cannot expect a place in the peace."[3]

A meeting with Salo Baron, the distinguished professor who held the Miller Chair of Jewish History, Literature and Institutions at Columbia University and an acquaintance of several members of Arendt's circle in Berlin and Paris, resulted in an offer to help her prepare an article in English to be published in the journal *Jewish Social Studies,* which Baron edited. As he predicted, the essay, entitled "From the Dreyfus Affair to France Today,"[4] which appeared in July 1942, became Arendt's *"carte de visite"* to the academic world.

Despite its focus on France, the article was motivated by contemporary debate about the "German question." Lord Vansittart, one of Winston Churchill's closest advisors, had published a widely read book arguing that a continuous record of German aggression since the time of ancient Rome was explained by such inherent elements of the Teutonic character as cruelty, envy, self-pity, and an inborn spirit of militarism. The destruction of Germany as a nation (although not the actual genocide of the German people) would be necessary, Vansittart argued, in order to secure a lasting peace.[5] In America, President Roosevelt's secretary of the treasury, Henry Morgenthau, took a similar position; and on both sides of the Atlantic alliance there was a widespread sentiment that "the only good German is a dead German."[6] Arendt, reacting to this as a kind of racism, set out to distinguish German tradition from the excesses of the Nazi regime. Her argument turned on the observation that anti-Semitism, at the center of Nazi destructiveness, was not an exclusively German phenomenon, as demonstrated by the extent to which anti-Semitism had been continuous in France from the time of Dreyfus to the Vichy Republic. The subtext of her argument was that any kind of racism—including the idea that either Jews or Germans are different than other people—is misleading and dangerous. We may see a judgment here of the type that characterized so much of Arendt's subsequent career as a public intellectual: independence of mind operating around a love of humanity that requires people to be judged only as individuals and not as members of a group.

Arendt held to this position even after learning in early 1943 about Hitler's death camps and crematoria, the existence of which was not widely known or discussed in the media until 1945. At first she and Heinrich Blücher dismissed the accounts they heard as anti-German propaganda; she told an interviewer on West German television twenty years later that even though they had always said that they expected anything from "that bunch":

> We didn't believe this because militarily it was unnecessary and uncalled for. My husband is a former military historian; he understands something about these matters. He said don't be gullible; don't take these stories at face value. They can't

> go that far! And then a half year later we believed it after all, because we had proof. Before that we said: Well, one has enemies. That is entirely natural. Why shouldn't a people have enemies? But this was different. It was really as if an abyss had opened. Because we had the idea that amends could somehow be made for everything else, as amends can be made for just about everything at some point in politics. But not for this. *This ought not to have happened.* And I don't mean just the number of victims. I mean the method, the fabrication of corpses and so on—I don't need to go into that. This should not have happened. Something happened there to which we cannot reconcile ourselves. None of us ever can.[7]

Unwilling to attribute causality for the great crime to Teutonic genes or culture, Arendt struggled to comprehend what had happened to the Germans. How had they, in the variety of their ways of being and thinking, been reduced to a nation of culpable murderers, torturers, accomplices, and yes-men? It was not until years later that Arendt began to recognize the "banal" aspects of evil, but writing in the 1940s she had only Kantian "radical evil" as a starting point: something apart, rooted like original sin in metaphysical foundations of human nature, a force isolated from and contrary to the principles of human goodness. Even then, however, she struggled for a better understanding of the overpowering reality of the evil that had broken all preexisting standards, and sensed that it was no longer possible to comprehend evil simply as the absence of good. Even the devil, she noted, is thought to have a celestial origin.

Her essays "Approaches to the 'German Problem' "[8] and "Organized Guilt and Universal Responsibility,"[9] published in 1945, continued to press the theme that not all Germans were

Nazis, not all Nazis were German, and that the great crimes were not a product of German nature or the German way of being, but rather that German totalitarianism had demonstrated what humanity is capable of bringing about. The culture, thought, and traditions of Germany were not causes of the Nazi movement, but were among its first victims: bastardized, destroyed, or transformed. Modern wars, she saw, are no longer between nations so much as between political ideologies. It was fascism, not Germany, that was responsible for what had happened; there had been plenty of quislings and fascist collaborators all over Europe. The principal force driving this evil had been an unprecedented form of total government—something new emerging in the twentieth century—that subsumed and overpowered the will of individuals. How, she wondered, did a totalitarian system seize control and achieve conformity to its will? How did fascism arise from all that came before, with which she was so familiar? How could it turn the sorts of people she had known, people like Martin Heidegger, who were by no means monsters, into instruments of evil?

13

IN THE LAST YEARS OF THE war Hannah and Heinrich grieved over reports and newsreels from behind the lines of advancing Allied armies documenting Nazi war crimes and crimes against humanity, including the death camps at the dark heart of the Holocaust. They mourned together not only for the dead and the still-displaced suffering survivors, but also for the German tradition, the world into which they had been born, now irreparably broken. Blücher in particular, having for a while imagined that it would be possible after the defeat of the Nazis to return to Germany and live as Germans, teetered on the edge of depression with anger, anxiety, and humiliation over what Germans had done and allowed to be done in their name, and he lost all desire ever to return.[1]

Immediately after the war Hannah's mood began to lift with the experience of joy and relief occasioned by reestablished contact with Karl Jaspers, who had been dismissed from his professorship in 1937 because of his opposition to the Nazi takeover of the university system and his steadfast loyalty and love for his Jewish wife, Gertrud. At the end he and Gertrud were both alive and still in their own home, although it seemed ghostly, he wrote to Hannah, since the world of which it had been a part no longer existed.[2]

Hannah and the Jasperses were put into contact through Melvin Lasky, an international journalist who worked for the U.S. Army and had frequent occasion to be in Germany beginning immediately after the unconditional surrender. Military defeat and total war—of the type the Nazis had pioneered—left German cities and towns in ruins along with the connecting infrastructures of transportation, markets, and services. Millions were homeless, hungry, and transient, including refugees from the east who wandered westward hoping to fall into the hands of American soldiers instead of Russians. In this time of hardship, when there were pervasive shortages of necessities, before there was a working postal service, Lasky brought gifts of food, books, and papers from Arendt to Japsers, who wrote back a delighted note of thanks. For a long time he and Gertrud had worried about her fate, and had little hope that she was still alive: "And now not only do we have your reappearance but also a lively, intellectual presence from the wide world!"

"Dear, dear Karl Jaspers," Hannah wrote back through Lasky (with another package of food), "Ever since I've known that you both came through the whole hellish mess unharmed, I have felt somewhat more at home in the world again." Thirty letters were exchanged between them in the next two years, and each read the other's recent publications and manuscripts. The communication between them was lively and loving, characterized by a shared feeling of solidarity in the effort to comprehend what had happened, how the Jews had become victims and the Germans perpetrators, and to chart a course forward.

Reading Arendt's wartime essays, Jaspers felt admiration for her openness, honesty, passion for justice, and especially her independent judgment and courage in coming forward to say that it was fascism and not the traditions of German culture that had caused so much destruction, especially in light of the fact that so much of the world, including the Jewish community, were unified in blaming the Germans. Jaspers, more eminent than ever, not only because of his work but also because of his honorable record of noncooperation with the Nazis, made arrangements to have several of Arendt's essays published in German, contributing to her rise to prominence on both sides of the ocean. He also sent a copy to her of his own small book *The Question of German Guilt*,[3] to which she and Blücher had a mixed response.

Jaspers was concerned with how the Germans might overcome their guilt, but his thinking was principally psychological rather than political. He saw that it was difficult for Germans to talk to one another, let alone anyone else, about what happened but observed that there was a thin line between dignified silence and denial. He worried that many people did not want to think, but only to have slogans and to be obedient to new masters.

The tens or perhaps hundreds of thousands of Hitler's unrepentant henchmen who had done the dirty work of the regime deserved punishment for their criminal guilt. This, Jaspers noted, would be administered by the victorious Allies at venues such as Nuremburg. Moral guilt, he pointed out, extended further: not only to the perpetrators of the worst crimes, but to all those who knew or could have known but conveniently looked away or permitted themselves to be intoxicated, seduced, or bought; to those who approved of the initial prosperity and order the Nazis brought without seeing it as fruit of a poisonous tree; to those who rejoiced in early victories, or obeyed out of fear, or thought of duty as a higher value than human decency; and to those who were blind to the misfortune of others, were indifferent to evil, lacked imagination of the heart, or ran with the pack to maintain their comfortable existence, get or keep a job, advance a career or gain other personal advantages. Almost certainly Heidegger was in the foreground of Jaspers's thought when he wrote about the moral guilt that attached to intellectuals who thought that they could guide the party and preserve old values, but deceived themselves, failing to see that their fine points and shadings were permitted only after they had already given themselves up to the movement. Their scholarly discourse was a mirage, encouraged by the Nazi leadership because it helped to entomb the German spirit.

No doubt overt resistance to the regime was dangerous, and Jaspers agreed that there is no moral obligation to choose certain doom or sacrifice one's life if it seems clear that nothing will have been gained, but there is nevertheless, he asserted,

> a claim of metaphysical guilt arising beyond moral duty from the necessity of absolute solidarity with others, and this is violated by one's mere presence at a wrong or a crime. It is not enough [thinking here perhaps of his own position] that I cautiously risk my life to prevent a crime; if it happens, and I was there, and if I survive where the other is killed, I know from a voice within myself: I am guilty of being still alive.[4]

The true signs of a German genuinely aware of his own guilt, of whatever type or degree, Jaspers thought, would be an impulse to help others anywhere in the world who suffer with the arbitrary despotism of a lawless regime. He advocated an unending inner struggle to become better people, to do better in the future, aware that everyone comes again and again to forks in the road and choices between the clean and the murky.

Jaspers was not only a philosopher; his initial profession was psychiatry. His two-volume *General Psychopathology*,[5] published in 1913, ten years before he turned his attention to philosophy, still guides techniques for the diagnosis of psychoses; and his method of focusing on biographical data of patients as well as their symptoms forms the mainstay of modern psychiatric practice. It was as a psychiatrist as well as a philosopher that Jaspers advised Germans to undertake an honest confrontation with their guilt in public discourse and private reflection in a spirit of "humility and moderation." This, he thought, was necessary not only for personal well-being, but also as a precondition for the reestablishment of political liberty, the revival of a German consciousness of solidarity with the world, and responsible participation in the community of nations.

By and large, however, Germans were not ready for Jaspers's morality or advice. They were busy rebuilding cities and infrastructure, looking to the future, embarrassed by their embrace of Nazism, and falling into a pattern of silence that lasted until the 1960s.[6] *The Question of German Guilt* attracted relatively little attention in Germany. Jaspers's disappointment that his fellow citizens avoided the challenge of moral regeneration through engagement with the past may have inclined him in 1948 to accept a professorship at the University of Basel in Switzerland, where he hoped to find peace of mind and time to think about philosophy.[7] Hannah was vacationing in New Hampshire with her childhood friend Julie Braun-Vogelstein, an art historian, when she received a copy of Jaspers's little book. Her initial response was warm; but when she sent a copy to Blücher with a note asking him to read it so that he could see "how amazingly this fellow, in just nine months [since the end of the war], has learned to come to an understanding of the new reality," he responded critically.

While honoring Jaspers's "truthfulness and honesty" as "marvelous," and recognizing that his behavior had been exemplary and that he deserved Hannah's respect and loyalty, Blücher was nevertheless put off by the book. He wrote to Hannah that Jaspers's monograph, despite its beauty and noble-mindedness was anathema:

> a Christianized/pietistic/hypocritical nationalizing piece of twaddle . . . allowing Germans to continue occupying themselves exclusively with themselves for the noble purpose of self-illumination . . . [serving] the purpose of extirpating responsibility. . . . This has always been [the function of guilt], beginning with original sin. . . . Jaspers's whole ethical purification-babble leads him to solidarity with the German National Community and even with the National Socialists, instead of solidarity with those who have been degraded. It seems that . . . he wishes to redeem the German people.

In the freshness of his anger and indignation, Blücher was not ready for reconciliation with the Germans as a people; with individuals on the basis of their individual records yes, but he thought that the Nazis had revealed the true nature of the "real civil war of our times, republicans against Cossacks, in other words the battle of the *Citoyen* against the Barbarian." The Cossacks had had their day in Germany. "What's stopping us," he asked Hannah,

> from throwing our chains in the Cossack's ugly faces? Instead Jaspers is calling for loving understanding and discussion, in order to establish the essence of the real German. The debate can keep going on till the Cossacks gain strength once more and smash our heads in, once and for all clarifying what the true nature of the German is: Germanness equals inhumanity. We shouldn't be asking what is German, but what is right. We shouldn't give a hoot for the inner transformation of the German . . . [but for] actions of solidarity with those who have been degraded. . . . A good battle [against the Barbarians] is the best cleaner for soiled souls. . . . Afterward one can still turn to Jaspers for an individual inner cleansing. For me, outer cleansing is more important. The Germans don't have to deliver themselves from guilt, but from disgrace. I don't give a damn if they'll roast in hell someday or not, as long as they're prepared to do something to dry the tears of the degraded and the humiliated. . . . Then we could at least say that they have accepted the responsibility and made good, may the Lord spare their souls.

A few weeks later, after several conversations with Blücher, Arendt wrote to Jaspers that both she and her husband, the only person to whom she could talk about such things, had a problem with the book. Writing in what she called "the first person plural," Arendt expressed concern that Jaspers had overlooked the fact that taking responsibility consists of more than accepting defeat and its consequences, or spiritual purification; the highest priority was not introspection, but action on behalf of victims. "We understand very well," she and Blücher thought Germans ought to say to Jewish survivors, "that you want to leave here and go to Palestine, but, quite apart from that, you should know that you have every right of citizenship here, that you can count on our total support [and that] mindful of what Germans have inflicted on the Jewish people, we will, in a future German republic, constitutionally renounce anti-Semitism. . . ."

As for herself, Arendt continued, she had additional things to say. Jaspers's characterization of Hitler's henchmen as having criminal guilt struck her as questionable:

> The Nazi crimes, it seems to me, explode the limits of the law; and that is precisely what constitutes their monstrousness. For these crimes, no punishment is severe enough. It may well be essential to hang Göring, but it is totally inadequate. That is, this guilt, in contrast to all criminal guilt, oversteps and shatters any and all legal systems. . . . And just as inhuman as their guilt is the innocence of the victims . . . in the face of the gas chambers [even the most repulsive usurer was as innocent as the newborn child because no crime deserves such a punishment]. We are simply not equipped to deal, on a human, political level, with a guilt that is beyond crime and an innocence that is beyond goodness or virtue. This is the abyss that opened up before us as early as 1933. . . . I don't know how we will ever get out of it, for the Germans are now burdened with thousands or tens of thousands or hundreds of thousand of people who cannot be adequately punished within the legal system; and we Jews are burdened with millions of innocents, by reason of which every Jew alive today can see himself as innocence personified.

Jaspers responded very warmly to her argument that action on behalf of victims was more important than introspection, but not to her characterization of what the Nazis had done as transcending criminal guilt. This, he argued, suggests a demonic aura of "satanic greatness" about Hitler and the Nazis, which it was necessary to reject. "We have to see things," he wrote to her, "in their total banality, in their prosaic triviality, because that's what truly characterizes them. Bacteria can cause epidemics that wipe out nations, but they remain merely bacteria."

Arendt wrote back that she could see that what she had written to Jaspers came "dangerously close" to the "satanic greatness" position that she, like he, rejected. She continued to think that what the Nazis had done was worse than ordinary murder, but one thing was certain, she wrote: "We have to combat all impulses to mythologize the horrible, and to the extent that I can't avoid such formulations, I haven't understood what actually went on."

In their friendship, communication, and openness to each other, both Arendt and Jaspers refined their own thinking by embracing the thought of the other. We see a hint of this in the fact that fifteen years later Jaspers's insight—that it is possible for great evil to arise from banal circumstances—was at the center of Arendt's immensely controversial report on the trial of Adolf Eichmann, one of the principle architects of the Holocaust.

Another sign of the openness and receptivity of Arendt to Jaspers is that she drew on her connections with publishers—she was, by then, a senior editor at Schocken Books, and her articles in *Partisan Review, Commentary,* and *The Nation* were attracting the attention of prominent New York intellectuals—to arrange for the translation and American distribution of *The Question of German Guilt*. Despite her reservations about his effort to reestablish the true German character (in which she did not believe) and his emphasis on introspection over politics and power (which she considered misguided), Arendt appreciated the brilliance and sensitivity of Jaspers's characterization of the moral state of the German people, shared his concern that they were falling into silence and denial, and wanted to assist in establishing an international discourse about judgment and responsibility for the recent past.

14

A BREAK BETWEEN HANNAH ARENDT AND THE Jewish leadership had been brewing for some time. As far back as the 1920s when she was working on her Rahel Varnhagen project, Arendt had been drawn to the thought of Bernard Lazare, Theodor Herzl's turn-of-the-century Zionist adversary from whom she appropriated the distinction between parvenus and pariahs. Like Arendt, Lazare had not seen anti-Semitism as an isolated example of hatred of one people, but as part of a broader pattern of racial and ethnic hatred associated with a larger collapse of moral values in Europe; like Arendt, he had been intensely critical of the Jewish leadership, and like her he was eventually ostracized by them.

In her first English-language essay, published in 1942, Arendt distinguished Herzl from Lazare.[1] Herzl created Zionism as a political movement when he was in Paris in the late nineteenth century to report on the Dreyfus case for the *Neue Freie Presse* of Vienna. The anti-Semitism of the French political and ruling elites and the mob shouting "Death to the Jews" gave him the idea that the solution to the Jewish problem was escape or deliverance to a homeland. In a sort of epiphany, this assimilated, secular Jew, who had many positive experiences among gentiles, suddenly came to the conclusion that the whole world was hostile, that there are only Jews and anti-Semites, and that a Jewish exodus from Europe would serve the interests of both groups. Arendt thought it an absurd conclusion that every Christian (including, like Karl Jaspers or Heinrich Blücher, every Christian living with a Jew) is a conscious or subconscious Jew-hater. If there is a divide in the world at all, Arendt believed it is not between one ethnic or national group and another, but between people who are drawn to diversity and people who are repulsed by it. Herzl had hoped for the support of anti-Semites who, wanting an ethnic cleansing of Europe, would help Jews make their way to Palestine. Arendt, on the other hand, like Lazare, who thought the core of the matter was that the Jews were poor, downtrodden, and demoralized, hoped to find real allies among all oppressed groups to oppose every form of racism, fascism, and imperialism.

Lazare had been hostile to the Jewish leadership and eventually withdrew from the Zionist movement because he found it patronizing toward ordinary Jews, who were excluded from the councils of policy. He felt that wealthy Jews offered charity in exchange for political control of the community, and that this meant that poor Jews, the bulk of the people, were oppressed from within as well as without. "I want no longer to have against me," Lazarre wrote, "not only the wealthy of my people who exploit me and sell me, but also the rich and poor of other peoples who oppress and torture me in the name of my rich."[2]

Arendt believed that Lazare had put his finger squarely on the double slavery that characterized Jewish life: not only a hostile environment, but also "highly placed brethren" who are in league with elements of that environment in order to maintain their own position, power, and wealth. What was necessary from Lazare's perspective (and Arendt's) was for ordinary Jews to enter the arena of politics as rebels resisting all forms of oppression and all categories of oppressors.

Lazare died in obscurity at the age of thirty-eight, having been unable to find work. Arendt placed the blame for his death squarely with the wealthy Jews he had attacked, who refused to support newspapers or publishers that would print what he wrote. She cited the eulogy for Lazare written by the socialist and Christian humanist Charles Péguy, who wrote that Lazare's "heart bled for the suffering of the Jews in all the ghettos of the world," that he had been "a prophet of Israel" when the Jewish leadership had been silent during the Dreyfus trial, and that their strategy of ostracism to silence his criticism "set things in motion to assure that he would die quietly of hunger." Little remembered within the Zionist movement, Lazare was nonetheless one of Arendt's favorite historical figures: a conscious pariah who did not believe that the Jewish people could solve their problems by withdrawing from the larger world or by separating themselves from the oppression of others.

Despite her friendship with Kurt Blumenfeld and more than a decade of active work on behalf of Zionist organizations, Arendt's suspicion of the leadership and her disapproval of the increasingly anti-Arab direction of the movement led her toward ever more critical positions. The World Zionist Organization had long campaigned for the creation of a Jewish homeland, a place to which all Jews could come and where they could live as free and equal citizens. Until the end of the Second World War, however, the call had never been for an explicitly Jewish state with an official religion and a culture into which minorities would have to fit themselves with less than equal rights. Historically many Jews had opposed Zionism. The most Orthodox, believing that the restoration of Zion had to await the coming of the Messiah, objected to the creation of Israel through mere human effort; and many politically sophisticated secular Jews, like Arendt's grandfather, for example, had considered the whole idea a pipe dream, preferring instead to concentrate their energies on improving the place of Jews in the Diaspora. Arendt was not at all anti-Zionist in either of these ways.

Prior to the war, the dominant position within the Zionist movement, with which Arendt identified, favored the creation of a secular Palestine as a democratic federation of Jews and Arabs working together to establish peace and prosperity in the region. Of course, there were Zionists who wanted an explicitly Jewish state (especially in England), but they were restrained by a general recognition that their rhetoric and strategy would elevate the hostility of Arabs and make the goal of a Jewish homeland more difficult to achieve.

All this changed in October 1944, with the world war drawing to an end and the magnitude of the genocidal crime against the Jewish people in Europe emerging from the shadows of the Nazi empire into the light of world awareness. The Zionist Organization of America, the largest and most influential section of the World Zionist Organization, partially in outrage over what had been done to European Jewry and partially in recognition of worldwide shock and sympathy, adopted a resolution calling for a "free and democratic Jewish commonwealth to embrace the whole of Palestine, undivided and undiminished."[3] There was no mention of the Arabs already living on the land, not even a guarantee that they would receive assurances of minority rights.

Arendt, who identified as a "general Zionist," a supporter of a Jewish homeland (as opposed to the new majority of "revisionists," who called for a Jewish state), was by then beginning to think of herself as the "loyal opposition" within Zionist politics. She objected to the ancient idea of a chosen people with a promised land as a justification for the resolution of conflicts not on the basis of politics, but of theological assertions about claims of God-given superiority, which she saw as a form of racism. She rejected Theodor Herzl's dream of transporting "the people without a country to the country without a people" on the basis that the million or so Palestinian Arabs were people and that it did not matter whether they were formally constituted as "a people" in a nation or state.

By seizing what seemed to them like an opportune moment arising from the European tragedy, "the Revisionists," Arendt wrote, "had forfeited for a long time to come" any chance of being trusted by the Arabs, and had gone a long way in a single day to create an "insoluble tragic conflict." How could this possibly work out well, she wondered: an explicitly Jewish state hated by 100 million neighbors from Morocco to the Indian Ocean, a client state of some superpower generally distrusted or disliked in the region, compelled to direct its intellectual and material resources largely into military strategies and campaigns. The British, Americans, Russians, all would eventually leave the region; the Arabs—with whom peace was essential and with whom common interests could have been found, but who were now hopelessly alienated—would be there forever.

Arendt argued that if anything might have been learned from the Nazis it was the error of treating any people as second-class citizens; this, she thought, would be inevitable in a Jewish state with a majority or a substantial minority of Arabs within its borders. She feared that the demand for an explicitly Jewish state marked the ascendancy of a new politics of exclusion and that this would be a "deadly blow to those Jewish parties in Palestine [like her friend Judah Magnes, the president of Hebrew University of Jerusalem and leader of the Jewish-Arab peace group Ihud] that have tirelessly preached the necessity of an understanding between the Arab and the Jewish peoples." Now the Arabs would pay for what the Germans had done, even though "no code of morals can justify the persecution of one people in an attempt to relieve the persecution of the other." The status of victim does not inoculate a people against the possibility of also becoming perpetrators.

Jewish nationalism, Arendt wrote in a 1944 essay entitled "Zionism Reconsidered," was no better than any other variety of nationalism, and perhaps worse because instead of trusting nothing but the "rude force" of the nation, which is bad enough, it "depends upon the force of a foreign nation." She anticipated with a degree of prescience that this would be the fate of a "Jewish state, surrounded inevitably by Arab states and Arab peoples."

> Even a Jewish majority in Palestine—nay, even a transfer of all Palestine Arabs . . . would not substantially change a situation in which Jews must either ask protection from an outside power . . . or come to a working agreement with their neighbors.

In the absence of such an agreement, Arendt feared that Jewish interests would clash with those of all other peoples along the southern Mediterranean, who would inevitably demand a "*mare nostrum*," and oppose any outside power.

> These outside powers, however powerful at the moment, certainly cannot afford to antagonize the Arabs, one of the most numerous peoples of the Mediterranean basin. . . . The Zionists, if they continue to ignore the Mediterranean peoples and watch out only for the big far away powers, will appear as their tools, the agents of foreign and hostile interests. Jews who know their own history should be aware that such a state of affairs will inevitably lead to a new wave of Jew-hatred; the anti-Semitism of tomorrow will assert that Jews not only profiteered from the presence of foreign big powers in the region but had actually plotted it and hence are guilty of the consequences.

Furthermore, unlike the Jewish leadership, Arendt did not think that the remaining Jews in the world should all be encouraged to relocate to Israel to assure the spiritual unity and military strength of the Jewish people, nor to assure a Zionist majority in the event of a plebiscite and partition. She observed that

> readers of the Yiddish press from the Bronx to Park Avenue down to Greenwich Village and over to Brooklyn . . . [who for decades] had been sincerely, if naïvely, convinced that America was the promised land . . . are united today in the firm conviction that a Jewish state is needed.

But she also noted that most American Jews did not plan to start life anew in the Middle East, and she did not think that should be the only viable option for European Jews either. Arendt would have preferred for the victorious allies and liberated peoples of Europe to renounce fascism and embrace pluralism by welcoming Jews back into their communities with full rights of citizenship and restoration of their well-being. Instead, the first impulse on all sides, where little had been done to rescue Jews before or during the war, was to complete the work of ethnic cleansing by sending the surviving remnant to Palestine.

In 1946, early in their postwar correspondence, Karl Jaspers inquired about what it was like to work for Zalman Schocken, the famously imperious owner of the world's premier publisher of Judaica. Hannah wrote that she got on well with "the old man," respected his intelligence, and appreciated his respect for intellectual and scholarly accomplishment. Furthermore, as her recent criticism of Zionist policy had placed her outside the new mainstream of Jewish politics, there was no longer anything of significance she could accomplish within the official world of Zionist organizations. She had no choice, Hannah wrote, other than to content herself "with a modest cultural-political opportunity," which was what a Jewish publishing house like Schocken offered.

Her alienation from the Jewish leadership grew more intense after May 14, 1948, when the Jewish Agency, the governing council of the Jewish settlement in Palestine under the British Mandate, which was coming to an end, promulgated a Declaration of Independence, announcing the existence of the new State of Israel. The first Arab-Israeli war, "the war of independence," broke out almost immediately thereafter. Arendt, concerned about the war's costs and general destruction, responded with an essay published in the May 1948 issue of *Commentary* entitled "To Save the Jewish Homeland: There Is Still Time." She noted that Israel's early victories demonstrated military superiority; but time and numbers, she cautioned, were inevitably against the Jews. It was possible to win many battles and still lose the war, since

> [t]he "victorious" Jews would live surrounded by an entirely hostile Arab population, secluded inside ever-threatened borders, absorbed with physical self-defense to a degree that would submerge all other interests and activities. . . . The nation no matter how many immigrants it could still absorb and how far it extended its boundaries . . . would still remain a very small people greatly outnumbered by hostile neighbors.

It has been a precept of Israeli policy that Palestinian refugees who evacuated whole towns and cities during the 1948 war did so voluntarily, and that Arab leaders are responsible for this because they encouraged it for the cynical purpose of motivating other Muslims with an image of the suffering of homeless Palestinians. Certainly there is a degree of truth in this, and Arendt saw that the "evacuation policy" of the Arab Higher Council represented a declaration clearer than all proclamations of intent to expend whatever time and numbers might be necessary to achieve eventual victory; but she did not think that culpability for the new refugee crisis lay only with the Arab leadership. It was doubtful, she argued, that the Arab leadership could have persuaded tens of thousands of city dwellers to abandon their earthly possessions on a moment's notice if massacres, rapes, and bombings organized by Irgun, an Israeli terrorist group, had not struck fear into the Arab population. Recent studies by Israeli historians Benny Morris and Ilan Pappé demonstrate that brutality directed at Palestinian civilians was greater than Arendt or anyone else realized at the time. It was not only terrorist groups but also the

Israeli Defense Forces that organized massacres. Roughly 1,000 victims were systematically murdered in twenty-four Palestinian villages pursuant to explicit but concealed expulsion orders originating at the highest levels of the fledgling Israeli government.[4]

The solution Arendt advocated, the same one she and Judah Magnes had always advocated, was now distinctly unpopular in Jewish circles. She called for a turn away from the dangerous and in her opinion inherently defective goal of a Jewish state with a disenfranchised or displaced minority Arab population in favor of a secular, democratic, federated state of Palestinian Arabs and Jews—a homeland for both constituencies. She had no illusions that this would be easily achieved. It was clear that there would be distrust and militant opposition on both sides. President Truman had suggested that statehood be postponed and that a United Nations Trusteeship be established. This, Arendt knew, could only be a temporary solution, but she thought it would establish a truce, suppress hostilities, allow time for the "fickle" mood of the public to change, provide opportunities for Jewish-Arab collaboration on infrastructure projects involving agriculture, industry, and local government committees under the supervision of an international authority, and could thus give shape to a modern nation state based on peaceful coexistence and mutual prosperity.

Peace with one's neighbors, she thought, ought always to be the most fundamental objective. "The real goal of the Jews in Palestine, she wrote, is the building up of a Jewish homeland. This goal must never be sacrificed to the pseudo-sovereignty of a Jewish state." Success and peace could only be achieved through a solid basis of Jewish-Arab cooperation aimed at building bridges between the Jewish and Arab peoples. Writing in 1948, Arendt thought there was still time—it was not yet too late.

◆ ◆ ◆

Arendt's call for the active pursuit of peaceful coexistence with Palestinian Arabs provoked a response from the self-proclaimed Israeli partisan Ben Halpern in the *Jewish Frontier*. He called Arendt a "collaborationist," meaning a traitor, one who deals with the enemy. Arendt wrote back saying that Halpern had restored the word to its original noncommittal and literal meaning: one who favors cooperation. Popular Jewish sentiment, however, was turning against her; a new unanimity of opinion (which she viewed as always a dangerous phenomenon) in support of a Jewish state was taking hold. Arendt's continued support for a secular federated state and her Cassandra-like warnings of potential disasters ahead left her increasingly marginalized.

A few months later Arendt was a signatory along with David Riesman, Sidney Hook, Albert Einstein, and others of a letter to the *New York Times* that cited acts of terrorism by Jewish groups as a basis for opposing the upcoming visit to the United States of Menachem Begin, the leader of the paramilitary group Irgun, which had led a violent resistance to the British mandate in Palestine, including blowing up the King David Hotel in Jerusalem. This visit, they wrote, was calculated to give the impression of American support for terrorist activities, offering as an example a massacre in the Arab village of Deir Yassin:

> The village, off the main road and surrounded by Jewish lands, had taken no part in the war, and had even fought off Arab bands who wanted to use the village as their base. . . . (Yet) terrorist bands . . . attacked this peaceful village, which was not a military objective . . . killed most of the inhabitants—240 men, women and children—and kept a few of them alive to parade as captives through the streets of Jerusa-

> lem. Most of the Jewish community was horrified at the deed, and the Jewish Agency sent a telegram of apology to King Abdullah of Transjordan. But the terrorists, far from being ashamed of their act, were proud of this massacre, publicized it widely, and invited all the foreign correspondents present in the country to view the heaped corpses and the general havoc at Deir Yassin.

Within the Jewish community, the letter continued, Irgun had preached a mixture of "ultra-nationalism, religious mysticism, and racial superiority," and like the fascist parties in Europe, they had been used to break strikes and destroy trade unions. They beat up teachers for speaking against them, and parents were shot for not letting their children join their group. "By gangster methods, beatings, window-smashing, and widespread robberies," Begin and his terrorist organization, they wrote, "intimidated the population and exacted a heavy tribute."

Arendt worried that, following upon the European catastrophe, Jews now tolerated or even secretly applauded terrorist acts and totalitarian methods on the basis that the moment had come to get everything or nothing, that Arab and Jewish claims were irreconcilable, that the Arabs—all Arabs—are enemies, that "only outmoded liberals believe in compromises, only philistines believe in justice, and only schlemiels prefer truth and negotiation to propaganda and machine guns," that Jews must look out only for themselves because everyone else is against them, "that this alone is reality and everything else is stupid sentimentality." Her other concern, besides the deterioration of the moral position of the Jews themselves, was that the new Jewish politics—either we will achieve a Jewish state or we will go down fighting—was a recipe for disaster, if not necessarily in the short run, then certainly over time. Eventually, she feared, the internal pressure of continuous militarism, the weight of superior Arab numbers, the eventual diminution of support from outside powers, would make a Jewish state untenable. Identifying herself as one who believed that the building of a Jewish homeland was the great hope and pride of Jews all over the world, Arendt worried that it would be catastrophic for all Jews, individually and collectively, if this hope and pride were extinguished in another disaster: "This would become the central fact of Jewish history and it is possible that it might become the beginning of the self-dissolution of the Jewish people. There is no Jew in the world whose whole outlook on life and the world would not be changed radically by such a tragedy."

Arendt's disapproval of the direction of Zionism did not detract from her concern about the fate of the Jews. The first thing she did every morning was to open the newspaper "to see what's going on in Palestine," and in answer to Jaspers's question about whether she felt more German or more Jewish, she wrote: "To be perfectly honest, it doesn't matter to me in the least on a personal or individual level . . . (but) politically I will always speak only in the name of the Jews whenever circumstances force me to give my nationality." She also told Jaspers that she worked and wrote under her maiden name rather than as Hannah Blücher because it identified her as a Jew. But at the same time, she worried about the impact of Israeli militarism and military successes on the character of the Jewish people. As the hostilities precipitated by the declaration of statehood died down with the first (and at the time genuinely surprising) demonstrations of Israeli military prowess, Hannah noted in a letter to Jaspers that Heinrich asked half-jokingly: "If the Jews insist on becoming a nation like every other nation, why for God's sake do they insist on becoming like the Germans?" Alas, she concluded, worrying about Israeli expansionism and reliance on discipline and force as the principal means to achieve objectives, "there is some truth to that."

By 1950 it was clear that Arendt's initial fear of an immediate Jewish disaster in the Middle East had been averted. Israel, despite its small size and precarious position, dominated its neighbors militarily. The war of independence that began in May of 1948 established regional air and ground supremacy for the Israeli Defense Forces, and ended in a series of separate armistices in 1949: with Egypt in February, Lebanon in March, Jordan in April, and Syria in July. Within its new borders the State of Israel, defined by what came to be known as the "Green Line," was about 50 percent larger than when independence had been declared. Nevertheless, Arendt published an essay highly critical of Israeli politics, which she dedicated to Judah Magnes, recently deceased, who was "from the close of the First World War to the day of his death in October 1948 the outstanding Jewish spokesman for Arab-Jewish understanding in Palestine."

An armistice, she warned, is not the same as peace; and Israeli victories in the war had done nothing to change or solve anything. The Arabs, she argued (in what has so far turned out to be a misreading of historical development), would eventually mend their rivalries and modernize their social, economic, and political systems. The only question was whether this would crystallize around revenge and a common hostility to Israel, or an understanding of common interests and cooperation with the Jews, the most advanced and Westernized people in the region. Arab reluctance to begin direct peace talks and Israeli intransigence about the return of Arab refugees suggested, she wrote, that the first course was more likely, "but all considerations of the self-interest of both parties speak for the second."

A "mere" armistice, Arendt worried, would force the new Israeli state to organize the whole people for permanent military mobilization. The Israelis would do well to be cautioned by the example of Sparta that even a highly effective and dedicated tribe of warlike people can dominate their neighbors for only so long.

Peace, she argued, is the only guarantor of a secure and prosperous future; and the achievement of peace would require from Israel a humane response to the Arab refugee problem. Even if it could be argued that Palestinian Arabs had left their homes at the beginning of the war "voluntarily" in a panic produced by Arab propaganda, atrocities such as the massacre at Deir Yassin (and as we now know at many other Palestinian villages as well) established a degree of Jewish culpability. It was disquieting that the very men who pointed to the tragedy of Jewish displaced persons in Europe as the chief argument for mass immigration into Palestine were now helping to create an additional category of displaced persons in the Holy Land.

From Arendt's perspective, Jews and Arabs were both oppressed people, both badly served by their own leadership. The role she envisioned for the Jewish people in a new homeland in the Middle East involved the pursuit of justice, freedom and prosperity in league with moderate elements among the Arabs, against the interests of the leadership on both sides if necessary. Zionist leaders, wanting a Jewish state with the smallest possible Arab population, were abandoning traditional Jewish humanitarian values and thus assuring a legacy of war for coming generations; and neither time nor numbers were on their side.

In 1952, Arendt delivered a final tribute to Judah Magnes,

whom she imagined as one of the thirty-six unknown righteous men of ancient Jewish legend without whose existence the world would go to pieces. In it she noted that, despite military victories, nothing had really changed in Israel since his death. The Arab problem was still what it always had been, "the only real political and moral issue in Israeli politics," and not a single peace treaty had yet been concluded with any of Israel's Arab neighbors. Who a man is, she wrote, is not clear until he is dead: "The eternity into which we say that a man passes when he dies is also the eternal essence that he represented while he lived and which is never clearly revealed to the living before his death. *Magnes was the conscience of the Jewish people,* and much of that conscience has died with him—at least for our time."

Having no illusion that she could play such a role among the Jewish people, or that she could be effective in the maelstrom of international politics, Arendt withdrew from the arena into a deep public silence and did not write on Jewish politics or Zionism again until a decade later (when she reported on the trial of Adolf Eichmann), although she did visit Israel in October 1955.

Hannah was happy to see cousins and was impressed by the building up of cities and the agricultural transformation of the desert that had been accomplished by the Jews "in this pigsty that calls itself the Near East;" but she was nonetheless deeply disquieted by a pervasive attitude of sadness and fear that left her feeling the situation was hopeless. "Everyone, with very few exceptions," she wrote to Heinrich, "is idiotic, often to an outlandish degree."

> And the idiocy is right in front of everyone's eyes. Here in Jerusalem I can barely go for a walk, because I might turn the wrong corner and find myself "abroad," i.e., in Arab terri-

> tory. Essentially it's the same everywhere. On top of that, they treat the Arabs, those still here, in a way that in itself would be enough to rally the whole world against Israel. When they see a United Nations car, which makes things easier here, they curse. Everyone is afraid of war *and* is a warmonger. . . . [T]here's also the internal terrorism of Orthodoxy. Amazingly enough nobody is really against them, and so this . . . power-hungry pack is becoming more and more insolent. And this despite the fact that the majority isn't even devout.

She wrote to Heinrich from Istanbul at the end of her visit that she had "escaped, relieved and sad from a hysterical, half-panic-stricken, half-boisterous war-spirit" that engulfed the whole of Israel. It seemed to her a madhouse where no one really wants war, "but with all the shouting going on, needless to say, the whole thing can explode quite easily. . . . I really feel sorry for those people," she ended, "and . . . worried for them."

At about the same time, Hannah received a letter from Karl Jaspers saying that he had recently had a visitor from Tel Aviv, an old doctor from Berlin who declared, among other strange claims about the Israeli situation, that due to shootings along the border, "more Jews have died since the cease fire than during the war." Jaspers found it "bizarre" that these claims came from a man who was clearly an admirable person, decent, open, and helpful, but whose militarism, seemingly unhinged from objective reality, gave him the appearance of an "exemplary Prussian."

15

Arendt's writing about the Jewish question and the German question, much of which appeared in relatively obscure journals during her years in exile, came to fruition in *The Origins of Totalitarianism*, a sort of grand synthesis of a decade of thinking about the destruction of the world and civilization into which she had been born. This book, which the *New York Times* reviewed as "the work of one who has thought as well as suffered" and which impressed Raymond Aron "by the strength and subtlety of its analyses," established her prominence as a political thinker and public intellectual. It was only indirectly relevant to the discourse on Zionism in which Hannah was such an active participant, because its focus was principally on events that had transpired in Europe. Heinrich Blücher, to whom the book is dedicated, was her principal thinking partner in this effort, and assisted with the research. Still in grief and sorrow, and with a tendency to lament, "but no longer in speechless outrage and impotent horror,"[1] they focused together on questions about the immediate past with which their generation had been forced to live: "*What happened? Why did it happen? How could it have happened?*"

The term *totalitario* was coined by Giovanni Gentile, the leading theorist of Italian Fascism, to refer to the totalizing structure, goals, and ideology of a state directed at the mobilization of entire populations and control of all aspects of social life including business, labor, religion, and politics.[2] Arendt adopted this term to characterize a new form of political mobilization of the masses that had emerged in the twentieth century, not just in Italy and Germany, but in the Soviet Union as well; something that could emerge in other places too, and without which humanity "might never have known the truly radical nature of Evil."[3]

Totalitarian regimes differ from the dictatorships of the past in which tyrants used brute force to oppress the masses. The totalitarian leader draws his legitimacy and inspiration from the love of the people, and they receive their position within the nation and their way of being from him. Hitler's popularity arose from a sort of *danse macabre* involving the leader and the led in gradual steps forward and back guided by utopian populist themes, ideological self-justifications, propaganda, and the use of terror to exterminate "enemies" and frighten opponents—ultimately to render the masses docile and obedient, making all men equally superfluous in a system dominated by a single man, bringing a final end to all diversity of opinions and interests among individual human beings, and thus an end to politics.

By "origins" Arendt specifically did not mean causes, because she did not believe that human affairs are governed by destiny, but rather that antecedents are crystallized into origins only after events have materialized (otherwise it would be possible to predict the future). For us it is only possible to trace history backward.[4] In making sense of what had happened to the Germans, Arendt focused on two related antecedents of totalitarianism: imperialism and anti-Semitism, both of which also played a role in shaping the Israeli experience.

Late-nineteenth-century imperialism promoted the development of brutal modern industrialized and bureaucratic technologies of exploitation and mass murder. Capitalism promoted personal initiative, individuality, liberty, democracy, and a degree of prosperity at home, but brought with it an insatiable, destructive appetite for precious stones and metals, ivory, rubber, timber, and other resources, including slaves. All were abundant in Africa, where natives were defenseless against Europeans waging total war with modern weapons. If there had not been earlier traditions of race thinking on which to build, Arendt wrote, the scramble for Africa would have had to invent racism to explain and excuse its reign of mass murder and exploitation.

The years of pan-European genocide in Africa at the beginning of the twentieth century were the golden period of German-Jewish enlightenment and emancipation, but the place of the Jew in society remained problematic in nationalist and racist thinking. The existence of the Jews in the Diaspora demonstrates that a "nation" requires a sense of affiliation among its people more than even territory. That the Jews are the sole surviving "people" of the ancient world suggests that in (an imagined) competition among the races, the Jews are formidable competitors.[5]

Anti-Semitism was of particular interest to Arendt, not only because of what it had produced in Europe, but also because the fear and memory of it had become the driving force in Jewish politics. It seemed outrageous to her that "so small (and in world politics, so unimportant) a phenomenon as the Jewish question and antisemitism could become the catalytic agent for, first, the

Nazi movement, then a world war, and finally the establishment of death factories." The catastrophic defeats suffered by the whole community of European nations began with the catastrophe of the Jewish people. It was particularly easy, she wrote, for the Nazis to begin the dissolution of the precarious European balance of power with the elimination of the Jews, and particularly difficult for non-Jews to understand that more was involved in this elimination than an unusually cruel nationalism, or an ill-timed revival of "old prejudices." When the catastrophe began with the Jews, all the other peoples of Europe were prepared to consider them a "special case" whose history follows exceptional laws; they did not perceive the underlying commonality between anti-Semitism and the intense nationalist competition of imperialism with its concomitant doctrines of racial inferiority.

It distressed Arendt greatly that the breakdown of European solidarity that began with the persecution of the Jews was mirrored in a breakdown of Jewish solidarity. When the persecution of German Jews began, Jews of other European countries clung to a myth that they were safe on the basis that German Jews constituted an exception. "Similarly the collapse of German Jewry was preceded by its split into innumerable factions, each of which believed and hoped its basic human rights would be protected by special privileges" such as "having been a veteran of World War I, the child of a veteran, or the proud son of a father killed in action." The annihilation of all individuals of Jewish origin, she wrote, "was preceded by the bloodless destruction and self-dissolution of the Jewish people." In Arendt's view, the absence of solidarity among Jews—and between them and other oppressed peoples—was a necessary condition for the success of the radical evil of Hitler and his accomplices. Yet she also made clear that the victims were not responsible for the suffering imposed upon them, and that ethical judgments about the behavior of individuals caught up in the final solution are almost impossible. When a man identified as a Jewish leader was given the alternative of betraying and thus murdering his friends or having his wife and children sent to their death—when even suicide would mean the immediate murder of his own family—how can he decide? "The alternative is no longer between good and evil, but between murder and murder. Who," Arendt wondered "could solve the moral dilemma of the Greek mother who was allowed by the Nazis to choose which of her three children should be killed?" No one touched by fascism—even as a victim—is exempt from having to think about what they did or did not do, or might have done.

Arendt counted the Jews among the nations of European people and did not consider them exempt from political responsibility for what had transpired. She rejected the idea that eternal anti-Semitism was simply a fact of history, and argued that a degree of responsibility for the persistence of anti-Semitism lies with the leaders of Jewish communities—the privileged parvenus with wealth and access to power who had governed their impoverished brethren through economic power and philanthropy, consistently aligning themselves with the wrong and ultimately losing side in national and European politics. They preferred monarchies to republics because they instinctively mistrusted the mob. They did not understand, Arendt argued, that over time, as various classes of society came into conflict with the state, ordinary people became anti-Semitic because the Jewish leadership invariably aligned their communities with whoever was in power. She did not offer this as a justification for what happened, but as part of an effort to understand how it could have happened.

16

ALMOST IMMEDIATELY AFTER THE WAR, HANNAH and Karl Jaspers had begun corresponding about the possibility that she would come for a visit, although it was not a real possibility at the time; not only because Hannah lacked the resources for international travel, but also because travel to occupied Germany was complicated, particularly for a stateless person. Even after Jaspers had accepted a faculty appointment in Switzerland at the University of Basel, where he was received with great honor, Hannah still did not have the necessary funds, and was too busy completing the 700-page manuscript of *Origins*, to be able to travel. By the fall of 1949, however, with the book in press and travel restrictions eased, Arendt, now past forty and rising to distinction as an editor, author, and public intellectual, was able to make a visit to Europe, where important work awaited her.

At the end of the war American troops discovered depots filled with millions of books and artifacts that had been seized by the Nazis in their effort to eradicate Jewish life in Europe, and to which the Germans now referred euphemistically as abandoned or "ownerless" property. A tremendous effort undertaken by the United States Army in collaboration with the Library of Congress resulted in the return of vast amounts of this property to rightful owners, but by 1948 there were more than half a million books and thousands of religious objects whose owners could not be identified or found. The Commission on European Jewish Cultural Reconstruction, a group of scholars organized and led by Professors Salo Baron and Jerome Michael (both at Columbia University) was invited by the Library of Congress to play a role in continuing to search for rightful owners or their heirs, or failing that, to distribute these materials in ways that would make a contribution to Jewish communities in the United States and abroad.[1] Baron and Michael created a subsidiary organization for this purpose, Jewish Cultural Reconstruction, Inc., and invited Arendt to serve as its executive director.[2]

In this capacity Arendt made her return to Europe. She set in place mechanisms to continue searching for rightful owners and for the distribution of hundreds of thousand of books, Torahs, and ritual objects for which ownership could not be established to institutions of Jewish learning in Israel, the United States, western Europe, and other places where Jewish communities survived. This trip also provided a first opportunity to survey the wreckage of her earlier life, forever disrupted by eighteen years of exile and statelessness, to reestablish and rebuild old friendships, and to make a first halting and imperfect reconciliation with Martin Heidegger.

She flew to Paris at the end of November, writing to Heinrich Blücher from there that air travel was "indescribably marvelous," and that Paris was still beautiful and lively. Then at the beginning of December she moved on to Wiesbaden and Bonn to begin work on the reclamation of Jewish property. Her first impressions were of the gray shortness of the winter day in Germany compared to New York (which, despite the differences in climate, is on the same latitude as Naples, Italy), and the reluctance of the Germans to confront the past, yielding instead to the very silence Jaspers had anticipated and feared. She wrote to Heinrich (her "Dear Snubby") that a new Jewish question seemed to reside behind every polite conversation: "How many did you kill?" even though she knew the honest answer in most cases would have been none. Heinrich was right, she told him, to want never to go back:

> The lump of sentimentality that begins to rise gets stuck in one's throat. . . . After one has spent a week here reading every newspaper, all the way from right to left, one is ready to go back home. And everything is written in a tone of gloating. What's true is, that *everyone's* against [rearmament for participation in NATO and the Cold War]. The newspapers express it more or less like this: You see, now you suddenly want us to become soldiers –but ha ha, now we're pacifists. . . . Yet there's this deceptive familiarity in everything, above all the landscape (an indescribably wonderful reunion!), towns which one suddenly remembers because one's feet know so well which way to go.

Silence about the past—about what had happened, how it had happened, who had done what—was oppressive: the proverbial elephant, unspoken of, in the room. Everyone knew there were Nazis among them, but no one spoke of it because it was Uncle Willi or Fritz and Käthe next door, and why make trouble? Arendt sensed that Nazi political influence was gone and that few Germans remained true believers, but she also saw that among the many new Christian and Social Democrats there were quite a few who missed the good old days of Hitler's rule before the war. The West Germans were too focused on the future—establishing democracy, rebuilding and improving the infrastructure and economy, salvaging what could be salvaged of a German way of Being—to grieve over their own losses or the evil they had brought about. They were all "living off lifelong illusions," she wrote to Heinrich, and "working like mad." The towns were still in ruins after bombings of unprecedented magnitude in the air war, but the ruins had already been swept clean.

> The sight of Germany's destroyed cities and the knowledge of German concentration and extermination camps have covered Europe with a cloud of melancholy. . . . But nowhere is this nightmare of destruction and horror less felt and less talked about than in Germany itself. . . . Amid the ruins Germans mail each other picture postcards still showing the cathedrals and market places, the public buildings and bridges that no longer exist. And the indifference with which they walk through the rubble has its exact counterpart in the absence of mourning for the dead or in the apathy with which they react, or, rather, fail to react, to the fate of the refugees in their midst. This general lack of emotion . . . [and] apparent heartlessness . . . is only the most conspicuous outward symptom of a deep-rooted, stubborn, and at times vicious refusal . . . to come to terms with what really happened.[3]
>
> Watching the Germans busily stumble through the ruins of a thousand years of their own history, shrugging their shoulders at the destroyed landmarks or resentful when reminded of the deeds of horror that haunt the whole surrounding world, one comes to realize that busyness has become their

> chief defense against reality. And one wants to cry out: But this is not real—real are the ruins, real are the past horrors, real are the dead whom you have forgotten. But they are living ghosts, whom speech and argument, the glance of human eyes and the mourning of human hearts, no longer touch.[4]

In mid-December, Arendt arrived in Basel, where she stayed for more than two weeks, celebrating the New Year at mid-century with Karl and Gertrud Jaspers, feeling as if she were a member of the family; and there she recaptured something of the German *Gemütlichkeit* (comfortable hominess) she had known in youth. Basel—a fortified center of commerce and trade since the Middle Ages controlling both banks of the Rhine at a favorable location just above the Lake of Constance—is Swiss, but shares borders with the heavily German-influenced Alsace region of France, and the Schwartzwald in Germany. The city is close to Freiburg and Heidegger's *hütte* at Todtnauberg, and not more than four or five hours by car from Heidelberg, where Arendt had been Jaspers's student in the 1920s. Even the predominant language in this multilingual Swiss city is a German dialect, *Schweizerdeutsche*. Basel had never been bombed, had never experienced Nazi control or suffered defeat. Here, what had been seemed still to exist.

In moral and historical terms Swiss innocence turned out to be something of a deception. Switzerland is honored for its neutrality in all wars since 1815, and the Swiss did not participate in the burden of guilt that fell on Germany and other Axis and even occupied countries. What was not clear at the time was the extent to which the Nazis benefited from Swiss neutrality. Hitler called Switzerland his "little porcupine," and historians have since shown how the nation's vaunted banking system was a conduit for German access to world markets and a repository for Nazi plunder. After the war the privacy provisions of Swiss law allowed the banks to continue profiting by retaining and shielding stolen property (vaults full of currency, precious metals, jewels, antiques, and masterpieces of art), denying access and information to the victims from whom it had been stolen.[5]

All of Europe played a part in the extreme horrors of the Nazis, but only Germany was completely unable to avoid public guilt and shame. The Austrians presented themselves as first victims rather than willing participants through *Anschluss*; the Italians denied their Fascism was serious, pointing to their having turned on Mussolini and welcomed the Allies; the French remembered the glorious Resistance more than ignoble Vichy. Neutral Switzerland was also running from its past, but this was not obvious to anyone in 1950. In Basel, Arendt found an undestroyed Germanic city where there was no sense of oppressive silence because there was no public awareness of the extent of Swiss complicity; in this setting, things may have seemed normal to both Arendt and Jaspers. It was not until forty years later that historical scholarship and a few lawsuits began to raise fresh questions about the meaning of Swiss neutrality in the face of Nazi genocide.

To her great relief Arendt found Jaspers flourishing in splendid condition in his new environment, "completely natural and unforced, without inhibitions, totally young and alive, and ready to tackle anything;" and Gertrud's kindness, gracious hospitality, and intelligent conversation left Arendt feeling very much at home in her house. Every day Arendt and Jaspers spent many hours talking, not only about philosophy, literature, publishers, and world politics, but also very intimately, with Jaspers mostly listening and Arendt talking without inhibition. Jaspers had, after all, first achieved distinction as a psychiatrist, and though he became even more distinguished as a philosopher, he never lost his interest in people or his gift for encouraging them to talk about themselves. In this way he learned that the ease and speed with which doors had opened for her in America left Hannah feeling that there was something a little "uncanny" about her successes. They also talked about the bad years with their horrors and miraculous strokes of luck, of which the single greatest was that she had met Heinrich Blücher, with whom she found love and security in a time of belligerence and destruction. Jaspers, ever committed to the idea of the "good German," whose very being contradicts the possibility that the Nazis were the natural outgrowth of German tradition and culture, wrote a note to Blücher (whose picture he also studied under a magnifying lens)[6] saying that Hannah revealed little about him in direct conversation, but her indirect communication made it clear that the two of them had survived and overcome everything through their togetherness. Blücher appealed to him, Jaspers wrote, as one of the very rare "true Germans in whose existence one rejoices," and expressed his hope they would meet one day.[7]

Martin Heidegger was also a topic in Hannah's conversation with Jaspers. She confessed her affair twenty-five years earlier, and he replied with what she described in a letter to Heinrich as totally inimitable matter-of-factness: "How very exciting." But she did not confess that she was thinking about visiting Heidegger, or that Blücher, from whom she had no secrets about the past, admired the quality of Heidegger's writing, and knowing that public humiliation and depression were interfering, encouraged Hannah to do what she could to help him to work in peace. Arendt had been thinking and writing about Heidegger during her years in exile. He was in some ways emblematic for her of what had happened to the Germans. Arendt often said that for her every thought was an afterthought, a reflection on earlier experience; Heidegger's role as a Nazi was part of the experience about which she had been thinking. What had happened to him and what he had done were illustrative of the phenomena she was struggling to comprehend. Right after the war Arendt published two essays in which she discussed Heidegger critically.

In "What Is Existential Philosophy?" Arendt traced the development of existentialism from Kierkegaard through Husserl's phenomenology to Jaspers, Heidegger, and the generation of postwar French writers like Sartre and Camus who built on them. Kierkegaard began by setting against Hegel's system "which presumed to comprehend and explain the 'whole,' . . . the single human being, for whom there is neither place nor meaning in a totality controlled by the world spirit."[8] Kierkegaard's point of departure is the individual's sense of subjectivity and of being lost and alone in a world in which nothing is certain but death.

> Death is the event in which I am definitely alone, an individual cut off from everyday life. Thinking about death becomes an "act" because in it man makes himself subjective and separates himself from the world and everyday life with other men. . . . On this premise rests not only the modern preoccupation with the inner life but also fanatical determination, which also begins with Kierkegaard, to take the moment seriously, for it is the moment alone that guarantees existence. . . .

Only Nietzsche and Jaspers, she wrote, had used the fact of death as a starting point for a life-affirming philosophy, in which man's existence is not simply a matter of Being, but rather a form of human freedom, not something given so much as an ensemble of possibilities. For Jaspers "man achieves reality only to the extent that he acts out of his own freedom rooted in spontaneity and 'connects through communication with the freedom of others.' " Man has the capacity to make choices, and becomes himself through the decisions he makes in each moment.

Heidegger, on the other hand, like Kierkegaard himself, interpreted death as proof of man's "nothingness"; and Arendt made clear her preference for the "playful metaphysics" of Jaspers over Heidegger's embrace of death as the guarantee of each man's individuality. Heidegger's self-centered egoism, she wrote, replaced the Kantian notion (and the fundamental principle of the French Revolution and of modern democracy) that each man represents humanity and that the debasement of any individual debases all, and misses completely the fact that man inhabits the earth together with others. Humanity, she argued, is not a collection of atomized individuals coexisting on a common ground that is alien to their self-centered nature. In a long footnote she inquired whether Heidegger's philosophy has been taken "unduly seriously because it concerns itself with very serious matters"; she notes that it is his political behavior as a Nazi that deserves to be taken seriously, concluding that his "complete lack of responsibility is attributable to a spiritual playfulness" stemming from delusions of genius in conjunction with despair.

Heidegger is also mentioned critically in an essay published just after the death camps had been liberated and the world had its first vision of the corpses, survivors, and instruments of torment and mass murder, in which Arendt assessed the culpability of various elements of German society for the deaths of millions of Jews through a method of accumulated terror:

> First came calculated neglect, deprivation, shame, when the weak in body died together with those strong and defiant enough to take their own lives. Second came outright starvation, combined with forced labor, when people died by the thousands but at different intervals . . . according to their stamina. Last came the death factories—and they all died together, the young and the old, the weak and the strong, the sick and the healthy; not as people, not as men and women, children and adults, boys and girls, not as good and bad, beautiful and ugly—but brought down to the lowest common denominator of organic life itself, plunged into the darkest and deepest abyss of primal equality, like cattle, like matter, like things that had neither body nor soul, nor even a physiognomy upon which death could stamp its seal."[9]

Characterizing this monstrous equality without fraternity or humanity, "an equality in which cats and dogs could have shared" as the image of hell, Arendt observed that some outstanding scholars went out of their way to aid the Nazis; she named the jurist Carl Schmitt, the theologian Gerhard Kittel, the sociologist Hans Freyer, the historian Walter Frank, and the existential philosopher Martin Heidegger, "whose enthusiasm for the Third Reich," she wrote, "was matched only by his glaring ignorance of what he was talking about."[10]

If her thinking about Heidegger had not exactly been filled with longing or affection, it was nevertheless the case that Heidegger held a continuing fascination for her, and also for Jaspers, who knew a great deal about his activities in the Third Reich. As a leading and highly esteemed figure in continental philosophy, Jaspers had been consulted by the authorities and been asked to review documents and make recommendations about whether there could be a role for Heidegger in a denazified university. He had counseled patience, a wait-and-see attitude over several years before it would be possible to determine whether Heidegger might be permitted to teach again;[11] but in his own life, despite his gentle nature and belief in the importance of communication, time was no healer. Jaspers was never able to find a path to reconciliation with Heidegger.

17

ON NOVEMBER 27, 1944, FREIBURG WAS devastated by British and American bombers. The philosophy faculty withdrew to Castle Wildenstein near the small Black Forest town where Heidegger had been born. When Heidegger returned to Freiburg in 1945, his house and library had been temporarily commandeered by Allied troops, who demanded a purge of Nazi leaders from teaching and other public professions. Elfride, now in the role of Heidegger's staunch defender, argued with the authorities that Heidegger had never really been a Nazi and that he needed his library in order to make a living.[1]

The faculty senate reconvened on April 25, immediately after the city fell to the allies. A new rector and vice rector were elected, and the Führer principle of governance established by Heidegger twelve years earlier was explicitly rejected. Discussions were initiated about the university's failure to resist the Nazis right at the beginning, and a denazification commission was established to review cases and determine who was and was not fit to teach.

The members of the commission had mostly been political

prisoners of the Nazi regime or men like Adolf Lampe, an economist whose tenure at Freiburg Heidegger had opposed on the grounds of political unreliability, and Friedrich Oehlkers, a friend of Karl Jaspers's, who was also married to a Jew and had lived in a state of constant fear during the Third Reich.[2] Heidegger, summoned before the commission, submitted a statement declaring his innocence and put forward a disingenuous image of himself as a victim of the regime, concealing details about his past—strategies that he never abandoned except to retreat into long periods of silence.

He only took on the position of *Rektor*, he told the commission, because the university needed him. He only joined the party, he said, because it facilitated his efforts to protect the university and because he hoped that the participation of intellectuals would deepen and transform National Socialism. He accepted the Jewish Proclamation reluctantly and passively only to keep the university from being closed (and did not see even after the fact that it would have been better to close universities in protest and perhaps awaken broader resistance throughout society). If his public statements in 1933 and 1934 were filled with enthusiasm for the Führer, it was because Hitler did seem at the time to be the man who would lead Germany out of crisis and toward its national destiny. These sentiments, he pointed out, were widespread among leading political, business, and religious leaders at the time, and proved neither that he was an ardent Nazi in 1933 or a Nazi at all after that. No references were made to his efforts to destabilize the old regime at the university, or of his ambitions to achieve greatness within the National Socialist revival. He claimed that by 1934 he had seen that there was an unbridgeable gap between himself and the Nazis based on his rejection of their materialist race-based explanation of the greatness of the *Volk*, which departed from his own view of the dominance of spirit, and that he withdrew from public life rather than accommodate to Nazi thought. After 1934 he placed himself among the victims of the Nazis, spied upon, marginalized in academic and intellectual circles, his work denied the national and international visibility it deserved.[3] Now that the war was over, Heidegger felt victimized by the hypocritical judgment of the West, which treated him as a Nazi for having lent intellectual prestige to the movement in 1933, but which embraced industrialists and rocket scientists who in the 1940s were working slave laborers to death in order to develop Nazi armaments and weapon systems.[4]

Heidegger never acknowledged that by consciously placing the full weight of his academic reputation and distinctive oratory in the service of the National Socialist revolution, he did a great deal to legitimize the Nazis in the eyes of educated Germans, to raise the hopes of ordinary people that there might be something of value in the new regime, and to make it much more difficult for German science and scholarship to maintain its independence during the period of political upheaval. His denial of responsibility exhibited precisely the type of unreflective thoughtlessness among Germans about which Jaspers despaired in *The Question of German Guilt.*

When the denazificaton commission approached Jaspers for an assessment of Heidegger's guilt and a recommendation about how to proceed, he began by identifying the fundamental dilemma raised by Heidegger's case. On the one hand, Heidegger was so tainted by association with the Nazis that it would have been unthinkable to leave his position at the university unchanged; but at the same time, it would be a serious and lamentable loss to the academic community and to the very concept of academic freedom if a renowned and brilliant philosopher were silenced because of his political past. Jaspers characterized Heidegger as a sort of mixture of nihilist and magician:

> In the torrent of his language he is occasionally able, in a clandestine and remarkable way, to strike the core of philosophical thought. In this regard he is, as far as I can see, perhaps unique among contemporary German philosophers. Therefore, it is urgently to be hoped and requested that he remain in the position to work and to write. [Yet] it is absolutely necessary that those, like Heidegger, who helped place National Socialism in the saddle, be called to account. . . . Exceptional intellectual achievement can serve as a justifiable basis for facilitating the continuation of scholarly work, but not for the resumption of professorial position and teaching duties.
>
> In our situation, the education of youth must be handled with the greatest responsibility. . . . Heidegger's manner of thinking, which seems to me in its essence unfree, dictatorial, and not directed at open communication, would be disastrous in the current environment. As long as he does not experience an authentic rebirth that is evident in his work, such a teacher cannot in my opinion be placed before the youth of today.[5]

He did go on, however, to recommend that any decision not to allow Heidegger to teach be subject to reassessment after several years depending on Heidegger's own development and evidence about the resilience of the university and larger society in recovering from the damage done by the Nazis.

In January of 1946 the faculty senate granted emeritus status and a pension to Heidegger, refusing to allow him to teach, and pointedly making no provision for periodic review of the decision. The public minutes went on to say that the senate requested the *Rektor* to inform Professor Heidegger that he would be expected to maintain a low profile at public functions and gatherings of the university. This was a harsh blow for Heidegger, who was hospitalized for several weeks in the spring of 1946 for depression and a physical and mental breakdown. Heidegger's friend, the psychologist Robert Heiss, wrote to Jaspers that even after his release from the sanitarium Heidegger was remote and seemed to have entered a state of internal exile "as if he were reaping what he had sown."[6]

Jaspers continued to think about Heidegger. In a letter written to Heidegger in 1948, but never sent, Jaspers offered an explanation of the comments he had made to the commission in 1945: "In the cool detachment of my observations you cannot perceive what was in my heart. My letter was conceived with the intention of letting the inevitable come into effect and to help you to achieve the best possible in a dangerous situation, to enable you to continue your work."

Jaspers did finally initiate an exchange of letters with Heidegger in 1949, which he shared with Arendt when she visited. In these letters each man recognized the gap that had developed between them, and each expressed the wish that their friendship might be restored. They greeted one another, as Jaspers put it, "from a distant path, from beyond an abyss of time, holding steadfast to something that was and that cannot be nothing." Heidegger thanked Jaspers for initiating the correspondence, but did not apologize for his conduct in 1933. He said that he had gone into a state of inner resistance and opposition to the regime when he resigned the rectorship. The correspondence was cordial, holding forward the promise of a reconciliation that never materialized. Jaspers confessed to Hannah that it was Heidegger's discourtesy toward Gertrud in 1933 that troubled him most and caused him finally to stop writing back. Hannah wrote to Blücher that she found Heidegger's letters touching, but false, a mixture of "genuineness, mendacity and cowardice. . . . Poor Heidegger," she recorded Jaspers as having said, "here we are, the two best friends he has, and we see right through him."[7]

The widespread view of Heidegger as an unrepentant Nazi is reflected in a letter he received in 1947 from Herbert Marcuse, an ardent communist who had been Heidegger's student between 1928 and 1932. Marcuse implored him to renounce his early association with National Socialism, denounce the actions and ideologies of the regime, and make a public avowal of changed views:

> Because you are still today identified with the Nazi regime, many of us have long awaited a statement from you, a statement that would clearly and finally free you from such identification, a statement that honestly expresses your current attitude about the events that have occurred. But you have never uttered such a statement. . . . A Philosopher can be deceived regarding political matters; in which case he will openly acknowledge his error. But he cannot be deceived about a regime that has killed millions of Jews—merely because they were Jews—that made terror into an everyday phenomenon, and that turned everything that pertains to the ideas of spirit, freedom, and truth into its bloody opposite.[8]

Marcuse ended by saying that he was sending a package of food to Heidegger as Germany was in a state of postwar poverty and devastation, but that his friends opposed this gesture of friendship and accused him of helping a man identified with a regime that sent millions of his fellow Jews to the gas chamber.

Heidegger wrote back that he had received the package, and in an effort to reassure Marcuse's friends had distributed its contents among former students who had no association whatsoever with National Socialism, and thanked Marcuse on their behalf. Pointing to the fact that Marcuse had not yet renounced Stalinism,[9] he said:

> To the serious, legitimate charges that you express about a regime that murdered millions of Jews, that made terror into an everyday phenomenon, and that turned everything that pertains to the ideas of spirit, freedom, and truth into its bloody opposite, I can only add that if instead of "Jews" you had written "Germans of the eastern territories," then the same holds true for one of the allies, with the difference that everything that has occurred since 1945 has become public knowledge, while the bloody terror of the Nazis in point of fact had been kept a secret from the German people.[10]

In light of Stalinist atrocities and purges in the Soviet Union, the murder and rape of German citizens by the Red Army, the brutal expulsion of ethnic Germans throughout central and eastern Europe after the war, and the fact that the Soviet Union was still holding German prisoners of war (including both of Heidegger's sons) under brutal conditions, one cannot say that Heidegger's observation was mistaken; but "you too" is not a defense. Even if Heidegger was right about the Russians, he failed to see that the Red Army established a sphere of control that extended as far west as Prague, Budapest, and Berlin only because it had been pushing the Wehrmacht back across central Europe, and that this would have been avoided had the Nazis been stopped at the beginning.

Furthermore, while there were indeed many secrets in Nazi Germany, Heidegger's assertion that the German people did not know they were governed by murderers, or that something bad was being done to the Jews, defies reality. Heidegger was disingenuous in his usual manner to deny that great horrors were already evident in every word of the Nazi leaders and every gesture and deed of their storm troopers before he joined the party in 1933, even if it was not yet obvious they would bring about total war and the liquidation of European Jewry.

Nevertheless, in 1949 a movement arose to reconsider Heidegger's relationship to the university. One of the prime movers was Max Müller, a liberal democrat whom Heidegger had banned from a university career during the Third Reich, but who now argued that in a state founded on freedom of speech, it was unacceptable that a man of Heidegger's stature should be denied a public voice indefinitely.[11] A former student, Hans-Georg Gadamer, organized a Festschrift in honor of Heidegger's sixtieth birthday, and a parallel publication, *Martin Heidegger's Influence on the Sciences*, was edited by Wilhelm Szilasi, who now held Husserl and Heidegger's old chair at Freiburg. If the academic world had not yet brought Heidegger out of the closet, a door had at least been opened in acknowledgment that such a mind should not be silenced by a democracy.

By a narrow vote the faculty senate reinstated Heidegger's right to teach beginning in the winter of 1950. Students turned out for his classes in great numbers, and his first public lectures in Bremen, Munich, and Freiburg on such topics as "Who Is Zorathustra?" "On Things," "On Thinking," and "The Arts in the Age of Technology" were all great successes. The shadows were receding, even if the "Heidegger affair" remained unresolved. The crisis was over. Heidegger celebrated New Years, 1950, with both of his sons, recently returned home from Russian prisoner-of-war camps.

18

ON JANUARY 3, 1950, AFTER TWO weeks with the Jasperses in Basel, Hannah was in London making arrangements to travel to the British Zone in Germany on behalf of Jewish Cultural Reconstruction. She wrote to Heinrich that the feeling of familiarity and intimacy with Jaspers kept growing up to the very last minute of her visit to Basel and that she felt "spoiled" by the two of them, full of admiration for their loving relationship. She wrote to Heinrich that as she conversed with Jaspers her interest in contacting Heidegger when she returned to Germany at the end of the month had diminished: "I don't know yet—I'll leave everything up to fate . . . with Jaspers I lost a little of my keenness for Heidegger. It always comes back to the same thing: the principle by which relationships are entered into. What is important, of course, is that, on the whole, Jaspers is pleased with me." Above all, she wrote, she was eager to return to America and to Heinrich, with whom she felt secure, wherever they were, as within her own "four walls."

At just this time, however, there was a break in her correspondence with Heinrich that frightened Hannah. She wrote from Paris in mid-January that she hadn't had a letter from him in two weeks and that she couldn't go roaming around the world without feeling protected at home. As it turned out, Heinrich had been unable to write, sick and in great pain with stomach flu and bouts of kidney stones for several weeks before and after New Years, and did not want that communicated to Hannah. Their friend Hilde Fränkel, who was dying of cancer, wrote to Hannah frequently during that time with nondescript assurances that Blücher was fine; but Hannah was worried that his silence signaled that something was wrong in their marriage.[1]

There had been a crisis eighteen months earlier. Heinrich, who liked women and was liked by them, seems to have had a few discreet trysts over the years, and since both he and Hannah abjured bourgeois conventionality, this had not threatened their love and trust in one another. But in the summer of 1948, when she went to New Hampshire for two months to have quiet time to write, Blücher had an affair with a vivacious and sensuous young woman who was known in their circle of friends in New York. Hannah felt publicly humiliated, and it took some time for them to reach a new understanding. During these months she formed a close friendship with Hilde Fränkel, the secretary and adored mistress of the theologian Paul Tillich. Hannah described Fränkel as "gifted with erotic genius," and wrote that with Fränkel she enjoyed an intimacy "like none she had ever known with a woman," expressing her gratitude for the good fortune of their nearness.[2] This friendship, perhaps because of the perspective it offered on men, was a conduit back toward Blücher.

But now in the winter of 1950, when letters were not forthcoming from Heinrich (he had written to Arendt twice by then describing his illness and with news of their friends, but those letters missed her at various locations and were forwarded to Basel), Hannah feared that he had wandered again. She wrote to him angrily from Heidelberg at the end of January about her concern:

> I simply can't understand your complete lack of sense about the most primitive human responsibilities and obligations. I cannot believe that you have so little imagination that you can't imagine how I feel careening about the world like a car wheel that has come off, without a single connection to home or anything I can rely on. . . . I write all this to you . . . bitterly . . . and embittered. If our relationship is not even worth your forcing yourself to send me news regularly, what can I say? Or do? I have often told you my view about how things stand—never wrote it to you, because I didn't want written words to stand between us. But this time I can't hold back. I have no choice.

He wrote back that her "hard" letter following upon the experience of kidney stones left him upset too, because she was upset and he was supposed to have caused it. He insisted that he hadn't wanted to burden her with news of his illness or her friend Hilde's fast-advancing cancer. He spent time with Hilde, begging her to stay alive long enough so that she and Hannah could see each other again. "Don't be unsettled and unhappy" about us, he wrote; "your home is standing waiting for you," and then—referring to the woman in the closet in Strindberg's play—assured her that "there is no ghost sonata being staged here."

She got his letters at the beginning of February when she returned to Basel for a second visit with Jaspers. "You got my bitter and angry letter right in the middle of your kidney stone attack," she wrote. "I'm terribly sorry, terribly." The crisis Hannah had imagined and feared was a phantom. She was secure at home: loved and understood by the man she loved. Clearly the reconciliation Hannah would initiate with Martin Heidegger in the following days did not arise from melancholy, loneliness, or dissatisfaction with the state of her life or marriage.

Hannah was in Freiburg a few days later. She had written to Heinrich about rumors (which turned out to be untrue) that Heidegger was speaking disparagingly of Jaspers, saying that she therefore no longer had "the slightest wish ever to see that man;" nevertheless, when she arrived at her hotel, she sent a note to him. Heidegger received it the following day and, not having a telephone, came that afternoon to the hotel to deliver a reply inviting her to visit at his home that evening. The clerk recognized the famous philosopher, knew that Arendt was in the dining room, and had the waiter bring Heidegger to her table. "This evening," she wrote to Heidegger the next day, was

> the confirmation of an entire life. A confirmation that, when it comes down to it, was never expected. When the waiter spoke your name (I had not actually expected you, had not received your letter, after all), it was as if time suddenly stood still. Then all at once I became aware of something that I would not have confessed before, neither to myself nor to you nor to anyone—how . . . the power of the impulse [to contact Heidegger] had mercifully saved me from committing the only really inexcusable act of infidelity and forfeiting my life. But one thing you should know (as we have had relatively little to do with each other, after all, and that not as openly as we might have), if I had done it, then it would only have been out of pride, that is, sheer crazy stupidity. Not for reasons.

This was the joyous moment of reconciliation, an instant recognition of continuity of interest, affection, and attraction in a shattered world. They talked until late in the night; and the next morning there was a meeting with Elfride at the Heidegger home, about which Heidegger was euphoric, even though Elfride had spoken harsh words. "The morning light," he wrote to Hannah that afternoon, had "taken away something dark that hung over our early encounter and over our long-distance waiting." He was ashamed of his original dishonesty with Elfride, which he called an abuse of trust and a grievous failure. Now he hoped to put things right so that "a lively harmony and genuine mutual understanding" might emerge among the three of them, the four actually, because he also hoped to meet Blücher.

The meeting with Elfride, however, had not gone well. There is no record of the words spoken that morning, but it appears from hints and references in subsequent letters that Elfride expected an apology from Hannah, and when it was not forthcoming, she suggested that "a German woman" would know how to behave more appropriately. The next day Heidegger wrote to Hannah saying that Elfride's words were aimed only at clearing the air and not as a demand for an apology or confession of guilt, nor "to infringe on the fate of our love."

Hannah wrote to Martin that she was "shaken by the honesty and urgency" of Elfride's reproach, and that she felt "a sudden feeling of solidarity with her . . . and . . . a sudden surge of sympathy," but had remained silent not just as a matter of discretion and pride, but "also as a matter of love for you—and not to make anything more difficult than it must be."

At Heidegger's request she also wrote to Elfride:

> Martin and I have probably sinned just as much against each other as against you. This is not an excuse. You did not expect one, after all, and I could not provide one, either. You broke the spell, and I thank you for that with all my heart. I could not have realized that you expected something from me, because I did things later in connection with this affair that were so much worse that I did not remember the early things at all. You see, when I left Marburg, I was quite firmly determined never to love a man again, and then later I married, somehow indifferent to whom I was marrying, without being in love. Because I thought I had everything completely under control and that everything was at my disposal—precisely, in fact, because I expected nothing for myself. All this changed only when I met my current husband. . . .
>
> Please believe one thing: what was and surely still is between us was never personal. . . . You never made a secret of your convictions, after all, nor do you today, not even to me. Now, as a result of those convictions, a conversation is almost impossible, because what the other might say is, after all, already characterized and (forgive me) categorized in advance—Jewish, German, Chinese. . . .

Nevertheless, Hannah concluded, "we will see each other again soon. Until then please accept this as a greeting and a thanks."[3]

Hannah wrote to Heinrich (her dearest Snubby, who had been encouraging her to see Heidegger) the next day, saying that shortly after she arrived in Freiburg, Heidegger had appeared at the hotel:

> The two of us had a real talk, I think, for the first time in our lives, with the result that I had to think of my darned Snubby,

> who is such a good judge of things. . . . For God's sake, you are my four walls.

She went on to describe her encounter with Elfride, "which might have hit the mark precisely twenty-five years ago, but was conducted as if time didn't exist," in much more severe terms than she had used with Heidegger:

> On top of everything, this morning I had an argument with his wife. For twenty-five years now, or from the time she somehow wormed the truth about us out of him, she has clearly made his life a hell on earth. And he, who always, at every opportunity, has been such a notorious liar, evidently (as was obvious from the aggravating conversation the three of us had) never, in all those twenty-five years, refuted that I had been the passion of his life. His wife, I'm afraid, for as long as I'm alive, is ready to drown any Jew in sight. Unfortunately she is absolutely horrendous. But I'm going to try to defuse things as much as I can.

There was a flurry of correspondence between Hannah and Martin after this, including seventy letters and poems between 1950 and 1952. Her visit lifted Heidegger's mood. He wrote to her almost every day for the next few weeks, and urged her in the most earnest terms to come back to Freiburg for a second visit before returning home.

Hannah and Martin spent two days in Freiburg at the beginning of March. One afternoon, walking through a beautiful Black Forest valley dotted with white birch trees and wildflowers making their first appearance from under thinning snow, they talked about the nature surrounding them and about language itself, which was at the center of Heidegger's interest, not only as an instrument of communication, but as the framework for how we think about nature and everything else. He wrote a poem to Hannah about the power of the most basic units of sound in language:

"Oh!"
you dash of delight,
sound of sorrow,
innocence or intimacy;
splitter of silence
. . . .
You "Oh!"
the unspoken's poorest legend,
but the word's asylum:
the first reply
and the last question.

Two months later, recalling aspects of their conversation while walking in the valley, Heidegger wrote to Arendt, "You are right about reconciliation and revenge." We cannot know what was said, but notes in Arendt's *Denktagebuch* reveal that she was beginning to think that forgiveness contains the potential "to destroy the fundamental equality of human relations by setting those who forgive apart from and above those who are forgiven." The alternative is to forgive in the Christian spirit that we are all sinners, but this contains "the possibility that the one who is forgiven may interpret forgiveness as a release from moral culpability—which can perhaps be earned but not bestowed." Revenge, paradoxically, with all of its negativity and destructiveness, "nevertheless preserves relationships because the person seeking vengeance always stays close (at least in a psychological sense) to the other, with no pretense of superiority—sharing perversely in the solidarity of sinners, wanting to do to the other what was done to him." Arendt wondered if there might be a third way—a path of reconciliation, "like an averted glance, a silent passing over of injustice, an acceptance of suffering as destiny that does not require self-reflection about one's own potential to be among the guilty."[34]

Another topic that we know Hannah and Martin discussed during these days together was his sadness at being unable to reestablish a friendship with Jaspers. Hannah revealed to Heidegger that Jaspers was still indignant over his failure to say good-bye properly to Gertrud the last time he visited their house in 1933, and then never coming back, Jaspers felt, in order to avoid contact with a Jewish woman. "Heidegger," Hannah wrote to Heinrich, "was totally taken aback" that Jaspers thought he had "boycotted" Gertrud; the truth of the matter, according to Heidegger, was that he realized what he had done "and was ashamed."

The evening after the walk in the valley, Heidegger wrote to Jaspers: "I no longer came to your house after 1933, not because a Jewish woman lived there, but *because I simply felt ashamed*. Since then, not only have I not entered your house, but I have also never again entered the city of Heidelberg, which is what it is to me only because of your friendship. . . . I would not like to enter Heidelberg before being received by you again in the kindly manner the memory of which *always remains painful* for me."

Jaspers responded to Heidegger's letter: "I thank you warmly for your candid explanation . . . it means a great deal to me that you said frankly you were ashamed. . . . You will forgive me," he wrote, "when I tell you that I sometimes thought that you seemed to behave with regard to the national-socialist events like a boy who dreams, does not know what he is doing . . . and soon stands helpless facing a heap of rubble and lets himself be driven even deeper." Jaspers ended with the suggestion that the two might now look for an occasion to see one another and speak again. "I am with you in my good wishes and greet you sincerely." Jaspers wrote again a few days later, saying that he kept thinking about Heidegger's use of the word "shame;" and that he was enclosing copies of three recent publications including *The Question of German Guilt,* which he hoped, might be of interest.

Heidegger was delighted by Jaspers's renewed interest. In a letter to Arendt after her return to New York, recalling the walk in the valley and their play on language and sound, he wrote, full of the German informal: "You, you [du, du] Hannah are the real 'and' [und] between 'Jaspers and Heidegger.' It is beautiful to *be* an 'und,' it is the secret of the goddess. It happens *before* all communication. Its sound rings from the same depth as the 'u' in 'du.' "

But Heidegger's hope for reconciliation with Jaspers was quickly frustrated. His response to Jaspers's letter began well enough with the observation that the word "*shame* was, and is, often spoken by my wife as well." Heidegger offered a broader, more general apology for his misconduct: "I immediately fell into the machinery of the office, the influences, the power struggles, and the factions. I was lost and fell, if for only a few months, into what my wife describes as an "intoxication of power." Later on, he was cautious and frightened because he knew that there were hostilities against him in the regime; after the war he was puzzled by the hostility against him, and only slowly came to see "what my step into the public domain in 1933 had meant."

But then came a paragraph of almost paranoid anticommunism that struck Jaspers as tinged by the sort of hatred that had made the Nazi experience possible. "*Now* it is *our* turn," Heidegger wrote; "I have no illusions. I know, from our son who has returned from Russia, that my name even now stands at the front again, and that any day the threat can have its effects. Stalin doesn't need to declare war any longer. Every day he wins a battle, but one doesn't see it." This strain of egocentric belligerence was a recurring theme with Heidegger. He had written to Hannah too that he was sure his ideas put him near the top of Stalin's list of people to be eliminated. He doubted American resolve to stand firm and worried that Germany, perhaps all of western Europe, could be overrun in a matter of days. After that, it would "no longer be possible to pass on what is great or recover what is essential; then there would no longer be even hope for a future that will reveal what is now hidden, that will preserve what is original." For Heidegger that original essential thing was still the pre-Socratic sense of awe in the face of Being; and this, dimmed and faded by centuries of misunderstanding, was nevertheless the last best hope for humanity.

Although Jaspers was not sympathetic to communism, he found Heidegger's attitude of hostility and fear alienating—he read it as pointing the way toward the next war and of avoiding responsibility for what had been done in the name of Germany. He did not write back to Heidegger for more than two years; and when he did write, it was to say that he was horrified by grand world visions that promote destruction: Is not the power of evil something for each of us, he wondered, to come to grips with individually? Had not the power of evil also grown in Germany, and had it not in fact prepared Stalin's victory through "the concealing and forgetting of the past, the new so-called nationalism, the return of the old ruts of thinking and of all the ghosts which destroy us, even though they are empty. . . . Is Stalin not victorious precisely through all of this?" Didn't Heidegger's philosophy, summarized in his last letter, produce visions of something monstrous, and was this not "something that prepares the victory of totalitarianism by separating itself from reality?" When Hannah inquired about his breaking off the correspondence with Heidegger, Jaspers responded that Heidegger's confession of guilt was not genuine and contained no real understanding. "Somewhere in life," he wrote, "one must, reluctantly, let things fade out of sight (but not forget them)."

Despite the failure to reconcile Jaspers and Heidegger, her own stable relationship with Jaspers and reconciliation with Heidegger seemed to Hannah like a promise of new beginnings in the world—a symbol of continuity with a past that had been almost entirely destroyed, and of the endurance of what is real between people. For his part, Heidegger seemed suddenly and unexpectedly unburdened. There was a spring in his step and an outpouring of feeling in letters and poems, with lines like these:

May the name
you and I
be one jewel here:
to grasp the late
ripening
of early seeds
we never attained . . .

or these:

Your "yes" with a great moan
out of pain so lightning-close,
reconciled in what's most
dear,
is still here.

Even without knowing the content of their letters, Elfride knew that they were writing, and that Hannah's return had lifted Heidegger's mood. If Elfride was angry and jealous of a woman 3,000 miles away, perhaps it was because her husband's letters characterized this distance as an "abyss of longing" across which he was nonetheless happy simply to have Hannah back in his life: "Though I often wish I could run the five-fingered comb through your frizzy hair, especially when your loving picture looks straight into my heart with the *same* gaze that leaped towards me on the lectern [during the Sophist lectures] . . . that same gaze whose light shines back from your countenance, letting the woman appear."

"I dream," he wrote in one letter, "that you would like living here after all, walking down forest paths, bearing the silent reign of things, and existing amidst the ultimate joy, but be at home abroad, you—most trusted one, you have returned and arrived—Hannah—du."

19

HEIDEGGER WAS MISTAKEN TO THINK THAT Hannah might have been happy returning to Germany. The German world into which she had been born no longer existed. She appreciated the beauty of the countryside, and the cities or parts of cities that had not been destroyed were familiar and comfortable to her, but she felt too much indignation about what had been done and not done, and about what was remembered or forgotten and denied. In addition to all that, there was the fact that Hannah was genuinely happy with her life in New York, where her energies were absorbed by extraordinary intellectual productivity, teaching, and immersion in a group of friends in which she and Heinrich were central, and who were so close that they referred to themselves as a tribe. This tribe was at first mostly German-speaking émigrés, but in the mid-1940s this began to change as she and Heinrich became more comfortable among American intellectuals and artists.

By 1952 both Hannah and Heinrich had become American citizens. While they were still puzzled by elements of the culture and uncomfortable with the materialist elements of mass society, both appreciated the democratic tradition and openness of American life, both were grateful for safe harbor in the New World, and neither took the obligations or the opportunities associated with citizenship lightly. The most fundamental human right, Arendt wrote after years of statelessness, is the right to citizenship; everything else follows from that.[1]

By the time Hannah and Heinrich had become Americans, their friendships and associations had already brought them deeply into an American way of being. The visibility of Arendt's writing and her position as an editor at Schocken Books facilitated contacts with a community of prominent left-leaning New York intellectuals centered around such journals of opinion and political thought as *Partisan Review, Commentary*, and *The Nation*, among them: Dwight Macdonald, Philip Rahv, Irving Howe, Sidney Hook, Clement Greenberg, Fred Dupee, William Phillips, Harold Rosenberg, Daniel Bell, Delmore Schwartz, William Barrett, Diana and Lionel Trilling, and Alfred Kazin. Many warm friendships emerged, but two in particular, with Randall Jarrell and Mary McCarthy, illuminate Hannah's (and Heinrich's) acculturation into American life and language.

In 1946, Arendt was approached by Randall Jarrell, a poet who had taken up the position of book review editor for *The Nation* for a year while Margaret Marshall was on leave. Jarrell had been impressed by Arendt's essay "Approaches to the 'German Problem'," which appeared in the Winter 1945 edition of *Partisan Review*, and asked her to submit book reviews. Over the next few years the two became close friends, and by 1951, when he had an appointment at Princeton (which he found so stuffy that he described it as "much more Princetonian than—than Princeton even"),[2] Jarrell was a regular visitor to the Blücher household in New York. He wrote to his wife, Mary, that Hannah and Heinrich were "a scream together," that sometimes they had "little cheerful mock quarrels," that they shared household duties such as washing dishes, and that "she kids him a little more than he kids her. They seem a very happily married couple." It was he who characterized the relationship between Hannah and Heinrich as a "dual monarchy."[3]

Language was part of the bond between Arendt and Jarrell.[4] Arendt, who loved poetry, was by the time she met Jarrell already familiar with a great deal of English-language poetry, the meaning of which she grasped better than the sound. Her own spoken English was heavily accented, and when she read English poetry, she did not have the sense for what she called "the specific gravity of English words, whose relative weight, as in all languages, is ultimately determined by poetic usage and standards." There was a bilingual collaboration between Arendt and Jarrell. He loved German poetry, and published quite a few translations (especially of Rilke), with which Arendt helped; and she benefited from his service as one of her "Englishers" (Alfred Kazin was another at the time) who transformed her long, complicated, awkward Teutonic sentences into long, complicated, beautiful English sentences. After Jarrell's death Arendt wrote that "whatever I know of English poetry, and perhaps of the genius of the language, I owe to him."

In the late 1940s and early 1950s, Jarrell would come to visit Hannah and Heinrich from wherever he happened to be teaching for what they all referred to as "American Poetry Weekends." He would read to her for hours, sometimes following her into the kitchen when she prepared something for them to eat, sometimes staying in the living room to argue with Heinrich about such questions as whether Rilke or Yeats was the better poet. Blücher preferred Yeats, and Jarrell, Rilke. For Jarrell, the pleasure of visiting with Hannah and Heinrich involved being in the presence of such great erudition, and joy at the opportunity to hear German spoken. German, he wrote (not Germany), was the country he liked best.[5]

Jarrell's arguments with Heinrich about poetry often devolved into shouting matches as both men had tendencies to zealous enthusiasm. After one of their weekends Jarrell wrote to Hannah that he found Heinrich awe-inspiring because encountering a person even more enthusiastic than himself was like "the second fattest man in the world meeting the fattest."

In Jarrell's satiric novel *Pictures from an Institution*, there is an immigrant couple, Gottfried and Irene Rosenbaum, modeled on the Blüchers: "very like you in some of the big general things," Jarrell wrote to Hannah, but "quite different" in smaller things. In Gottfried Rosenbaum's heavily accented English, characterized as "a pilgrimage towards some *lingua franca* of the far future," Jarrell captured Heinrich's voice: Rosenbaum declares that the way he speaks is "vot ve all speak ven de Shtate hass viderdt away."[6] The novel's narrator describes its protagonist Gertrude Johnson (an acerbic writer whose books are condemnations of mankind) as always able to fault clever people for being bad and good people for being stupid; then the voice of God, straight out of Job and Goethe's *Faust* (and reflecting Jarrell's admiration for Blücher): "Hast thou considered my servant Gottfried Rosenbaum . . . a kind and clever man."[7]

The closing essay in Arendt's collection *Men in Dark Times*, was written after Jarrell's death in 1965 at the age of fifty-one. It may have been a suicide; he seemed to be recovering from the depths of a depression when he went walking in dark clothing along a country road at night. The driver who hit him claimed that Jarrell jumped in front of his car, although the autopsy concluded that he had been sideswiped.[8] One way or the other, Hannah felt that the last time she saw him, not long before his death, that the laughter in him was almost gone and he was almost ready to admit defeat; but it was his laughter, exuberance, and cheerfulness that she recalled at the end. "He would have been a poet if he had never written a single poem," she wrote, describing him, even to the details of his physical appearance, as "a figure from fairyland . . . blown down by some charmed wind into the cities of men," or emerging perhaps "from the enchanted forests in which we spent our childhood, bringing with him the magic flute, and not just hoping but *expecting* that everybody and everything would come to join in the midnight dance."

Hannah's friendship with Mary McCarthy was of a whole other order of magnitude. From the late 1940s until her death in 1975, Mary McCarthy was Hannah's closest friend other than Blücher, her lover and husband, and Jaspers, her mentor and father confessor. As it happens, though, their friendship did not begin smoothly. Hannah and Mary were both guests at a party in the spring of 1945 at the home of Philip Rahv, an editor of *Partisan Review,* the leading journal of a renowned group of left-wing anti-Stalinist New York intellectuals. Neither woman had achieved the degree of public prominence that lay only a few years ahead, but both already stood out in the crowd: Arendt for the authority, breezy insouciance, skeptical wit, and easy erudition with which she conveyed mastery of European culture, and for an "extraordinary electric vitality" that filled Mary McCarthy "with delight and wonder."[9] McCarthy, for her part, was a dazzling intellect and daring iconoclast with an acerbic manner and vivid good looks.

The conversation that evening turned to the hostility of the French to their German occupiers, and McCarthy joked that she "felt sorry" for Hitler, who was so absurd as to long for the love of his victims. Arendt, incensed by any expression of sympathy for Hitler, and perhaps not reading the subtlety of McCarthy's wit quite properly, snapped: "How can you say such a thing in front of me, one of Hitler's victims, a person who has been in a concentration camp." She stormed out of the apartment, but not before telling Rahv that he ought not to allow such things to be said in his home.

After that, the two women saw each other from time to time at various meetings at which politics and literature were discussed. Each noticed the shared elements of their world-views, but the estrangement between them was not overcome until three years later when, after one such meeting, they were waiting on an otherwise empty subway platform and Hannah approached Mary: "Let's end this nonsense," she said, "we think so much alike."

Mary apologized for her flippant comment, which she had not intended to be hurtful, and Hannah confessed that she had not been in a concentration camp, but only an internment camp in France. Thus began a friendship that Carol Brightman, Mary's biographer and the editor of the Arendt-McCarthy correspondence, has characterized as a romance, not sexual, but not entirely platonic either, in the sense that each longed for the companionship and presence of the other.[10]

Hannah's first and very short letter to Mary, written in March of 1949 congratulated her on the publication of *The Oasis,* a satirical novel about the utopian intellectuals of the 1930s and

'40s, which Hannah called a "veritable little masterpiece." Mary's first letter to Hannah, was written in April of 1951, just after the publication of *The Origins of Totalitarianism*; Mary said she had been "absorbed" for two weeks, reading it in the bathtub, riding in the car, waiting in line in the grocery store:

> It seems to me a truly extraordinary piece of work, an advance in human thought of, at the very least, a decade, and also engrossing and fascinating in the way a novel is: i.e., that it says something on nearly every page that is novel, that one could not have anticipated from what went before but that one often recognized as inevitable and foreshadowed by the underlying plot of ideas.

This letter also proposed that Hannah and Heinrich come to visit Mary and her third husband, Bowden Broadwater, who were living at the time near the beach in Newport, Rhode Island. That was the first of many visits, and of an intimate correspondence of more than two hundred letters over the next twenty years.

In the years before their friendship began, when Hannah, who was six years older than Mary, was experiencing exile and statelessness first in France and then in New York, Mary was outgrowing the Catholicism of her childhood and adopting a radical stance among a community of largely Jewish New York intellectuals. Her parents died in the great influenza epidemic of 1918, when she was six, and Mary had been raised first under conditions of considerable emotional deprivation by her father's Catholic parents in Minneapolis and then, still as a Catholic schoolgirl, under conditions of greater prosperity and affection by her Jewish grandmother and protestant grandfather in Seattle.[11]

In September of 1929, when she was seventeen, Mary came

east and began school at Vassar College. Although her family remained financially secure during the Great Depression, Mary became interested in socialism and gravitated into circles associated with the American Communist Party. Mary never joined the party, in part because her interest was less a matter of political conviction than the fascination of a literary person with the politics of the intellectuals in New York, among whom she was living in a rather extended sequence of romantic liaisons. Her association with a group of anti-Stalinist Trotskyists who espoused a sort of democratic socialism without totalitarian overtones brought her into contact with the editors of the *Partisan Review,* which was established in 1934 as an alternative to *New Masses*, the official publication of the American Communist Party. In December 1937, when *Partisan Review* reappeared after a year's hiatus, it was with a regular feature of "Chronicles of the Theater" by Mary McCarthy, who was by then living with the *Review*'s editor Philip Rahv; soon she would abruptly abandon Rahv to marry Edmund Wilson, perhaps the preeminent American literary critic of the twentieth century. Mary's marriage to Wilson (her second and his third) lasted eight years and produced Mary's only child, but it was an unhappy relationship, with fights so intense that Wilson would lock himself in his study, and on at least one occasion Mary, who was in and out of psychotherapy during those years, shoved pieces of burning paper under the door.[12]

Both women had turbulent lives, at least through midlife: Hannah was the steadier, more stable personality, maintaining equilibrium even while displaced and threatened by world history; Mary was emotionally labile, "her slashing wit and amatory wanderings [four marriages and countless love affairs] were the subject of 'red-hot gossip'."[13] This represented a difference of attitude about which neither of them made judgments, but about which they were keenly aware. In December 1954, for example, when Mary was writing her novel *A Charmed Life*, she wrote to Hannah:

> I have you horribly on my conscience every time sex appears. You are tugging on my elbow saying "Stop" during a seduction scene I've just been writing. And your imagined remonstrances have been so effective that I've rewritten it to have it seen from the man's point of view, instead of the heroine's. But you still won't like it, I'm afraid. I'm not joking, altogether; I have misgivings about the taste of this novel, which localize around your anticipated or feared reaction.

Both women lived with controversy: Arendt accepted it as the price one had to pay for unflinching truthfulness; McCarthy seems to have embraced it as a matter of personal and literary style. Arendt was a political theorist and philosopher. McCarthy was a political activist and an artist; during the Vietnam War she traveled to Hanoi and was outspoken in her support for the Viet Cong. Arendt was an exemplar of the *vita contemplativa*, committed to the life of the mind, but comfortable too in the world of action. McCarthy was an exemplar of the *vita activa*, fully engaged in social action, but comfortable in the world of thought. Both women were writers by habit and disposition: Arendt was erudite, a careful scholar immersed in her sources; McCarthy was a storyteller and stylist, meticulous with words and meaning.

In their friendship, Hannah was for Mary a brilliant teacher whose subjects ranged from antiquity to existentialism and contemporary politics; Mary was for Hannah a quick study who could follow and challenge her thinking, and also a brilliant editor. "As far as I know," Mary wrote after Hannah's death,

> all of Hannah Arendt's books and articles were edited before reaching print. . . . Sometimes several hands, unknown to each other, went to work on her manuscripts, with her consent and usually, though not always, with her collaboration; those she learned to trust, she tended to leave rather free with the blue pencil. She referred to all this wryly as her "Englishing." She had taught herself to write English as an exile, when she was over thirty-five, and never felt as comfortable in it . . . as she had once felt in French. . . . Though she had a natural gift, which would have made itself felt in Sioux or Sanskrit. . . .[14]

Mary enjoyed working on Hannah's projects because it was a "collaboration and exchange," and because Hannah "accepted correction with good grace." Sometimes they argued over how best to translate a German word or phrase. Mary would sometimes catch a contradiction, or argue that readers needed more information to be able to follow a thought, but there was never a substantive difference, and such disagreements as they had were usually settled by compromise or cutting. Arendt seems to have viewed McCarthy as a perfectionist and was inclined to humor and benefit from that tendency.[15] "She did not like fussing over details. 'You fix it,' she would finally say, starting to cover a yawn."

20

IN FEBUARY 1950, WHILE ARENDT WAS traveling in Europe, Blücher, still less well integrated into American life than she, went to an artists' club at 39 West Eighth Street in Greenwich Village with his friend Dr. Alfred A. Copley, a research physician at New York University (who also painted under the name Alcopley), to attend a lecture about André Malraux's work on the psychology of art.[1] By then, the Village, in Lower Manhattan, had been a lively art colony, indeed the preeminent hub of the arts in America, for a century or more, with art schools, galleries, museums, clubs, and studios. It enjoyed a reputation as a bohemian enclave, tolerant of political radicalism and social nonconformity, and as a nurturing milieu for the avant-garde in poetry, literature, and theater as well the visual arts. After the Second World War, the coffee houses and jazz clubs of the Village became the epicenter of the Beat Movement.

Alcopley had helped to found the Eighth Street Club as a venue for conversation, lectures, and panel discussions. Members of "the Club" were mostly Abstract Expressionists, including Franz Kline, Willem de Kooning, Barnett Newman, Ad

Reinhardt, Mark Rothko, and Jackson Pollock.[2] There were more than forty people at the club to hear the lecture on Malraux, but the speakers never arrived: one had been called out of town at the last moment, and the other chose not to make the presentation alone. Blücher's friends, knowing his familiarity with the subject, pressed him to stand in. He agreed, but only after introductory remarks made clear that he did not really want to do it and that he was totally unprepared. The unconventionality of modern art, he began, makes it the common enemy of all forms of tyranny. Blücher wowed the audience with his advocacy for cosmopolitan style, drawing examples from the "new world" discovered by artists like Cézanne, Picasso, and Kafka. His accent, though heavy, was no barrier to communication, and the discussion after the lecture went on late into the night. Taken by Blücher's originality, intensity, and style as a lecturer and discussion leader, the club immediately commissioned two follow-up lectures. Shortly thereafter, Günther Stern decided to return to Europe and arranged for Blücher to take over his course at the New School for Social Research, where his reputation as a teacher grew quickly. These events were seeds from which Heinrich's own highly successful academic career began to grow over the following years.

In July 1952 (when Arendt was again traveling in Europe) the president of Bard College, a progressive liberal arts school not far from New York City, approached the head of the philosophy department at the New School saying that he was looking for a "Socratic" man to develop a core course for freshmen on "ultimate questions." He was referred to Blücher. Within a matter of weeks, and with the enthusiastic approval of the Bard faculty,

Blücher, who had no formal higher education, was hired to create, lead, and supervise a team of instructors in a seminar (the only required course at Bard) that was intended to be the cornerstone of the school's curriculum, at the very substantial salary of $7,000. After a decade of having been largely dependent on Hannah's income, Heinrich wrote: "I'd love nothing more than being your patron." Blücher's very happy association with the faculty and students at Bard continued for the rest of his life (and that, in fact, is where he and Hannah are buried).

At about this same time, while Hannah was in Europe, Heinrich, reflecting their increasing involvement in American political issues, wrote to Hannah that a recent conference of one hundred writers, artists, and scientists, including many of their New York associates, organized under the auspices of the American Committee for Cultural Freedom (he called them "the fatherland-savers"), failed to pass a resolution condemning Senator Joseph McCarthy. Mary McCarthy, he wrote, had done very well speaking in favor of the resolution to condemn, and told him later that she felt she had to make a good job of it because she was standing in for Hannah. At the end of that letter Heinrich urged Hannah to "keep loving me as I love you. These are lousy times."

In these lousy times, when fear of disapproval and the danger of guilt by association restrained many Americans from criticizing Senator McCarthy, not many of the writers and critics known collectively as the New York Intellectuals, with whom Hannah and Heinrich were associated, had the courage necessary to sustain active public dissent. Some who had been communists in youth and then anti-Stalin Trotskyists in the 1930s became increasingly conservative during the Cold War, and began writing as anticommunist advocates for American culture and values. For several of them, such as Sidney Hook, Irving Kristol, and Norman Podhoretz, this was the beginning of a long march toward a new identity near the century's end as "neocons."[3]

By 1952, *Partisan Review* was becoming increasingly centrist and was joined in this by *Commentary*, a magazine established in 1945 by the American Jewish Committee. Arendt, who had long recognized and opposed the totalitarian aspects of communist thought and Soviet practice, was not uncomfortable with this development; but she grew increasingly concerned as McCarthyism and the work of the House Un-American Activities Committee threatened to raise anticommunism into a full-fledged attack on traditional American conceptions of civil liberties. Her experience of Martin Heidegger and the German intelligentsia in the 1930s left Arendt with little confidence that intellectuals would have the courage or foresight to stand up for fundamental values.

Almost immediately upon returning home at the end of that summer, Arendt began work on an article that was published in the March 1953 issue of *Commonweal*, a progressive journal of opinion edited and managed by a committee of lay Catholics who she thought had more clarity about the threat than "the boys from Brooklyn" who edited *Partisan Review* and *Commentary*. Her essay, "The Ex-Communists,"[4] focused on the controversy surrounding Whitaker Chambers's admission that he had been a communist agent and his revelation that Alger Hiss and others had infiltrated the State Department and various branches of the government as Soviet spies. Arendt observed that the ex-communists still had communism at the center of their lives, opposing it now with the same dangerous zeal with which they had once embraced it. She argued that fighting totalitarianism with totalitarian methods, which people like Chambers knew all too well, would be disastrous. America, she wrote, is a living republic, and like all living things is imperfect, but efforts to shape it along the lines of some ideal model or to "make America more American" can only destroy it.

Publishing this essay was an act of courage. The McCarran-Walter Act, recently passed into law over President Truman's veto, authorized the deportation of immigrants and naturalized citizens who were or had been members of the Communist Party or fellow travelers. In 1955 and 1958 Supreme Court decisions, relying in part on arguments Hannah had made in *The Origins of Totalitarianism,* ruled that denationalization is a cruel and unusual punishment prohibited by the Eighth Amendment because it involves "the total destruction of the individual's status in organized society."[5] But in 1953, when Hannah and Heinrich Blücher had just become citizens, this was a real danger; less for Hannah whose background was "clean," than for Heinrich, who had been a member of the German Communist Party in the 1920s—and had denied it on his immigration papers in 1941. This left him vulnerable to informers, of whom there were a great many afoot during the McCarthy, Nixon, McCarran "red hunt." Hannah and Heinrich faced this danger with equanimity and took heart from the fact that their McCarthy (Mary) was also publicly outspoken against the dangers of extreme anticommunism and was talking about giving up her writing career in order to go to law school and become an advocate for civil liberties in the courts.[6]

In May 1953, Hannah wrote a long letter to Jaspers characterizing the rise of McCarthyism in the United States as a disintegration of American culture and politics taking place with "breathtaking speed," and "hardly any resistance," and weighing so heavily on her and on Heinrich that it takes away all desire to do anything. "Everything," she wrote, "melts away like butter in the sun." All elements of society were involved: the entertainment industry, philanthropic foundations, schools and universities. This was not a matter of terror or force coming from the government, Hannah explained, but in a society of jobholders no one will be given a job unless their "unquestioned loyalty" is clear; thus everyone censors themselves and becomes afraid to speak up or be critical. Of major importance were the totalitarian methods of the ex-communists. Other, "decent" ex-communists did not come forward voluntarily, but were under pressure to divulge the names of former comrades in order to demonstrate that they were not still loyal to the party; for if that was so much as suspected, they joined the ranks of the unemployable. The Fifth Amendment guarantee against self-incrimination, she wrote, had become a sham because anyone who invokes it becomes guilty in the eyes of society, if not of the law. At a public discussion, the president of Brooklyn College, "an idiot with an important job," said to Hannah that because he was born and raised in Iowa he "therefore didn't need to think or read anymore to know what was right," and told her that it was un-American to quote Plato. Her worst fear, Hannah explained to Jaspers, was that Senator McCarthy would become president in 1956. If that did not happen, she thought, "there's a good chance that things will be all right again. But we're seeing now what is *possible* here."

Arendt's letter noted the prominence among intellectuals of the international Congress for Cultural Freedom, which she felt had never done much to advance either culture or freedom (and which it was later learned had been financed by the CIA). Jaspers had recently agreed to serve as a member of the "honorary presidium" of the organization, and she warned him to be careful about his involvement.

He wrote back thanking her for her words of caution, telling her that he had begun to examine the activities of the Congress for Cultural Freedom more carefully and agreed that politically the group seemed to be primarily opposed to Russia and "not to the principles of totalitarian methods in general." He remembered that she had prophesied correctly in 1931 what lay in store for Germany, and that he didn't believe her then, but still he clung to the hope that what happened in Germany was less likely to happen to America or else "what a wretched and despicable end that would be to a great and honorable human venture." What Jaspers saw most clearly was the personal element of the crisis for Hannah, and the support that she had in Heinrich Blücher: "How much your husband must share your agitation. The two of you together—I see you as a real intellectual force. All the more so because, in this great game of existence, you both speak with voices of calm dependability against overblown, self-important stupidity, and also because you are able to enjoy the present moment by moment."

A few weeks later Hannah wrote to Jaspers that Albert Einstein had taken a public position on McCarthyism, encouraging intellectuals to risk contempt of Congress rather than testify. "Politically that is the only correct thing to do; what makes it difficult on the practical level isn't the legal implications but the loss of one's job." She complained that Sidney Hook, a major figure in the Congress for Cultural Freedom, had called Einstein's suggestion "ill considered and irresponsible." "Irresponsible," she told Jaspers, "is the only critical thing the Hook group has ever called McCarthy: Ergo: McCarthy and Einstein are equally irresponsible."

Then, over a period of nine months in 1954, the threat of McCarthyism dissolved in full public view. On March 9 of that year, Edward R. Murrow of CBS News televised a report on Senator McCarthy's methods of half-truths and innuendo; taking positions very close to Arendt's, Murrow admonished viewers not to confuse dissent with disloyalty:

> We must remember always that accusation is not proof and that conviction depends upon evidence and due process of law. We will not walk in fear, one of another. We will not be driven by fear into an age of unreason, if we dig deep in our history and our doctrine, and remember that we are not descended from fearful men—not from men who feared to write, to speak, to associate and to defend causes that were, for the moment, unpopular.
>
> We can deny our heritage and our history, but we cannot escape responsibility for the result. There is no way for a citizen of a republic to abdicate his responsibilities. . . . We proclaim ourselves, as indeed we are, the defenders of freedom, wherever it continues to exist in the world, but we cannot defend freedom abroad by deserting it at home.[7]

A few days later Senator McCarthy announced that the United States Army was sheltering high-ranking officers who were communists, and that he had a list of 130 subversives working in defense plants. The army responded that this was untrue and that the senator had used threats and bullying tactics to try to secure special treatment for David Schine, a friend of his chief counsel, Roy Cohn. Thirty-six days of televised hearing ensued, and the total audience that watched at least parts of these hearings was estimated at 80 million people. The most dramatic moment came on the thirtieth day of the hearings, June 9, 1954, when the army's lawyer, Joseph Welch, challenged McCarthy to turn over his list of subversives to the attorney general of the United States "before the sun goes down." McCarthy responded by saying that if Welch was so concerned about persons aiding the Communist Party, he should check on a man in his own Boston law office named Fred Fisher, who had once belonged to a left-wing organization called the National Lawyers Guild (which was never shown to have been associated with the Communist Party). Welch responded: "Until this moment, Senator, I think I never gauged your cruelty or recklessness. . . ." When McCarthy resumed his attack, Welch cut him short: "Let us not assassinate this lad further, Senator. . . . You've done enough. Have you no sense of decency, sir, at long last? Have you left no sense of decency?"[8]

From this point on, polls began to show declining support for Senator McCarthy. Even before the two-thirds majority vote of the Senate in December of that year to censure him, Hannah had written to Jaspers saying: "McCarthy is finished. The historians will no doubt busy themselves someday writing about what has happened here and how much extremely valuable china got smashed in the process. . . . What I see in it is totalitarian elements springing from the womb of society, of mass society itself, without any 'movement' or clear ideology."

21

ARENDT WAS IN EUROPE IN THE spring and summer of 1952; again under the auspices of the Commission on European Jewish Cultural Reconstruction, but this time also as an American citizen and a Guggenheim Fellow visiting libraries and extending her research into the totalitarian elements of Marxism. Her goal, never fully realized as a book, was to demonstrate through details of the Soviet case that totalitarianism was a terrifying new political institution in the twentieth century, something that was possible anywhere, and not just an aberrant German excess.

In had been almost two years since her first trip back to Europe. Between visits she maintained active correspondence with Jaspers and Heidegger. While Heidegger's letters in these months were full of loving feeling, Jaspers's reflect the greater interest in Arendt's life, work, and friendships.

In one letter Jaspers described a dream in which he was back in the salon atmosphere in Max Weber's apartment in Heidelberg, and then Arendt arrived late. Weber had just returned from a world trip and brought back documents and artworks, particularly from the Far East: "He gave us some of them," Jaspers wrote, "you the best ones because you understood more of politics than I." Arendt replied that she felt "so idiotically flattered" by his dream that it made her feel ashamed, and she began reading Weber. She and Jaspers read each other's books, essays, and works in process. They shared ideas, discussed world affairs, history, philosophy, and their hopes for a unified Europe and a peaceful Middle East. Each helped the other to arrange translations and international publication of their work. Heidegger is mentioned in only one exchange of letters in which Arendt acknowledged a "guilty conscience" for having encouraged Heidegger to reinitiate the correspondence that Jaspers cut short, concluding that Heidegger showed "no real understanding."

Heidegger's letters to Hannah in the two years before her second visit are full of "unceasing joy" at her return. In September 1950 he thanked her for pictures and commented on one that he loved in particular because in it "you are as present as you were in my room in Freiburg. The days are preserved in it—with all your loving mischief." In April 1951 he notes that he "was recently in the valley by the birch which says hello to you, as do the first cowslips opposite the slope we walked along. The spring has been very reluctant. There are still two meters of snow in the Upper Black Forest." This letter ends, "All my love across the wide waves." In a letter in July he recalled the conversation they had about language on their walk in the woods, concluding: "the valley lies quietly between the mountains and says hello, hello."

There were also references in Heidegger's letters to his own work: slow progress on his "Kant book," his lectures on "Language," "Thinking," "Heraclitus," "The Nature of the Thing," his seminars and forced retirement from the university. What might be thought to be missing among these declarations of love and interesting accounts of his thought were any questions about her life or work.

Arendt arrived in Paris on March 28, 1952, made arrangements to meet with the Conference on Jewish Material Claims Against Germany, a union of thirteen organizations that negotiated reparations for Jews living outside of Israel; then made her way by the first of April for a visit with Jaspers in Basel, which she later described to Heinrich as "marvelous, a single conversation that went on for ten days." Shortly after this visit, Jaspers wrote to Blücher that Hannah seemed to have undergone an evolution in recent years, making more progress, he felt, than he himself had made in developing an attitude of detachment toward Germany. Her rage, he noted, was almost gone, and she was becoming more just and tolerant. At the end he expressed the hope that Blücher too would overcome his aversion to European travel and that "life will last long enough for us to meet here in Basel." He was particularly eager, Jaspers told Blücher, to meet him because the things Hannah said about him hinted at how much they had in common:

> your lectures, your mode of work, the factual details of your life. When I told her that I wanted to lecture on four major figures (crucial in the history of the world), she exclaimed with pleasure: just like Heinrich. The basic idea behind the lectures seems similar for both of us, though the names are not the same. Along with Socrates, Buddha, Confucius, and Jesus, you are also discussing Abraham and Moses. In the past I've spoken about the latter two only in connection with the biblical idea of God. Perhaps you are right to single them out

> for special treatment also. I'll reflect more on that. I'm glad that you take Abraham's reality as established fact. Someone like that can't possibly have been invented.

Blücher's response began: "Dear and most honored Professor Jaspers, It pleases me deeply that you feel I have in some sense been with you; and the opportunity to be with you in realty is, as far as I can see now, about the only thing that could lure me back to Europe again. . . . Yes," he went on to say:

> I too am planning to talk on prototypical human figures. But Hannah must have made a mistake in reporting the plan to you, because I don't count either Moses or Paul among them. . . . I am much more drawn to Solon, to whom you erected a truly Greek memorial tablet in your short essay on him. . . . I'm not really sure about Buddha, although in his Asiatic way he had much in common with Jesus. In place of Confucius I'm inclined to put Lao-Tzu, who looks more and more Socratic to me the closer I study him. And then of course Jesus and Socrates. Abraham seems to me utterly unique . . . the father of what is humanly possible . . . who . . . found the one God . . . the possible God. . . . I found this concept of the possible God and then I found Abraham, and yet I owe the concept to him.

Blücher noted that he had used Jaspers's *Introduction to Philosophy* with his students, for whom "your exemplary distinctions between science and philosophy are as urgently needed as daily bread." Americans have an intuitive recognition of competence, and in you, he told Jaspers, they found both a scientist and a philosopher committed to the purity of both, and quickly developed a sense of trust. What has always separated me from the Germans, he went on to say, "is that none of them, with a few major exceptions, have ever been seriously concerned about freedom; and, if you'll excuse me for saying so, that is what separates you from the Germans, too. And for that very reason you are a German who can speak to good effect in America."

Heidegger, as well as Blücher, was also a recurring topic of conversation between Jaspers and Arendt, but as a bone of contention. Hannah wrote to Heinrich that she could not get Jaspers to refrain from speaking dismissively about Heidegger, whose recent work, he insisted, all "sensible people" recognized as "nonsense." Jaspers strategy in discourse was endlessly to compare leading figures in the German intellectual tradition to determine their value against each other, finding Rilke, for example, beneath the highest standard through comparison to Hölderlin and finally "finishing off" Heidegger through comparison to Nietzsche.

After her reconciliation with Heidegger in 1950, Hannah's attitude about him was more nuanced and gentle.

Shortly after her visit with Jaspers, Hannah received a letter from Blücher, who understood her complicated feelings about Heidegger, addressed to "Dear Doctor Arendt;" how else, he asked, should he address his "famous Snuffy dearest," in light of the fact that she had just received an invitation to deliver a series of six well-compensated lectures at Princeton. Between that honor and the Guggenheim, he wrote, "Jaspers will be even prouder of you, and Heidegger will have new reason to regret women's breakthrough into philosophy." The totally unexpected news about Princeton left Hannah feeling happy and honored: "Yes," she wrote, "Jaspers will be pleased, and Heidegger I'm seeing tomorrow; he'll be less pleased, but I don't care;" and "as for you," she continued, "I had to laugh at how convinced we are of each other and each other's 'marvelousness.' "

The following days in Freiburg with Martin, she wrote to Heinrich, were "not exactly milk and honey, and quite a few times I was on the brink of throwing in the towel and leaving." Elfride, she wrote, "was half-crazed with jealousy, which had built up over the years, during which time it is obvious she constantly hoped he would simply forget me."

> She manifested this in a halfway anti-Semitic scene when he wasn't present. I must say, the woman's political beliefs (I must bring you or maybe send you her favorite newspaper, the worst political smear sheet I have ever seen in Germany) have remained untouched by all that has happened, and are of such a close-minded, vicious, resentment-laden stupidity that it isn't at all difficult to understand what is happening to him . . . In short, the whole thing ended with me making a scene in front of him, and since then things have been considerably better.

Nevertheless, she was encouraged to see that Heidegger's capacity for work was undiminished. He was in top form, writing and rewriting the text of a lecture subsequently published as "*Was heisst Denken?*" (What Is Called Thinking?),[1] which, Arendt told Heinrich, was delivered with great calm, quite unbombastically, with cool composure. The crowd was so large that the main auditorium of the university was filled to the brim, and the overflow was sent to two other large rooms where they were able to listen to a simultaneous radio transmission of the lecture.

"What Is Called Thinking?" is not an exercise in logic. It

reads like a long poem, repeating themes, drawing new themes out of old, tying them together in units of increasing complexity. Heidegger argued that thought is related more closely to poetry than to science or technology, because these human enterprises do not inquire into the meaning of things, but only into the way things work. We have not come face-to-face with Being, which calls out above all else to be thought about. Thinking the meaning of Being turns man's efforts away from efforts to dominate it through reason and technology.

"What is Called Thinking?" is full of wordplay. Not just, what is it that we call thinking, but what is a calling? We speak of some professions—the clergy, for example—or medicine, perhaps, as callings; but what is it that calls, what is it that calls us to think, and what sort of thinking responds to the call? In the end, the wordplay culminates in the relationship between thinking and thanking, *denken* and *danken* in German:

> How can we give thanks for this endowment, the gift of being able to think what is most thought-provoking, more fittingly than by giving thought to the most thought-provoking? The supreme thanks, then, would be thinking? And the profoundest thanklessness, thoughtlessness? Real thanks, then, never consists in that we ourselves come bearing gifts, and merely repay gift with gift. Pure thanks is rather that we simply think—think what is really and solely given, what is there to be thought.[2]

Hannah was delighted by the lecture and by the feeling that Heidegger "had found his center" and regained a degree of stability, and she was confident that so long as he could be productive there was no immediate danger. Nevertheless, she was concerned about his recurring bouts of depression. When she was together with Martin, Hannah felt certain of a fundamental goodness within him, an openness that she could not define any other way, and which she knew was not necessarily accessible to anyone else. "The moment we are together," she wrote to Heinrich, "all those artifices of his that otherwise surface so easily just disappear, and he is left in his true helplessness and defenselessness."

Arendt thought that she might arrange additional "surreptitious" meetings with Heidegger in June and perhaps in August as well, hoping that time together away from Elfride would lift his mood and help to prevent subsequent depressions when she was gone. Blücher supported this, encouraging her to do what she could to stabilize Heidegger. "Forget his wife," he wrote, "when foolishness turns obstinate it spills over into evil, or at least to where one can no longer tell the two apart." These subsequent meetings never took place; Arendt received a letter from Heidegger at the beginning of June: "It is best if you *do not write* now and do not *come visit* either. Everything is painful and difficult. But we must bear it." What havoc a nonentity of a woman can cause, she wrote to Heinrich, who responded in perfect Heideggerian terms, transfiguring nouns into verbs: "Nonentity nonentifies."

At the beginning of August, having completed her research in France and just before returning home to prepare for the Princeton lectures, Arendt vacationed in St. Mortiz with Karl and Gertrud Jaspers. Jaspers was again in marvelous condition, full of ideas and challenges, a little worried that his getting old meant they might never see each other again, and for this reason especially eager to meet Blücher. He had no more interest in Heidegger, whose condition, despite increasing public acceptance of his work, Arendt saw as unstable and emotionally disastrous. "Everything I thought I had accomplished for Martin," she wrote to Heinrich, referring to her desire to help him overcome his continuing bouts of depression and also to promote his reconnection to Jaspers, "has been for nothing."

Arendt was back at home in New York by mid-August 1952. It would be another three years before she returned to Europe. During that time her closeness with Jaspers continued to grow through correspondence, but her exchanges with Martin Heidegger dwindled almost to naught. She agreed to supervise and critique the translation of *Being and Time* into English. Now and then, there were personal notes between them. In December 1952, Heidegger lamented that "the world keeps getting darker," that "contentiousness dominates everything," and that "the essence of history keeps getting more and more enigmatic . . . so that all that remains is resignation." Although even then he recognized that the "forests and mountains are still standing and are not yet weary of their essence. They send you their best at this Christmas season into a world we can scarcely conceive of here. . . . All my best in sincere remembrance."

Despite her obvious affection for Heidegger, Arendt remained cynical about his character and his way of relating to the world and to his own past. She wrote a parable in her *Denktagebuch* (a writer's diary of notes and thoughts) in July 1953 that begins with a recollection of a snippet from one of their conversations in Freiburg:

> Heidegger says proudly: "People say Heidegger is a fox." This is the true story of Heidegger the fox.
>
> There was once a fox who was so utterly without cunning that he not only constantly fell into traps but could not even

> distinguish a trap from a non-trap. . . . After this fox had spent his entire youth in other people's traps . . . he decided to completely withdraw from the fox world, and began to build a den. . . . He built himself a trap as a den, sat down in it, pretended it was a normal den (not out of cunning, but because he had always taken the traps of others for their dens). . . . This trap was only big enough for him. . . . Nobody could fall into his trap, because he was sitting in it himself. . . . If one wanted to visit him in the den where he was at home, one had to go into his trap. Of course everybody could walk right out of it, except him. . . . The fox living in the trap said proudly: so many fall into my trap; I have become the best of all foxes. And there was even something true in that: nobody knows the trap business better than he who has been sitting in a trap all his life.[3]

In October 1953, Martin sent a note to Hannah responding to her greeting on the occasion of his sixty-fourth birthday: "Your loving remembrance was a great joy in the hourly and daily path of memory;" then, referring to the lines from Goethe that she had quoted at their first reunion in Freiburg ("to say that a thing endures means the beginning, the end, the same"), he asked: "How could it be otherwise—in what endures—" After this there was almost no further communication between them for a dozen years.

In May of 1957 her friend Mary McCarthy, whose witty, acerbic fiction analyzed the finer moral nuances of intellectual dilemmas, and who in her personal life was always having trouble with men, wrote to Arendt about an unhappy love affair she had with an Englishman about whom she still had tender feelings, but who turned out to have lied habitually about himself, his family and educational background. In response, Arendt wrote that men who lie about facts are better than men who lie about their feelings because with the former there is always the likelihood that facts will come out and show them to be liars no matter what they do, but as to lies about feelings, who can find out? Men who lie can sometimes be redeemed by a woman's love, but this, she thought, was rarely worth the effort except in the case of men with genius or a talent so compelling that it overrules everything else. She offered two examples. One was the avant-garde playwright Bertolt Brecht, a Marxist with a Swiss bank account, to whom she applied some lines of Auden's ("God may reduce you on Judgment Day to tears of shame, reciting by heart the poems you would have written, had your life been good.") to suggest that he might have been a better poet if he had been a better man. The other was Martin Heidegger.

22

WHEN THE GERMAN TRANSLATION OF *THE Origins of Totalitarianism* was published in 1955, Arendt was in Europe for the third time since the end of the war. Heinrich wrote to her that since the book had an introduction by Jaspers, Heidegger, who because of his past could never have been associated with such a project, would nonetheless feel that Arendt had aligned herself with Jaspers against him and consequently that there was no chance he would read it. Hannah responded that her relationship with Heidegger "could only exist according to the law under which it was begun": "I am, as you know, quite prepared to act with Heidegger as if I had never written a line and was never going to write one. And that is the unuttered *condition sine qua non* of the whole affair. But right now . . . I could only do this with the greatest of difficulty, and I have no wish to."

Heinrich wrote that he thought Hannah's attitude too severe and that it was a mistake for her to leave Europe without so much as letting Heidegger know that she was there, although this is what she did. It had been more than a year since she had received a letter from Martin, and this, she thought, was for two reasons:

on the one side because he had heard of her successes, and on the other because of the tension and animosity with Elfride, which made it impossible for both of them. She thought it likely that she would see him the following year,[1] but as it happened, they did not see each other again until 1967, more than a decade later.

She continued, however, to be very happy in her friendship with Jaspers, and the warmth of this relationship was extended to Heinrich. In November of 1955, between Hannah's visits to Basel, Jaspers wrote to Blücher that he and Gertrud and even their maid found that her presence enlivened their existence. He admired her high-spirited intensity and commented that Heinrich was present in the meeting of the minds that was taking place: "As on earlier occasions, you were present this time, too. Not that Hannah spoke of you—apparently she can't do that. But in response to our questions she communicated so much concrete information about your life and work in New York and Bard that I have a picture of it. And through that picture I always feel I can sense in you . . . a remarkably kindred spirit. . . ." Acknowledging that after persecution and exile "Germany will be no pleasure for you," Jaspers nevertheless encouraged Blücher to visit, reminding him that there are still "excellent individuals" here and that Europe has more to offer than just Germany. "It would be wonderful for us if you would decide to come sometime. I would very much like to meet you in person and not just in the way I have met you so far, extremely gratifying as that has been. Then, too, I would like to ascertain, with you, what the important thing is to us in the fact that we are German, which is our heritage, and to which we somehow ultimately belong."

Blücher did not write back until three months later, thanking Jaspers for his "good" letter which made "Hannah's visit with you both so vivid" that he felt he had been there himself, and this, he said, strengthened his desire "to be part of the next gathering of this kind." But he went on to separate himself from Jaspers's essentialist effort to identify positive aspects of national character that might have survived the Nazi experience. "This brings me again," Blücher wrote, to your old question to me: "How do I perceive myself as a German in these times? My answer has to be: not at all."

Everywhere in Europe, Blücher lamented, "The First World War represented the real betrayal of fatherland of which no one ever speaks. National societies betrayed their sons and delivered them up to the industrial slaughter of war, and then in Germany betrayed them a second time with inflation and for a third time with Hitler." The only hope, Heinrich wrote, lay in a great Atlantic Federation, but "everything national works against such a future." To want to become good Atlantic citizens, just as Nietzsche once wanted us to be good Europeans, is the only goal he considered worth striving for.

> Nationalism began when every individual, every small spirit, saw in it his chance to embody something higher than himself and to feel himself, as a German or whatever, to be greater than he could feel alone. What now marks the end of nationalism is that it has become impossible to be both a human being and a German, a Frenchman, or a Jew (in Israel, in any case) or whatever. On the contrary, as a representative of this or that nationality, one will be forced sooner or later to become an inhuman monster.
>
> So we are obliged today to try to become human beings only as ourselves—aided by those friends who have been moved to make this same decision and supported not by the "great spirits" of Romanticism but by the great human beings

> of all our national pasts. And one's own as well as other "nations" should be judged solely . . . in terms of the question: Where is the human being's person held inviolate?

Jaspers did not respond to this, but did write to Hannah that he understood better than ever the closeness between the two of them. "I have hardly ever been so powerfully struck with what true being together is as I have in the silence and calm that you (and Blücher) share. . . ."

In 1958, Arendt returned to Europe twice; the first time in the spring to lecture at the International Cultural Critics Congress in Munich, and the second time in September to have the opportunity she had hoped for some years earlier: to lead the world in honoring Jaspers. He was awarded the Peace Prize of the German Booksellers Association in acknowledgment of his lifetime contribution to humanity but also in recognition of his new book, *The Atom Bomb and the Future of Man*. Arendt was invited to deliver the major oration of the day, introducing Jaspers at the award ceremony in Frankfurt. The invitation made her nervous, she wrote to Heinrich, partially because of the venue of the event: the Paulskirche, Frankfurt's most famous Protestant Church, legendary as the seat of the *Paulskirchenparlament*, the first German National Assembly, and the cradle of German democracy and unity during the unsuccessful revolution of 1848. The place was so significant in Germany that it was the first building to be rebuilt in the bombed-out center of Frankfurt after the war, in time to be reopened on the hundredth anniversary of the Frankfurt Parliament. Hannah was concerned, she confessed to Heinrich, that she had been chosen, even though there were other more qualified possibilities such as Albert Camus or Reinhold Niebuhr, only because the committee found it desirable to have a woman in this role for the first time. She also worried that as a Jew and an emigrant her presence would be a source of controversy; and that with Jaspers and Heidegger (with whom she had had no contact at this point for several years) still unreconciled, her participation in the ceremony would create the impression that she was taking sides, which she did not wish to do. Heinrich (who was angered by the unhappiness Heidegger's silence was causing Hannah) advised her that for such a friend as Jaspers "one can even stand up in the Paulskirche, which actually is quite amusing. . . . National politics or partisan politics are not involved here at all. But there is something fundamentally political about this, namely, that both Jaspers and you are very much interested in the future of mankind and nothing else. Like Nietzsche. And me. You should really talk to them about the concept of the good European." What is more, he continued, it made no difference if Hannah's public display of loyalty, respect, and affection offended Heidegger: "that is just what Heidegger has coming to him anyhow, that little German shrimp!"

Hannah agreed to speak because it was clear that Jaspers enjoyed the idea and that the invitation provided a unique opportunity for her to do something nice for him. Citing Cicero as authority, she began by declaring that the sole consideration of a laudation is the greatness and dignity of the individual, which is something more than the sum total of what one has done or created. Jaspers, Arendt told the assembly, though he was alone and isolated, stood as a representative of *humanitas* in Germany during the Hitler years because his character was inviolable, untemptable, and unswayable:

> What distinguishes Jaspers is that he is more at home in (the) region of reason and freedom, knows his way about it with greater sureness, than others who may be acquainted with it but cannot endure living constantly in it. Because his existence was governed by the passion for light itself, he was able to be like a light in the darkness glowing from some hidden source of luminosity.[2]

Arendt's speech in honor of Jaspers is reprinted among the biographical essays she brought together under the title *Men in Dark Times*. She borrowed the title from Brecht's poem "To Posterity," which speaks of the time given him on earth as having passed away amid the disorder, hunger, massacres, betrayal, and slaughter of the Nazi years, "when there was only injustice and no resistance," but which encouraged those who would come after to think "when you speak of our weaknesses, also of the dark time that brought them forth."[3] Even in the darkest times, Arendt wrote, thinking of Brecht as well as Jaspers,

> we have the right to expect some illumination (which) may well come less from theories and concepts than from the uncertain, flickering, and often weak light that some men and women, in their lives and their works, will kindle under almost all circumstances and shed over the time span that was given them on earth. . . . Eyes so used to darkness as ours will hardly be able to tell whether their light was the light of a candle or that of a blazing sun. But such objective evaluation seems to me a matter of secondary importance which can be safely left to posterity.[4]

23

HEIDEGGER'S LETTERS TO ELFRIDE, PUBLISHED BY his granddaughter Gertrude forty years after his death, indicates that love affairs with younger women continued well into his later years. Elfride, perhaps still compensating for the imbalance in their relationship caused by her own affair and extramarital pregnancy when they were newlyweds, was the long-suffering wife.[1] Nevertheless, after the war, the balance in their marriage seemed to shift again. Heidegger was no longer young, and even after his official denazification he was subject to the disapproval of others and bouts of depression; he needed Elfride and the comfort and support of the home she provided more than ever. If she, as her granddaughter suggests, was able to tolerate his occasional infidelities on the basis that such moments of passion inspired his work without intruding on their relationship, she was nonetheless unwilling to accommodate herself to a continuing relationship with Hannah.

For her part, Hannah saw through Heidegger, saw him as the fox too clever for his own good and as disingenuous and manipulative. Though she was hurt by his silence, Hannah was no longer estranged from him in the way she had been between 1933 and 1950. She continued to support him in the way that Heinrich Blücher had encouraged, by helping to create an environment conducive to creative work; drawing on her network among publishers in New York, she arranged for the translation of his books into English, selecting translators and supervising their work. These efforts contributed to Heidegger's financial security, international stature, and peace of mind.[2]

Despite their absence from each others' lives, the years of this second hiatus in their relationship were good for both Hannah and Martin. It was a time of escalating public prominence and private contentment for her; and for him it was the period in which his reputation was rehabilitated and he was restored to a degree of dignity in the community of scholars. Nevertheless, despite all the successes in Hannah's professional life and in her private life as well during this period—her happy marriage to Heinrich Blücher, for whom things were all also going well, the esteem in which she was held on both sides of the ocean, her many friendships including her very close relationships with Karl Jaspers and Mary McCarthy—Hannah continued to think about Heidegger, and he remained an emotional and intellectual presence in her life.

There is no reference to Heidegger in Arendt's 1958 classic *The Human Condition*, not even in the index, but his presence is recognizable throughout, especially in their shared concern that the Being of man was increasingly threatened by technology—not only human existence but human nature, our way of thinking and of relating to the world. It was especially evident to her after *Sputnik*, when people started talking about one day leaving the Earth altogether, that humanity was losing its respect and affection for earthly nature, which is the quintessence of the human condition. "For all we know," she argued, "the Earth may be unique in the universe in providing human beings with a habitat in which they can move and breathe without effort and without artifice." Now people seemed to think that "human existence was a free gift from nowhere" and wanted to exchange it for something new and man-made.[3] Arendt's judgment that it makes more sense to love and care for the Earth than to abandon it anticipated the environmental and ecological movements of the next half-century.

Heidegger is also present in the obverse in *The Human Condition,* which counters his provincialism and German exceptionalism with a universalist appreciation of the Being of others. The book celebrates "action," which unlike "labor" (which sustains life) and unlike "work" (which is the expression of man's creativity), takes place only between human beings. *The Human Condition* begins with recognition of plurality and the fact that men—not Man—live on the earth and inhabit the world; no human life, not even the life of the hermit in nature's wilderness, is possible without a world that directly or indirectly testifies to the existence of other people. Being is not an isolated moment of existence in the face of nothingness; it is the condition of being with others. The signs of this are that love is possible, and that there is the endlessness of new beginnings, brought into the world by the ceaseless arrival of new people and by the endless spontaneity of human action.

Political activity, which is the way we participate in the socially constructed fabric of communal life, involves words and deeds with which we insert ourselves into the human world. The new beginning that came into the world when we were born gives rise to an imitative impulse to begin something new on our own initiative. In the ubiquitous possibility of unexpected new beginnings, Arendt found the source of human freedom, faith in the world, and hope for the future, of which the most glorious and succinct expression, she wrote, may be the few words with which the Christian Gospels announce their glad tidings: "A child has been born unto us."[4]

Thinking with and against Heidegger and also about him, Hannah comes late in the book to the problem of reconciliation, which, she argued, must be a possibility in a world in which action is capable of producing new beginnings. The predicament of action in an uncertain world, in which people can never foretell the consequences of what they do, is that it is impossible to undo what has been done. Reconciliation, she concluded, contra her first discussions with Heidegger after their initial reconciliation, cannot be achieved merely through an averted glance; the pain is too great to be denied and can only be overcome through forgiving. Only forgiveness can undo the deeds of the past, which otherwise "hang like Damocles' sword over every new generation."[5]

Forgiving, like love, derives from being with others—no one, Arendt thought, can forgive himself. Christian belief, so close to the center of the Western tradition, recognized that men must forgive each other before they can hope to be forgiven by God.

Arendt noted that in the Christian tradition, the principal characteristic of a "trespass" is not necessarily that it does less injury than willed evil, but that it arises from thoughtlessness, from men's acting when they "know not what they do." That is how she had come to see Heidegger's derelictions. Trespasses require forgiving and dismissing if the web of relationships in which life is enmeshed is to go on. "Only through this constant mutual release from what they do can men remain free agents, only by constant willingness to change their minds and start anew can they be trusted with so great a power as that to begin something new."

Revenge, which is the natural, expected, automatic reaction to transgression, never puts an end to the consequences of a misdeed, but instead keeps everyone bound to a chain reaction with no place for freedom or spontaneity. Forgiving, which can never be predicted, "is the only reaction which does not merely re-act but acts anew and unexpectedly . . . [thus] freeing both the one who forgives and the one who is forgiven."

Forgiveness, Arendt argued, "is always an eminently personal [though not necessarily individual or private] affair in which *what* was done is forgiven for the sake of *who* did it."[6] In Christian thought and the Western tradition forgiveness is associated with love: love as regard for another person from the distance that the world puts between us, love as awareness of shared humanity rather than as admiration or esteem. Such love, which Arendt thought rare in human life, opens us to extremes of self-revelation and clarity of vision "because it is unconcerned to the point of total unworldliness with *what* the loved person may be, with his qualities or shortcomings, achievements, failings, or transgressions." Love did not blind Hannah to what Heidegger had done but, along with gratitude for his thought and teaching, was part of the basis for reconciliation.

The Human Condition has no dedication. When the book was published in German in 1960, Hannah sent a note to Martin saying that her publisher would send him a copy, and that "if things had ever worked out properly between us—and I mean *between*, that is, neither you nor me—I would have asked if I might dedicate it to you." The book, she said, grew directly out of their talks in those first days when they were together again in Freiburg, and therefore owed practically everything to him in every respect. The absence of a dedication demonstrates that silence speaks; and Heidegger, whose silence had offended so many, was offended by it. Perhaps he felt, despite his own behavior, that she owed him a public display of her loyalty. In any event, he never acknowledged receipt of the book, and no copy of it was ever found in his library, although a note in Hannah's diary in November 1968 suggests that they had spoken about it.[7]

Just after publication of *The Human Condition*, W. H. Auden, the great poet and literary critic, introduced himself to Arendt with a telephone call that embarrassed her in its effusiveness.[8] The book, he said, left him with the impression that it had been written especially for him, to answer precisely those questions he had been putting to himself; but what he most differed with was precisely the phrase that seemed to summarize her experience with Martin: "we forgive what was done for the sake of who did it."

Auden approached the problem of forgiveness as a turn-the-other-cheek variety of Christian, believing one must practice charity and forgiveness for the sake of Jesus, for the sake of the good. Auden genuinely believed that if a man demands our coat we are to give him our cloak also.[9]

Arendt quipped that she did not know whether it would be more difficult to be the one who demands a coat or the one who gives a cloak also, but that she was sure it is easier to give forgiveness than to ask for it. No doubt this is how she understood Heidegger's silence. Nevertheless, Arendt was not satisfied with charity as a reason to forgive everything, including personal betrayal. To forgive in the spirit of "Who am I to judge?" was a great temptation, she admitted to Auden, "but I'd rather resist it."[10] Arendt preferred to forgive in the spirit of friendship, which (unlike friendliness and good manners) cannot be universal; friendship requires us to make distinctions among individuals.

Ultimately, Auden and Arendt had similar convictions. In her talk "On Humanity in Dark Times," on the occasion of receiving the Lessing Prize of the Free City of Hamburg in 1959, Hannah referred repeatedly to Lessing's *Nathan the Wise*, in which inter-ethnic friendship, modeled on Lessing's own friendship with Moses Mendelssohn, is the central theme. In the last scene of the play there is a powerful exhortation for fraternity, universal tolerance based on "confirmation of human nature common to all men:"[11] Nathan's adopted (Jewish) daughter and the (Christian) Knight who rescued her from a fire are revealed to be siblings, the orphaned son and daughter of a noble German woman and the Sultan's adored younger brother. In the end, Jews, Christians, Muslims, however different they seemed to be, are united by bonds of blood and love. Nathan's wisdom, Arendt concluded, is shown to consist in his readiness to sacrifice truth to friendship.[12] Auden put the same thought better—catching all its ambiguity with more clarity and precision—in his poem "The Common Life," which ends:

And always, though truth and love
can never really differ, when they seem to
The subaltern should be truth.

24

IN THE AUTUMN OF 1945, A few months after Germany's unconditional surrender, Frédéric Towarnicki, a young cultural officer in the French army occupying the southwest territory, visited Heidegger. When Heidegger expressed a strong desire to rebuild his connections with France, but confessed that he had not had an opportunity to read *Being and Nothingness*, Towarnicki lent him a copy and proposed a meeting with its author, Jean-Paul Sartre, in Baden-Baden. Sartre originally opposed such a meeting but relented when Towarnicki assured him (apparently without a basis in fact) that Heidegger had protected Jewish professors. Towarnicki tried to persuade Albert Camus to meet Heidegger, but Camus declined because of Heidegger's Nazi affiliations.[1]

The meeting with Sartre did not come about, because it was difficult to secure travel papers and the few trains still running were full. Heidegger wrote to Sartre saying that in *Being and Nothingness* he had "for the first time encountered an independent thinker who, from the foundations up, has experienced the area out of which I think." He hoped that they could work together "to bring thinking back to a point from which it can be experienced as a basic event of history, and thus bring modern man back into an original relation with Being." Heidegger regretted that the meeting in Baden-Baden had not been possible and suggested a meeting at his *hütte* in Todtnauberg, which they could use as a base for cross-country ski tours in the Black Forest.

Sartre had been interested in Heidegger since the early 1930s when the constellation of thought that would later be known as existentialism began to gain currency in France. He was drawn to the conception of existence as finite, fragmented, contingent Being. In the absence of belief in God, or any conviction that reason can provide man with security or meaning, French thinkers were struck by the absurdity of life. Some, like Camus, were drawn to Husserl's rejection of unifying principles in favor of rich phenomenological description of the irregular diversity of the world.[2]

Sartre first learned about these philosophical developments talking with his friend (and later Arendt's friend, as well) Raymond Aron, who had studied in Germany. Phenomenology, Aron explained to him, makes it possible to philosophize about everything: a cup of coffee, the spoon with which it is stirred, the table on which it sits, and the waiter who brings it.[3] In this moment, Sartre wrote a few years later, he felt "electrified" because philosophy, which had grown arcane, was suddenly made realistic: "the phenomenologists have plunged man back into the world; they have given full measure to man's agonies and sufferings, and also to his rebellions."[4] Sartre arranged to study in Berlin in 1933 and 1934, and was so absorbed in the work of Husserl and Heidegger that he hardly noticed the rise of the Nazis.[5]

Sartre's work all through the 1930s was steeped in phenomenology. His novel *Nausea* derives its title from the experience of its narrator, Roquentin, who, sitting alone in a park, notices the root of a chestnut tree plunging into the ground beneath his bench but does not recognize it as a root, seeing it instead as a crude "black knotty mass," and experiences a revelation: without the meaning given to things by consciousness, they stand before us naked in the confession of their existence. Nothing is as it appears to consciousness. The very existence of things is contingent upon perception: "The essential thing is contingency . . . [which alone] is absolute . . . [everything else] is gratuitous, this park, this city, and myself. When you realize that, it turns your heart upside down, and everything begins to float . . . here is nausea."[6]

Horrified by the raw existence of things, the narrator is driven back to the world Kant discovered, in which consciousness creates illusions of order and meaning, negating the independent existence of the myriad things around us (such as the root in the park) by contextualizing them (for example, as an inconspicuous part of a tree). Thus man is the being whose consciousness selects things for being or nothingness. It is through this insight that Sartre's philosophy approaches the thought of Heidegger.

In the winter of 1940, during the "phony war," after the invasion of Poland but before the invasion of France, when the western powers were posturing militarily but not yet really fighting, Sartre was taken prisoner by the Germans. During nine months of captivity, he read *Being and Time*;[7] and with irony not lost on Sartre, it was under these conditions of confinement that he found in Heidegger a path of thought leading in the direction of personal freedom. Continuing on this path, Sartre published *Being and Nothingness* in 1943, intending it as a companion volume to Heidegger's masterwork. By the end of the war, this work, with its emphasis on freedom and commitment, had established

Sartre as a leading French intellectual. Yet rather than take the traditional stance of lofty philosophical remove from current events, he personified the life of the mind as political commitment, calling upon writers and artists to assume responsibility for the well-being of society by championing the oppressed and working class.

Edward Said has observed that in France, where postwar memory was organized around a myth of heroic resistance (while everyone knew the realities of collaboration and defeat), philosophical questions that had previously been debated only in the academy turned into an almost national obsession, with social, spiritual, and moral concerns. The war "made overt what had been stirring beneath the surface of French life, the conflict between . . . the stability of principles and the shifting variety of human experience."[8] In this environment, Sartre's public lecture at the end of October 1945, "Existentialism Is a Humanism," was the intellectual event of the year in Paris; and when it was published to wide distribution a few months later, Sartre became a European cult figure.[9]

The crowd awaiting the talk was so large and boisterous that when Sartre arrived he thought at first that there might be a protest taking place; it might have been either Marxists or Catholics, both of whom disliked the fact that his existential perspective denied God and historical determinism alike. Instead, it was a throng of enthusiasts greeting him like a star, with men fighting for seats and women swooning in the audience.[10] Such was the place of philosophy in French public life. The lecture was delayed for an hour while a semblance of decorum was established. When it was time to begin, the speaker had to be hoisted above the massed bodies and passed up to the podium, where he began by declaring that he intended to defend existentialism against the charge that it is an invitation to quietism and despair, a "bourgeois contemplative luxury." Rather, it was an invitation to a kind of heroic self-fashioning:

> there is no human nature since there is no God to have conceived of it. Man is not only what he conceives himself to be, but that which he wills himself to be, and since he conceives of himself only after he exists, just as he wills himself to be after being thrown into existence, man is nothing other than what he makes of himself. That is the first principle of existentialism.[11]

In the absence of God, there are no universal standards, but this, according to Sartre, does not negate the existence of singular universes in which each man, making his own choices, creates an image of what he believes man ought to be. A man who marries, Sartre asserted, not only commits himself to monogamy, but also fashions an image of monogamous man. People may think that they are committing no one but themselves to anything, or are too modest to think they are fit to impose conceptions of right and wrong on the whole of humanity, but failure to consider the Kantian imperative—what would happen if everyone did as I do—is a kind of bad faith.

The recognition that we are alone without God or excuses, Sartre told the crowd, "is what I mean when I say that man is condemned to freedom." We are abandoned in the universe, compelled to decide our own being, and we despair because we have nothing on which to rely except that which is within our own wills. Man is nothing but the sum of his actions; for the existentialist there is no genius or authenticity other than that which is expressed in action. In life a man draws his own portrait, and there is nothing but that portrait. The existentialist, he concluded, sees a coward as one who makes himself a coward through his deeds, and a hero as one who makes himself heroic. Existentialism defines man by action and sees no hope for man other than in action.

Viewed this way, existentialism is a humanism insofar as it places man at the center of the universe. The humanism of enlightenment—centered on man's reason and the progress of humanity—had been severely (if not mortally) wounded by two world wars. Reason (and its acolytes science and technology) had apparently led to new forms of brutal lethality: mechanized warfare, aerial bombings, and poison gas. The Nazi regime and the totality of the second war, with its attacks on civilian populations and its factories of death, went beyond the absence of reason to the presence of horrifyingly powerful unreason. A universe that earlier generations had perceived as lawful and benign now appeared absurd and evil. Kafka rose from obscurity to prophet, and Camus imagined humanity as its own plague. What could philosophy offer in a shattered world?

Sartre's effort was aimed at restoring the position of man as the measure of all things, but Heidegger thought he had failed at this; indeed, Sartre's approach to existentialism was almost directly contradictory to the direction of Heidegger's thought after his "turn" in the Nietzsche lectures, which he had not yet announced to the world. A few months later, after receiving a printed copy of "Existentialism Is a Humanism," Heidegger wrote "On Humanism" in the form of a letter to another of his French admirers, Jean Beaufret. Beaufret happened to have been reading Heidegger on D-day, June 6, 1944, when the Allies landed in Normandy, and felt that he understood him for the first time. Later he said that his happiness over this understanding overshadowed even his joy about the impending liberation of France. This rather excessive exuberance (combined with the fact that in later years Beaufret was sympathetic to a party of French Holocaust deniers)[12] may detract from the value of his judgment that Heidegger above all others advanced the dignity of philosophy by freeing it of platitudes.[13] It was Beaufret who had written to Heidegger asking whether it was possible after all that had transpired that the word "humanism" could once again be meaningful.

Heidegger wrote that he thought it unnecessary to retain the word "humanism," or indeed any of the "isms," which flourish only when original thinking has come to an end. Above all, he hoped that by deconstructing the word "humanism," which had become associated without reflection or independent thought with such values as humanitarianism and reason, that he might advance thinking about the "truth of Being . . . which alone reaches the primordial essence of *logo,*" and which had already been obfuscated and lost in the formal logic of Plato and Aristotle. Man does come into the world with a nature; it is the nature of man to be aware of existence and able to search for meaning within it. Sartre asserted that human nature is not given a priori but is shaped only by men's action ("existence precedes essence"). To Heidegger this was a disparagement of the "proper dignity of man" whose essence inheres in an "ecstatic" relationship to the truth of Being, which man alone in creation can comprehend. Sartre's view of man as self-creating, he argued, places humanity outside of nature. By making man the "lord of beings" Sartre reinforced the very attitudes of power, ambition, and control that had led to the recent disaster. It would be better, the chastened postturn Heidegger maintained, for man to see himself as the "Shepherd of Being," and to adopt a quiet attitude of expectant repose waiting for the meaning of existence to reveal itself.[14]

Sartre, seeing a path to authenticity and freedom in *Being and Time*, and deducing from it that the starting point of any philosophical enterprise is man's own life, made Heidegger the touchstone of his thought. Heidegger's rejection of Sartre's assertion that there is no transcendent human essence—his insistence on an essence that "de-centered" man and his will to power—had the effect of elevating his cachet among the younger generation of French philosophers, such as Gilles Deleuze, Jacques Derrida, and Michel Foucault. They were searching for a way to make places for themselves outside of Sartre's shadow, and embraced Heidegger's philosophical preference for "letting go" over the French master's call for purposive action to shape destiny—which, they agreed, the whole experience of the twentieth century had shown to be dangerous. They were drawn to Heidegger's preference for the language of poetry over the conventional language of formal reason; and they (especially Foucault) never averted their eyes from Heidegger's insistence on death as the only assurance of human authenticity, individuality, and truth. Thus, Heidegger, still a pariah at home, through Sartre's embrace of his thought and his critique of Sartre's, became a dominant figure in French philosophy in the second half of the twentieth century.

At home Heidegger's public esteem began to rise a few years later, phoenixlike out of the ashes of what had been. He was formally "denazified" at the university, the world of philosophy became aware of the importance of his work in France, and he gave a series of well- attended public lectures in which (like the mystagogue-cum-sorcerer that Jaspers claimed he was) Heidegger assumed a role resembling Nietzsche's Zarathustra. In 1949 in the first of several annual visits to the prestigious Bremen Club, he warned that technology was overcoming humanity, asserting that agriculture, for example, had been transformed into "a motorized food industry, in essence the same as the manufacture of corpses in gas chambers and extermination camps, the same as the blockade and starvation of countries, the same as the manufacture of atomic bombs."[15]

It is possible to see an unrepentant Nazi, or at least a painfully insensitive German, equating Auschwitz and even the most brutal poultry farms, slaughterhouses, or other forms of mechanized exploitation of the Earth; and yet Heidegger's turn away from man's will to dominate the world through science resonates as an early recognition of the increasingly apparent dangers of technology in an epoch of environmental degradation.

In March of 1950, Heidegger made the first of four annual appearances at the Bühlerhöhe, a famous Black Forest spa in the hills high above Baden-Baden, where a wealthy clientele from all over Europe participated in a *Kur* based upon the therapeutic effect of encounters with "creative minds." Scientists, artists, and politicians gave lectures and led discussions on "the great spiritual problems of the day." But no one, Dr. Stoorman, the charismatic director of the sanitarium, wrote in his notes, matched Heidegger for the "totally exceptional excitement" that arose when he appeared at the rostrum, and no one demonstrated a comparable power of thought and knowledge.

Later that year, Heidegger spoke at the Academy of Fine Arts in Munich, where there was some controversy about inviting a one-time prominent Nazi to speak, but he attracted a large crowd. When he was invited back three years later to speak on the question of technology, the room was full of Germany's leading intellectuals, from whom he received a standing ovation when he ended with his now-famous assertion that "questioning is the piety of thinking."[16]

During the early 1950s, Heidegger was visited not only by

Arendt, but also by Sartre, the American philosopher Walter Kaufman, and the Japanese Germanist, Tezuka Tomio. In 1955 he visited Paris and then Normandy, where he lectured on the theme "What Is Philosophy?" at the International Cultural Center at Cérisy-la-Salle and met the poet René Char and the painter Georges Braque. The following year he visited Lyon with Jean Beaufret and also lectured at the University of Vienna. As the decade advanced, Heidegger, now approaching the age of seventy, continued to write extensively and lecture widely and was honored increasingly not only in France, Vienna, Bremen, and Munich, but also at home in Freiburg and in Messkirch, where he had been born. In 1958 he delivered a lecture, "Hegel and the Greeks," in Aix-en-Provence, whose lush subtropical atmosphere he loved, and returned there several times in the following years to lead a seminar and visit with René Char amid the landscapes that had inspired Cézanne. In 1962 he made the first of four visits to Greece, which had always been the landscape of his imagination and the abode of his thinking about the awestruck beginning of humanity's awareness of Being.

Heidegger was back in the world. He had been rehabilitated without apologia or *mea culpa* through the singular force of his own genius.

25

ON MAY 24, 1960, ADOLF EICHMANN, the SS Jewish specialist, was kidnapped in Argentina and brought to Jerusalem by agents of Mossad, the Israeli intelligence agency. Eichmann had been the mastermind and master bureaucrat of the system of transport that herded millions of terrified and brutalized victims away from their homes all over Europe to slave labor and death camps. The nightmare train rides of the early 1940s recalled in horrifying detail by Elie Wiesel[1] and Primo Levi[2] were orchestrated by Adolf Eichmann: the overcrowded cattle cars without ventilation, food, or water; innocents tortured by thirst, unbearable heat, or cold; people hungry, threatened, bullied, intimidated, the doors nailed shut; here and there someone going crazy, or puking, or defecating, the space so crowded that no one could sit or lie down; the terminus full of the reek and contamination of crematoria, guards with tommy guns, abusive inmates with truncheons, and a process first for separating men from women and then for selecting who would have a chance to survive and who would be killed right away. Eichmann's guilt was not only in the brutality of the transport, but in that he knew the fate to which he was transporting these unfortunates.

When the Third Reich collapsed in the spring of 1945, Allied troops were everywhere. Millions of Germans were homeless in bombed-out cities or refugees fleeing west hoping to fall into the hands of the Americans or British rather than the Red Army advancing from the east. Hitler, Himmler, and Goebbels, increasingly acknowledged as "evil men," had all killed themselves. The search for surviving war criminals and collaborators was under way, and over the next few years there were thousands of trials and executions all over Europe; but Adolf Eichmann simply disappeared. His name came up at the Nuremberg Trials, but no one knew where he was, or if he was alive.

By 1948 revelations about the magnitude and brutality of Nazi abuses had given rise to broad international support for the United Nations' Universal Declaration of Human Rights. In almost every particular the declaration stands as a rejoinder to how the Nazis had treated people, but after this milestone in international law was achieved and the war crimes tribunals concluded, the world's attention drifted away from crimes against humanity. The new structure of international relations diverted focus from the recent past. The Cold War supplanted World War II as the pressing current crisis, and on both sides of the Iron Curtain the Germans were transformed from former enemies into new allies, and there seemed to be little point in stirring up old animosities. Among victims and perpetrators, the victors and the vanquished, each for their own reasons, silence (if not actually forgetfulness) about the Nazi past was the order of the day.[3] It was almost fifteen years after his liberation, for example, before Primo Levi was able to find a publisher for his book *Survival in Auschwitz* (which has since sold more than 10 million copies) because acquisition editors did not think there would be a market for it.

For Arendt too the focus of work had shifted from the Nazi past to the Cold War, with research projects on the totalitarian elements of Marxism. After the anti-Soviet rebellion in Hungary in 1956, she rewrote sections of *Origins of Totalitarianism* and a published a new book, *On Revolution,*[4] reflecting optimism that spontaneous rebellious action reveals that totalitarian regimes are not monolithic and that there is always potential for unanticipated sudden change. Zionism had also fallen away from the center of Arendt's professional (if not personal) interest because with Israel clearly established as a Jewish state with estranged Arab residents and neighbors, she could no longer influence its direction. The capture of Adolf Eichmann brought both the Nazi past and the Israeli present back to front and center in Arendt's thought.

When Eichmann's capture was announced in 1960, Arendt approached William Shawn, the editor of the *New Yorker*, suggesting that she be sent to report on the trial. He accepted her offer, and Arendt set about modifying (and when the trial was postponed, further modifying) a very busy schedule including a two-month visit to Northwestern University planned for January and February 1961, a seminar at Columbia University, a lecture at Vassar College, and completion of a project funded by the Rockefeller Foundation. She wrote to the people involved that attending the trial in Jerusalem was an obligation that she felt she owed to her past: "You will understand, I think, why I should cover this trial; I missed the Nuremberg Trials, I never saw these people in the flesh, and this is probably my only chance."[5]

Arendt's plan to visit Karl and Gertrud Jaspers that spring was also disrupted by the original schedule and subsequent rescheduling of the trial. She wrote apologetically to Jaspers, reminding him how soon after the Nazi rise to power she had left Germany and how little of the horror she had experienced directly. She would never be able to forgive herself, Arendt said, if she didn't go and look "at this walking disaster face-to-face in all his bizarre vacuity, without the mediation of the printed word."

Of course, Jaspers understood, but he told Arendt that he felt unsettled by the Eichmann trial and worried that it would be difficult for her personally and injurious to Israel. Noting that the State of Israel is not coterminous with the Jewish people, Jaspers questioned the legitimacy of Israel's claim to the right to try Eichmann for crimes committed before the existence of the state. He relented, though, when Arendt wrote back that no other jurisdiction showed any interest in undertaking such a trial and that Israel had the right to speak for the victims because a large majority of survivors were living there as citizens. For the sake of these victims, she pointed out, Palestine had become Israel.

Still, Jaspers would have preferred for the international community, by treaty or perhaps through the United Nations, to create a permanent international criminal court to hear cases involving crimes against humanity. He believed that Eichmann deserved to be executed, but since "what was done to the Jews was done not only to the Jews" but to all humankind, the sentence would best be imposed outside of Israel and in the name of all of humanity. Most of all, Jaspers worried that the trial would somehow backfire on Israel, making the state look vengeful and establishing Eichmann as a martyr for anti-Semites worldwide. The greatest positive potential of the event, he felt (anticipating what has since come to be known as a truth and reconciliation commission) was neither an attribution of guilt nor the imposition of punishment, but rather the establishment of a historical record for all generations.

Aware of Arendt's long-standing antipathy to the Jewish leadership and her disquiet over the direction of Zionism, Jaspers warned that she would see and hear a great deal in Jerusalem that would depress and outrage her. He admonished her not to launch verbal attacks on the state or the court, to cast as little shadow as possible on Israel, to refrain from passing judgment, and cautioned her not to judge harshly "where only a prophet would have such a right," especially as "the risk to one's self is not small here." In the end, however, Arendt believed in the necessity of human judgment; and her conclusions were harsh, not only about Adolf Eichmann, whom she judged to be a fool, but also about the way the trial was conducted, and about the ethical and political conditions prevailing in Israel and in the Federal Republic of Germany.

The historical effect of the Eichmann trial was to establish the Holocaust as central to international human rights law. Arendt's book, *Eichmann in Jerusalem: A Report on the Banality of Evil*, which appeared first as a series of articles in the *New Yorker* in the spring of 1963 (and which is still in print and has been translated into seventeen languages) compelled worldwide attention. In the last years of her life nothing caused Arendt as much pain as the hostile reception of the Eichmann book in the Jewish community, which Amos Elon characterized as amounting to a virtual excommunication.[6] Yet, this is perhaps the work for which she is now most famous. As Arendt understood, fame is a double-edged sword.

Arendt arrived in Tel Aviv on April 9, 1961, and though she was again happy to be surrounded by friends and family, letters to Heinrich, Mary McCarthy, and Karl Jaspers demonstrate that her mood was irritable and almost all of her first impressions were critical: "Jerusalem loud and horrible, filled with the oriental mob typical of the Near East," the super-Orthodox very visible among them in their peies and caftans, "making life impossible for all reasonable people here"; Eichmann in his glass cage like a "ghost with a cold," or "a materialization at a séance;" the prosecutor, a Galician Jew, immeasurably boring and talking "a blue streak, constantly repeating and contradicting himself like an eager schoolboy who wants to show how much he knows"; the defense attorney, "oily, adroit and corrupt," but concise and to the point, "much more clever than the public prosecutor." The police, who organized everything, gave her "the creeps," speaking only Hebrew and looking Arabic "with some downright brutal types among them who would obey any order." And on top of everything else, the city was swamped with "philosemitic Germans who find absolutely everything [about Israel] so wonderful" that it is enough "to make one's stomach turn." When a German reporter, sobbing, flung his arms about Hannah and declared that "we Germans are the ones who did this," Hannah felt as if she were in a theater. Only the three judges, all German Jews, "the best of German Jewry," towering high above the proceeding, impressed her favorably, especially the presiding judge, Moshe Landau, who she found "really and truly marvelous—ironic and sarcastic in his forbearing friendliness."[7]

To a considerable extent Arendt's writing about the trial was based on historical documents and thousands of pages of transcripts of police interrogations and court proceedings. She was also present in the courtroom every day for the entire first month of the trial, which was dominated by witness testimony. From May 8 through June 12 (when there was a weeklong recess) the court was mostly involved in procedural decisions involving the submission of documents. During this time Arendt returned to Europe, where she undertook library research related to the trial, and visited with Jaspers and other friends. She returned to Jerusalem on June 20 to be present for the first week of Eichmann's testimony; then flew back to Europe, where she vacationed with Heinrich, who had finally agreed to international travel.

They spent a very happy time in Basel with Karl and Gertrud Jaspers. Despite the closeness of their friendship, Arendt and Jaspers had always addressed each other using the German formal *Sie*. In their generation this was the polite way in which all but close friends and relatives communicated, and was certainly the way that children—even adult children—spoke to their parents and teachers. Hannah was delighted on this visit when Karl and Gertrud Jaspers offered her and Blücher the informal *du*, reserved for intimate friendships. Nothing could reflect more fully the attitude of mutual respect and camaraderie that prevailed among them.

All in all, Arendt was present for only a third of the trial, but this was long enough to form clear impressions of the key actors, and she was able to reconstruct the rest from thorough and complete court transcripts. Though she conceptualized her project as a report on the trial, Arendt proceeded more like a scholar than a journalist, and much of her time in Europe during those months involved writing up notes and collecting research materials on events with which Eichmann had been associated.

A year and a half passed between the end of the trial and publication of the book. Hannah's ability to concentrate on the project was undermined when Heinrich suffered a cerebral aneurysm in October 1961, and she stopped everything to help take care of him. Then, as he was recovering in the winter months at the beginning of 1962, she was hospitalized for two months after a serious accident in a New York taxi. After her release, she wrote to Mary McCarthy that immediately upon regaining consciousness she felt not that death was terrible, but that "life was beautiful and I'd rather take it."[8]

She began to write her report on the Eichmann trial. Despite her happiness at being alive, Arendt's writing reflected the irritation and frustration that she had felt in Jerusalem. She began with a few nice words about the judges, "so obviously three good and honest men."[9] But the judges alone, despite their integrity, Arendt felt, were not enough to keep the proceedings from deteriorating into a show trial.

She did not mean a show trial in the sense of the Soviets in the Stalin era when political enemies were railroaded and innocent men coerced to confess—for Arendt had no doubt that Eichmann was guilty and deserved to be executed—but in the sense that the proceedings were theatrical rather than strictly legalistic. Justice, Arendt wrote, demands that the accused be prosecuted, defended, and judged, and that all other questions—such as "How could it happen?" "Why did it happen?" "Why the Jews?" "Why the Germans?" "What was the role of other nations?" "How to understand the cooperation of Jewish leaders in their own destruction?" and "Why did the Jews go to their death like lambs to the slaughter?"—that all such questions be left in abeyance. These were not Arendt's questions, but were all raised by the prosecution. While she agreed that they were interesting and important issues for philosophers or historians, Arendt emphasized that, at a trial, justice demanded that attention be focused on the deeds of Adolf Eichmann, not on the sufferings of the Jews, the crimes of mankind or of the Germans, "not even," she wrote, "on anti-Semitism and racism."

A criminal trial begins and ends with the deeds of an alleged perpetrator; if he is to suffer, it must be for what he is shown to have done to cause the suffering of others. To show only that others suffered is not sufficient. Yet this, Arendt thought, was the goal of the prosecution and the government of Israel, not to demonstrate details of Adolf Eichmann's behavior but to show that the nations of the world stood by and permitted the destruction of 6 million Jews. The lesson that the government of Israel derived from the Holocaust, Arendt wrote, was that the world hates Jews, that security requires Jews to separate themselves from the peoples of the world and become strong so that generations of virile young Israelis would never succumb to a ghetto mentality the way the Jews of the Diaspora (which is to say, people like Arendt) had, debased and walking quietly to their deaths.

This angered Arendt as an affront to the memory of Jews in the Diaspora, whose destruction, she believed, owed more to the short-lived triumph of racist totalitarian ideology and the imperfect judgment of Jewish leaders than to any inherent weakness derived from Jewish involvement in the European Enlightenment. The "propaganda" inherent in the "show" trial also struck her as reckless insofar as it aimed at persuading young Israelis that their well-being depended on military prowess rather than efforts to find a path to peace with their Arab neighbors.

She was incensed by the hypocrisy of Gideon Hausner, the chief prosecutor, who denounced the infamous Nuremburg Laws of 1935 that prohibited intermarriage and sexual intercourse between Jews and Germans, even though he knew, as she pointed out, that Israel prohibited (as it still does) the intermarriage of Jews and non-Jews, although such marriages (like her own) concluded abroad were recognized. The better-informed correspondents, she wrote, were well aware of this irony but did not mention it in their reports. "This, they figured, was not the time to tell the Jews what was wrong with the laws and institutions of their own country." Arendt, however, felt no such constraint.

To religious Jews and Zionists, she wrote, the most important value is the survival of the Jewish people; assimilation is to them as much a threat as anti-Semitism, because in their fear it also points toward the end of the people as a people. They do not count on countercurrents that are, of course, always present. For Arendt the highest value even after the Holocaust (perhaps especially after the Holocaust) was the plurality of humanity. Any emphasis on separations among people inevitably leads in the direction of racism, totalitarianism, war, and disaster. The militant Zionists had not learned empathy for victims from the Nazi experience, but only that Jews had to be unified and strong so as not to become victims again. They did not seem to notice that in Europe even the strong had been brought to disaster. Working toward peace, with all its dangers, was the right, safer, and better choice for the Jewish people than preparing for war. Better, she thought, following Socrates, to be a victim than a perpetrator; for a person ultimately lives with one's self, and no one wants to live with a murderer.

As the trial progressed, witness after witness testified to the calamity of the Jewish people. Gideon Hausner pointed his finger at Eichmann and pronounced, "There sits the monster responsible for all this," without attending to the details of how "the monster" had done it all. At one point thirty-eight volumes of the diaries of Hans Frank, the Nazi governor-general of occupied Poland who was hanged as a war criminal at Nuremburg, were introduced into evidence to illustrate the fate of Polish Jewry.

Dr. Robert Servatius, the defense attorney, rose to ask whether Eichmann's name was mentioned in any of those volumes, and the answer was "No."

The prosecutor, eager to demonstrate the contrast between Israeli heroism and the submissive meekness with which the Jews of the Diaspora went to their deaths asked witness after witness: "Why did you not protest?" "Why did you board the train?" "Why didn't you revolt and charge and attack?" But as Arendt pointed out, no group in all of Europe had behaved differently once they had fallen into the terror and overwhelming force of Nazi killing squads. The reason for this was clear; she illustrated it with the example of a small rebellion in the old Jewish quarter of Amsterdam in 1941 after which

> four hundred and thirty Jews were arrested in reprisal and they were literally tortured to death, first in Buchenwald and then in the Austrian camp of Mauthausen. For months on end they died a thousand deaths, and every single one of them would have envied his brethren in Auschwitz and even in Riga and Minsk [where civilians were gunned down on the streets or in trenches which they were made to dig themselves]. There exist many things considerably worse than death and the S.S. saw to it that none of them was ever very far from the victims' minds and imagination.

Had the trial focused, as Arendt thought it should have, on the behavior of the defendant rather than the suffering of victims, it would have become evident that another reason the Jews of Europe had submitted passively to Nazi control, boarding trains to death camps without protest, was because they were badly served by their leaders:

> The Jewish Councils of Elders were informed by Eichmann or his men of how many Jews were needed to fill each train, and they made out the lists of deportees. The Jews registered, filled out innumerable forms, answered pages and pages of questionnaires regarding their property so that it could be seized more easily; then they assembled at the collection points and boarded the trains. The few who tried to hide or to escape were rounded up by a special Jewish police force.

The failure of the Jewish leadership, which was understood by Holocaust survivors, and had been examined by a handful of scholars, never entered into the prosecution case but did break briefly into public awareness toward the end of May during the testimony of Baron Philip von Freudiger, who had been prominent as a leader of the Hungarian Jewish community. People in the audience screamed at Freudiger in Hungarian and Yiddish; and he, visibly shaken, acknowledged that "there are people here who say they were not told to escape. . . . [But] where could they have gone to? Where could they have fled? What could we have done? What could we have done?" Half the people who escaped, he pointed out, were captured and killed; but Arendt notes that 99 percent of Hungarian Jews were killed in the camps, and that Freudiger managed to escape and make his way to Palestine.

Had the prosecution focused on Eichmann's actual behavior, it would have shown that he negotiated with leaders like Baron Freudiger and Dr. Rudolf Kastner, the vice president of the Zionist organization in Budapest, for "quiet and good order" in the transit camps from which hundreds of thousand of Hungarian Jews were deported to their deaths at Auschwitz. All this in exchange for the lives of a few thousand prominent Jews sent to Palestine on trains guarded by German soldiers.

"To a Jew," Arendt wrote, the "role of the Jewish leaders in the destruction of their own people," which had recently been documented in all its "pathetic and sordid detail" by Raul Hilberg in his seminal work *The Destruction of the European Jews,* "is undoubtedly the darkest chapter of the whole dark story."[10] They compiled lists of persons and property, distributed Yellow Star armbands and badges, secured money from deportees to defray the expenses of their transportation, kept track of vacated apartments, supplied police forces to help seize Jews and get them on the trains, and then handed over their assets in good order. In Budapest, the Jewish officials to whom the right of "absolute disposal over all Jewish spiritual and material wealth and all Jewish manpower" had been granted reported that they felt like captains of sinking ships who "succeeded in bringing them safe to port by casting overboard a great part of their precious cargo." Baron Freudiger and Dr. Kastner, for example, had saved 1,684 prominent community leaders by throwing overboard 476,000 innocent victims. In Lodz, Chaim Rumkowski, who called himself Chaim I, issued currency notes and postage stamps engraved with his portrait. In Berlin the chief rabbi, Leo Baeck, "scholarly, mild-mannered, highly educated," (but to whom Hannah referred in the *New Yorker* articles as the "Jewish Führer," a phrase that was redacted from the book) believed that Jewish policemen would make the ordeal easier by being gentle and helpful, whereas in fact, Arendt pointed out, they were more brutal and less corruptible, precisely because so much was at stake for them. Baeck, who knew what the fate of deported persons would be, chose to conceal it out of "humane" considerations believing that living in the expectation of death by gassing would only make things harder. The result of this was that individuals who were relatively safe at Theresienstadt, the show camp the Nazis allowed the Red Cross to tour (and at which Baeck was held), sometimes volunteered for deportation to Auschwitz thinking that those who tried to tell them the truth were insane.

Without Jewish help in administrative and police work, Arendt concluded, there would have been either complete chaos or an impossibly severe drain on German manpower; drawing on witness testimony and reports of the Dutch government, she estimated that perhaps as many as half of the victims might have survived. She offered a quote from Robert Pendorf's 1961 book *Mörder und Ermordete: Eichmann und die Judenpolitik des Dritten Reiches*: "There can be no doubt that, without the cooperation of the victims, it would hardly have been possible for a few thousand people, most of whom, moreover, worked in offices, to liquidate hundreds of thousands of other people. . . . Over the whole way to their deaths the Polish Jews (for example) got to see hardly more than a handful of Germans."

Arendt was not the first to reveal these sad facts about the extent to which respectable society collapsed not only in Germany but throughout Europe, and not only among perpetrators but also among victims. In addition to Pendorf's book,[11] Raul Hilberg's 1961 study of the destruction of European Jewry,[12] and H. G. Adler's book *Theresienstadt, 1941–1945*, published in 1955[13] (which even the prosecutor, when asked about it by one of the judges, admitted was based on irrefutable sources), there was also Dr. Kastner's own published report of his wartime activities and a court record arising from a slander action that Kastner brought against an Israeli newspaper that published an article in 1956 accusing him of collaboration with the Nazis. Judge Benjamin Halevi, one of the three judges at the Eichmann trial, had presided at that hearing and concluded that Kastner "had sold his soul to the devil."[14] In March 1957, while the slander case was being appealed, Kastner was murdered, and the Israeli Supreme Court subsequently vacated the judgment of the lower court, but the transcript and findings of fact remain. These issues had for years been widely discussed in Israel, where even schoolbooks, Arendt noted, discussed the problem openly and with "astonishing frankness."

The Holocaust survivors who gave testimony at the Eichmann trial, but who had never seen Eichmann or had seen him only briefly at a great distance, established a powerful record of the horror of Jewish suffering but offered no insight into the defendant's *modus operandi*, which was dependent upon the cooperation of the Jewish leadership. Nor was there any reference to the fact that it was not just the leaders in Europe but also in Palestine who for a while played ball with the Nazis' forced-emigration policies. They had hoped for a demographic boost to assure a Jewish majority in a plebiscite or in military action and were blinded at first to the full meaning of the persecution and destruction that overwhelmed European Jewry, viewing Hitler's rise to power as the decisive defeat of assimilation and the expulsion of Jews from Europe as a godsend for their own settlements.

Had the trial focused on how the great crimes were committed, Eichmann would still have been found guilty, but others, whom the Israeli regime wished to protect, would have been embarrassed: not just Jews in Israel but also Germans in Konrad Adenauer's government, which was supportive of Israel and paying reparations. Perhaps even more to the point, the image of Eichmann as a monster would have been thrown into question (for if he was a monster, what were these others?) and with it the assertion that the world is filled with murderous Jew-haters against whom the only protections are an in-gathering of Jews into Israel and fierce militancy. Arendt's differences with the

Zionist leaders were clear. She was not ashamed of the Diaspora and did not accept that it was destined to have ended in the Holocaust. She challenged the legitimacy, morality, and effectiveness of the Jewish leadership past and present. She was not hostile to Israel but was firmly in the loyal opposition, wanting Israel to adopt secular, multicultural values in support of a state based on the equality of all citizens; failing that, she would have liked a government with a less belligerent attitude, committed to working for peace by promoting projects of cooperation between Arabs and Jews. She did not feel that these judgments separated her from the Jewish people, but rather that she was thinking deeply about the Jewish people and participating with a sense of urgency in a discourse about their destiny.

26

◇◇◇◇
◆

ARENDT'S EPIPHANY IN JERUSALEM WAS THAT the greatest crimes and most profound evil did not require hate or even malice as it is commonly understood. This is part of what she meant when she called the trial "a long course in human wickedness" that taught the lesson of the "fearsome, word-and-thought-defying *banality of evil*." Eichmann was by all accounts a normal family man. The psychiatrists and clergymen who interviewed him in conjunction with the trial certified that he was normal in such things as his attitude toward his wife and children, parents, siblings, friends. He was not perverted, sadistic, or obsessed with dangerous urges to kill or insane hatreds. He was average, normal, not feeble-minded or indoctrinated: "more normal," one physician concluded, "than I am after having examined him."[1] What most surprised Arendt at the trial was her sudden insight that Eichmann was not actually a Jew-hater. She noticed, however, that Eichmann was unable to articulate complex thoughts, reverting inevitably to stock phrases, slogans, and clichés, as if he had trouble finding words of his own. She thought this derived from the fact that he did not think very deeply or well, and certainly never from the perspective of the other, which is a necessary condition for being able to distinguish right from wrong.

Eichmann pled "not guilty in the sense of the indictment," and maintained that "with the killing of the Jews I had nothing to do. I never killed a Jew, or a non-Jew, for that matter—I never killed any human being, I never gave an order to kill; I just did not do it." Not only did he not "personally" have any thing against the Jews, but Jewish relatives on his mother's side had always been good to him and to his family. He did not deny that he had aided and abetted the annihilation of the Jews, and even called this "one of the greatest crimes in the history of humanity," but he did deny that he had any animus against Jews, or harbored hatred in his soul. He was not, he said, an "*innerer Schweinehund,*" which Arendt translated for her readers as "a dirty bastard in the depths of his heart."[2] Perhaps this is so; certainly Arendt thought he gave the impression of a man more likely to be made ill by the sight of blood and gore than of one lusting for it, but she also recognized that all such distinctions were inconsequential. Eichmann knew from his own direct observations that genocide was being undertaken, and he understood the centrality of his own role and position. In criminal law such knowledge is regarded as the moral equivalent of "intention," and forms a sound basis for punishment. The man who organizes mass murder from his desk is just as culpable as the *Kommandant* who operates the gas chamber, though they may be different types of men.

Arendt did not absolve Eichmann of guilt, nor oppose his execution,[3] but thought the prosecution case against him was misleading insofar as it portrayed him as a monster, and exaggerated in its assessment of his individual responsibility for the totality of harm done to the Jewish people. This offended her and detracted from the important task of reconstructing what had happened and how it happened. A focus on the behavior of the offender rather than the suffering of the victims would have shown Eichmann, more frighteningly, to have been an ordinary man behaving with ordinary motives in a culture that produced an abundance of murderers and accomplices.

Arendt's understanding of "banal" evil was a radical revision of her thinking immediately after the war, when Karl Jaspers had to remind her not to fall into the trap of thinking of Nazi criminality as demonic or larger than life. It had broad implications. The phrase "banality of evil" is not merely, as some critics suggested, a catchphrase, but rather an acute insight that evil is neither, as Kant thought, a wholly independent phenomenon with its own independent roots, nor the total absence of good. Evil coexists with good, and individuals engaged in evil may believe in the moment that their behavior is justified and morally appropriate. Thus it was not only Eichmann's evil that Arendt perceived as banal, but also the complicity of the Jewish leadership, the passivity of the rest of the world in the face of the horror.

One does not need to find monsters in order to explain the existence of evil; it requires only normal, ordinary men and women. Shakespeare understood this when he had Marc Antony say of Brutus and his collaborators: "So are they all, all honorable men."

But can this really be said of Adolf Eichmann? Is it plausible to believe his denial that he hated Jews or wished to harm them? Critics who think Arendt misjudged him refer to an interview five years earlier with the journalist Willem Sassen, also a former Nazi and a fugitive from justice, in which Eichmann declared that he would jump into his grave happy to know that he had the blood of 5 million Jews on his hands. One possibility is that Eichmann was the sort of man who would say what people wanted to hear, and in the case of the Sassen document perhaps also what would sell, since both men needed money. As it happens, though, the interview did not sell at all until after Eichmann was kidnapped by the Israelis, when it was published in *Life* magazine[4] in the United States and *Stern* in Germany. Another possibility is that Sassen, exercizing literary license, may not have written precisely what Eichmann said: the published voice of Adolf Eichmann in *Life* magazine bears very little resemblance to the meticulously preserved record of his words in hundreds of hours and thousands of pages of transcripts of his speech in the courtroom in Jerusalem or in interviews with Captain Avner Less of the Israeli police, to whom he said that he would "gladly" hang himself in public "as a warning example for all anti-Semites on this earth."[5] Both comments, equally clichés, Arendt thought, might have served the purpose in different circumstances of giving Eichmann an emotional lift. It was the same in the last moments of his life after the trial, when the noose was being put around his neck: first he proclaimed emphatically that he was a *Gottgläubiger*, to express that he was not a Christian and did not believe in life after death.

> He then proceeded: "After a short while, gentlemen, *we shall all meet again*. Such is the fate of all men. Long live Germany, long live Argentina, long live Austria. *I shall not forget them.*" In the face of death, he had found the cliché used in funeral oratory. Under the gallows, his memory played him his last trick; he was "elated" and he forgot that it was his own funeral.

The greatest moral and legal challenge of the whole case, Arendt understood, derives precisely from the observation that

Eichmann was a normal man, neither hate-filled nor insane. To be normal means not to be an exception, and to be "no exception" within the context of the Nazi regime meant to be in complicity with evil and to accept without thought (or at least without thinking deeply or clearly) that being in conformity with the law was the moral equivalent of behaving appropriately. Under the conditions of the Third Reich, Arendt suddenly realized, only "exceptions" could have reacted "normally" if by that we mean as resistors to murder.

Karl Jaspers was such an exception, but Martin Heidegger, though he had no blood on his own hands, was not. Had Arendt's reconciliation with Heidegger prepared the ground of her understanding? Surely she went to Jerusalem to see Eichmann, the mass murderer, expecting something qualitatively different but, seeing him, was reminded of so much else that she had seen in Germany. She concluded that the harmony of all of German society "had been shielded against reality and factuality by exactly the same means, the same self-deception, lies, and stupidity that had become ingrained in Eichmann's mentality."

In the end, Arendt felt that everyone in the courtroom in Jerusalem could see that Eichmann was not a "monster," but that it was difficult "not to suspect that he was a clown." He had insisted, for example, that all his problems arose from having taken an oath of loyalty when he joined the SS, and that he learned from this never again to take an oath. No one, he said, could ever persuade him again to make a sworn statement; he would refuse to do it for moral reasons. "I have made up my mind once and for all," he said, "that no judge in the world or any other authority will ever be capable of making me swear an oath, to give sworn testimony. I won't do it voluntarily and no one will be able to force me." Then after being told that he could testify in his own case with or without being sworn in, declared that he would prefer to do it under oath as an assurance of his truthfulness.

Whatever Arendt had expected to find when she set out for Jerusalem, what she actually saw in the bulletproof box in which Eichmann appeared in court was a man who had perpetrated the greatest possible evil not out of hatred, sadistic impulse, or any preexisting inclination to mayhem, but because he had drifted more or less without purpose into the ambit of Nazism. He had been at best a mediocre student, had no political interests, seems never to have read *Mein Kampf* or much of anything else, and was, like many young men of the period, underemployed. When Ernst Kaltenbrunner (later hanged at Nuremburg), the son of one of his father's business associates, said to him, Why not join the SS? Eichmann replied, Why not?

The National Socialist Party offered employment, status, and the excitement, camaraderie, and sense of shared enthusiasm that Leni Riefenstahl captured so well in her film *Triumph of the Will*. Hardly anyone in Germany had proven to be immune to Nazi seduction; even so distinguished a scholar as Martin Heidegger had responded to the opportunities presented. Suddenly, Adolf Eichmann was somebody, with something important to do, and although it was another ten years before it was entirely clear what that was, he was determined from the beginning to honor his oath of loyalty to the Führer, and to demonstrate worth and competence to his new associates.

Eichmann, who assisted in organizing the Wannsee Conference at which Heydrich announced the "final solution" to a group of very senior dignitaries, noted that there were no objections to the plan. Indeed, these "Popes of the Third Reich," whose judgment and character he respected if for no other reason than by dint of their high positions in government and society, received it with "happy agreement" and "extraordinary enthusiasm."[6]

> Now he could see with his own eyes and hear with his own ears that not only Hitler . . . the S.S., or the Party, but the elite of the good old Civil Service were vying and fighting with each other for the honor of taking the lead in these "bloody" matters. At that moment [he] "sensed a kind of Pontius Pilate feeling . . . free of all guilt." *Who was he to judge*? Who was he "to have (his) own thoughts in this matter"?

The judgment of the court in Jerusalem was that Eichmann had "closed his ears to conscience," but Arendt did not think this was the case; it was not that Eichmann did not hear the call of conscience, but that his conscience spoke with the voice of respectable society, and this is the voice that seduces men to evil. When the devil comes to negotiate for our souls, he brings attractive gifts and rationalizations, and is more likely to be wearing a business suit or uniform of national pride than a fiery cape.

27

THE FIRST INDICATOR OF THE MAGNITUDE of the storm of indignation that Arendt's criticism of Israel and the Jewish leadership was about to produce was a sympathetic letter from Henry Schwarzchild, warning her that his organization, the Anti-Defamation League of B'nai B'rith, was preparing an angry response.[1] A few days later she received a less sympathetic note from Siegfried Moses written on behalf of the Council of Israeli Jews from Germany making a "declaration of war" on her and the Eichmann book.[2] Moses flew to Switzerland to meet with Arendt and demanded that she stop publication of *Eichmann in Jerusalem* in book form in order to quiet the storm. She refused, and warned Moses that "her Jewish critics were going to make the book into a cause célèbre and thus embarrass the Jewish community far beyond anything that she had said or could possibly do."[3]

Heinrich, writing from New York before he left to meet Hannah in Europe, warned that a great many letters of protest were arriving at their apartment and that the "Israelites seem to be gathering into a phalanx." William Shawn, the editor of the *New Yorker*, sent a telegram saying that "people in town seem to be discussing little else."[4] Hans Morgenthau, whose review in the *Chicago Tribune* lauded Arendt's work as "superb," "concise," "incisive," and "powerful,"[5] wrote to her in Europe that the Jewish community was up in arms and in a state of "psychological havoc."[6] A few weeks later the Anti-Defamation League distributed a memorandum informing its members about the *New Yorker* series and alerting them to "Arendt's defamatory conception of Jewish participation in the Nazi Holocaust."[7] This was followed by a public statement condemning the book and several critical reviews published in the Jewish magazine *Aufbau*,[8] where many of Arendt's first articles in the United States had been published in the 1940s. Irving Howe later described the bitter public dispute that ensued as "violent,"[9] and Mary McCarthy said at the time that it had assumed the proportions of a pogrom.[10]

Although Arendt had never been religious, and certainly she had been open in her criticism of the Jewish leadership, her involvement with Jewish issues had been such that Alfred Kazin characterized her as "a blazing Jew."[11] Now, however, she became a pariah among her own people. Leo Mindlin wrote in the *Jewish Floridian* that Arendt was a self-hating Jew who had turned her back on her faith and promulgated a hostile attack on the integrity of the Jewish leaders in Europe and a postmortem defense of Eichmann, concluding that she was "digging future Jewish graves to the applause of the world's unconverted anti-Semites."[12] Trude Weiss-Rosmarin, the editor of the *Jewish Spectator*, published a review under the title "Self-Hating Jewess Writes Pro-Eichmann Series for the New Yorker" arguing that "Miss Arendt should disqualify herself from writing on Jewish themes to which she brings the pathology and confusion of the Jew who does not want to be a Jew and suffers because 'the others' will not let him forget that he is a Jew."[13] The Anti-Defamation League followed its original denunciation with a pamphlet entitled *Arendt Nonsense* that identified the book as banal, evil, glib, and trite, appended a selection of hostile reviews, and encouraged rabbis to speak out in their congregations in opposition to the book, perhaps with the goal of persuading readers either to hate the book before reading it, or simply not read it at all.[14] Similarities of text and tone in several of the more scathing subsequent reviews suggest that some reviewers may have been more familiar with this pamphlet than with the book itself.

At the beginning of May, while still vacationing with Heinrich in Greece, Hannah went to Israel for four days to see Kurt Blumenfeld, who was hospitalized with the illness from which he died before the month was over. He had heard the criticism swirling around the *New Yorker* articles but had not read them. In their conversations Blumenfeld agreed that at least some of her critics were "idiots"; but after his death Hannah received a note from Siegfried Moses saying that on his deathbed Blumenfeld had been outraged by what she had written. Hannah was sure that Moses and others who saw Blumenfeld *in extremis* during his last days had swayed him with distortions and lies, and she was deeply hurt that her lifelong friend had been maliciously alienated from her at the end of his life.[15]

At about this same time Michael Musmanno, a justice of the Supreme Court of Pennsylvania and a former high-ranking naval officer who had been a judge at the second round of Nuremberg Trials published a highly critical review in the Sunday *New York Times Book Review.* Musmanno had been a witness for the prosecution at the Eichmann trial, and Arendt ridiculed his testimony that von Ribbentrop, the Nazi foreign minister, had told him at Nuremburg that Hitler would have been all right if he had not fallen under Eichmann's influence.[16] Now, he wrote that Arendt had been motivated by "purely private prejudices," and had "attacked the State of Israel, its laws and institutions, wholly unrelated to the Eichmann case."[17] He read Arendt's assertion that Eichmann was not a Jew-hater as an expression of sympathy, not recognizing her horror of the banal evil that could undertake mass murder even in the absence of the usual sordid motives. He interpreted her observation that an international system for containing and responding to crimes against humanity is necessary because punishment alone has never "possessed enough power of deterrence to prevent the commission of crimes" as a declaration that "it was a terrible mistake to try Eichmann at all," which she neither said nor believed.

Over the next few months the *Times Book Review* received over a hundred letters, the majority defending Arendt and attacking the review. How, one writer wondered, could a reviewer have missed the point of the book as completely as Judge Musmanno did? Another thought the review "childish," that Musmanno's intellect was clearly inferior to Arendt's, and that no intelligent person who had read the book could take him seriously. But others thought the judge had written a powerful rebuttal of an appallingly ugly and vicious book.[18]

The day after Musmanno's review appeared, the *Times* published a report of a meeting of the Bergen-Belsen Survivors Association in New York at which Gideon Hausner, the Israeli prosecutor, expressed "sharp criticism" of Hannah Arendt and others who "twisted and distorted" the facts of the Eichmann trial. Dr. Nahum Goldmann, the president of the World Zionist Organization, also present at this meeting, was quoted as saying that people like Hannah Arendt who charge Holocaust victims with their own destruction "are devoid of any psychological understanding and perspective of those terrible days, as well as all reverence for the unparalleled suffering and tragedy of the 6,000,000 who perished."[19]

In July, Hannah wrote to Jaspers that upon returning she found that her "whole apartment was literally filled with unopened mail . . . about the Eichmann business." Much of this bordered on hate mail, like the letter from a woman in New Jersey which began with the declaration that she had never read the Eichmann book and "would never read such trash," and concluded with the hope that "the ghosts of our six million martyrs haunt your bed at night."[20]

That summer, debate among the New York intellectuals began in earnest in the pages of *Partisan Review* with a scathing review by Lionel Abel, who had always found Arendt too self-assured: Hannah Arrogant is what he sometimes called her. Hannah never forgave the editors, who had published so much of her work in the preceding years, for choosing a reviewer who was widely known to dislike her. She wrote to Mary McCarthy (who twenty-five years earlier had been a founding editor of *Partisan Review*) that she was breaking her relationship with the journal not because of the content of Abel's comments, but because the editors showed an extraordinary lack of the most elementary respect for her and her work in choosing him as a reviewer.

Abel suggested that Arendt had called the Holocaust itself banal, ignoring that it was the motives and character of the Holocaust's operatives (Eichmann and others) and not the harm they had done that she identified as banal. It was preposterous, he wrote, for her to deny that Eichmann was a moral monster: How could a man who had murdered 5 million people (ignoring the point that however great his guilt, Eichmann had not personally killed anyone) be anything other than morally monstrous? "And all the more a monster if he did not know he was one." Then, opening the door to the calumny that Arendt was more German than Jewish, he declared that her portrayal of the Nazis made them more aesthetically appealing than their victims, which overlooks the fact that Arendt had been very severe in her judgment of the Germans both during the Third Reich and in the years after.[21]

She had pointed out, for example, that prior to Eichmann's capture the Germans had made no serious efforts to find or try the murderers in their midst, many of whom had not even felt it necessary to live under assumed names. The international publicity attached to the Eichmann trial prompted German authorities to post rewards and apprehend Nazi criminals, and for a while the German newspapers were full of accounts of trials of mass murderers; but the sentences imposed were "fantastically lenient": ten years of hard labor, for example, for the killing of 15,000 Jews, five years for the deportation of 1,200 Jews half of whom were killed, three and a half years for the liquidation of the Jewish inhabitants of two Russian towns, four years for a prominent postwar political leader who had participated in the murder of 40,000 Polish Jews. Six and a half years for having gassed 6,280 Jewish Serbian women and children in specially constructed vans. More than 100 judges with more than "ordinarily compromised pasts" were dismissed from service, but the fact remained that more than 5,000 members of the judiciary in West Germany had been active in the courts of the Third Reich. Arendt characterized the sudden rush of long-postponed denazification activity as a sop to world opinion:

> The attitude of the German people toward their own past, which all experts on the German question had puzzled over for fifteen years, could hardly have been more clearly demonstrated: they did not particularly mind the presence of murderers at large in the country, since none were likely to commit murder of their own free will; however, if world opinion—or rather what the Germans called *das Ausland*, collecting all countries outside Germany into a singular noun—became obstinate and demanded that these people be punished, they were perfectly willing to oblige, at least up to a point.

The government of Konrad Adenauer, Arendt pointed out, was full of ex-Nazis. Hans Globke, one of Adenauer's closest advisors, had been the author of the Nuremburg Laws. It had been his "brilliant idea" to compel all Jews to take "Israel" or "Sarah" as middle names. Wolfgang Immerwahr Fränkel, the chief prosecutor of the German Supreme Court had (despite his middle name, which translates as ever-true) lied about his Nazi past. Theodor Maunz, the constitutional law expert who had written in 1943 that the command of the Führer is the absolute center of the legal order, was the minister of education and culture in Bavaria. Wilhelm Harsten, the head of the Nazi security service in Holland, who had been sentenced to twelve years by a Dutch court, was given a position in the Bavarian civil service after his release from prison in 1957.

> It is one thing to ferret out criminals and murderers from their hiding places, and it is another thing to find them prominent and flourishing in the public realm—to encounter innumerable men in the federal and state administrations and,

> generally, in *public* office whose careers had bloomed under the Hitler regime. True, if the Adenauer administration had been too sensitive about employing officials with a compromising Nazi past, there might have been no administration at all. For the truth is, of course, the exact opposite of Dr. Adenauer's assertion that only a "relatively small percentage" of Germans had been Nazis, and that a "great majority (had been) happy to help their Jewish fellow-citizens when they could."

Mary McCarthy published a response to Abel in *Partisan Review*. Her essay, "The Hue and Cry," begins with the observation that the negative reviews were all written by Jews or special cases like Judge Musmanno who had been criticized in the Eichmann book or Hugh Trevor-Roper, "who has a corner on Nazi history in its popular form." Her own Gentile friends and family, Mary wrote, spoke of the book in hushed tones, asking, "Did you get that out of it?"

> The division between Jew and Gentile is even more pronounced in private conversation, where a Gentile, once the topic is raised in Jewish company (and it always is), feels like a child with a reading defect in a class of normal readers—or the reverse. It is as if *Eichmann in Jerusalem* had required a special pair of Jewish spectacles to make its "true purport" visible. Propagandists [such] as Lionel Abel . . . have been eagerly offering their pair to the reader for a peep into Miss Arendt's mind . . . [to expose] her as an anti-Semite. . . . More moderate parlor critics talk of "arrogance" or "lack of proportion" while conceding that Miss Arendt is of course not an anti-Semite or an admirer of Eichmann's.[22]

Of Abel's conclusion that Hannah had made Eichmann aesthetically palatable and his victims aesthetically repulsive, McCarthy wrote that he offered no evidence on behalf of this idea, which could be defended only as his personal impression of the book, and that this revealed more about him than about Arendt: "Reading her book, he liked Eichmann better than the Jews who died in the crematoriums. Each to his own taste. It was not my impression." McCarthy agreed that of course it was evil to send millions to their deaths, but it was Abel who by constructing Eichmann as a depraved and wicked creature like Richard III or Iago made him an object of aesthetic interest.

Mary's own position was that the Eichmann book, despite all the horrors in it, was morally exhilarating.

> I freely confess that it gave me joy and I too heard a paean in it—not a hate-paean to totalitarianism but a paean of transcendence, heavenly music, like that of the final chorus of *Figaro* or the *Messiah*. As in these choruses, a pardon or redemption of some sort was taking place. The reader "rose above" the terrible material of the trial or was born aloft to survey it with his intelligence. No person was pardoned, but the whole experience was brought back, redeemed, as in the harrowing of hell.

In April 1964 a review of *Eichmann in Jerusalem* in the London *Times Literary Supplement* turned these words against McCarthy, the reviewer claiming that the reference to the great choral masterpieces implied that she was exulting over the mass murder of Jews. Mary wrote to Hannah that her internal alarm system had warned her that there was something dangerous about the reference to Mozart and Handel, but she left it in specifically so as "not to be like *them*," who would never tell the truth if there was a possibility it might be used against them. She had not imagined that anyone could twist her words in quite that way, and wrote to Hannah: "I don't even mind that, what I do mind is that they have used it to compromise you. . . . I should have shown more caution. Please forgive me if you can."

Hannah wrote back that she thought it would have been better not to have included "the Mozart business . . . because the comparison even of effects is too high. But I always loved the sentence because you were the only reader to understand what otherwise I have never admitted—namely that I wrote this book in a curious state of euphoria." Writing *Eichmann in Jerusalem*, the exercise of intellect as a way of mastering the past, had been for Hannah a sort of *cura posterior*, a path of healing involving neither forgiveness nor forgetting, but of finding peace through the hard work of thinking.

28

THERE WAS HARDLY A PROMINENT INTELLECTUAL in the English-speaking world who did *not* review *Eichmann in Jerusalem* or write to Arendt about it in the two years after it was published. Bruno Bettelheim published a review in the *New Republic* lauding the book's powerful impact, drawing on Arendt's previous work to assert that the Holocaust was less a part of the ancient history of anti-Semitism than an aspect of totalitarianism, something new in the world. He agreed with Arendt that the stories of the ghettos would have been different had the leadership been less cooperative with the Germans, not restrained the small minority that wanted to resist, and been more forthcoming about their knowledge of what lay in store. He concluded that Arendt had furnished readers with rich material with which to form a personal understanding of events as they had actually transpired, which he called "our best protection against oppressive control and dehumanizing totalitarianism."[1]

The controversy continued into 1964. The Spring issue of *Partisan Review* contained over thirty pages of argument, counter argument and accusations much of it directed at Mary McCarthy who was accused by Marie Syrkin of intellectual irresponsibility and ignorance, and by Harold Weisberg as wholly lacking in charity and almost equally lacking in logic. The poet Robert Lowell defended *Eichmann in Jerusalem* as a masterpiece, characterizing Hannah's only motive as a "heroic desire for truth." Dwight Macdonald, a former editor of *Partisan Review* referred to the book as a masterpiece of historical journalism and defended McCarthy's "brilliant" observation in response to Lionel Abel's review that the split over the book was between Christians and Jews, especially "organization-minded Jews." He concluded by noting that he had known both Mr. Abel and Miss Arendt for many years and that "the notion of the former giving lessons in morality to the latter strikes me as comic." Abel responded that Mary McCarthy's defense of Arendt was "worthless," and that Macdonald's contribution, unable to advance any argument of his own, "is to abuse me. . . . It all comes down finally to calling people 'Jews.' " The last word at *Partisan Review* went to William Phillips, the editor, who regretted "the procession of polemics, with everyone arguing so cleverly, with so much wit and logic, as though those awful events were being used to sharpen one's mind and one's rhetoric." He thought the criticism of Arendt, about whom he had heard people say that she was worse than Eichmann, was excessive, but regretted that her defenders had turned the issue into a disagreement between Christians and Jews, arguing that whether a person was Jewish or Gentile should be of biographical and not intellectual interest.[2] The English historian Hugh Trevor-Roper, in the *Sunday Times* of London, wrote that Arendt was "unbearably arrogant." She was guilty, he declared, of bias, half-truths, loaded language, and double standards of evidence.[3]

Norman Podhoretz, the editor of *Commentary* (one of the journals in which Arendt published frequently), a deeply committed Zionist, and already well along the path from a socialist childhood to eventual prominence as a neocon leader of the Project for the New American Century and a hawkish advisor to George W. Bush, published a complex review entitled "Hannah Arendt on Eichmann: A Study in the Perversity of Brilliance." He applauded her portrait of the mind of a middle-echelon Nazi and of the world that produced him and gave him the power to do the things he had done. He also admired Arendt's scrupulous account of the almost total unwillingness of the Federal Republic of Germany "to prosecute and mete out adequate punishment to Nazi war criminals still at large and in many cases flourishing." But on balance he thought the weakness of the book was that "in place of the monstrous Nazi, she [Arendt] had given us the 'banal' Nazi; in place of the Jew as virtuous martyr . . . the Jew as accomplice in evil; and in place of the confrontation between guilt and innocence . . . 'collaboration' of criminal and victim." In the end, he declared with no supporting evidence, the banality of evil thesis "violates everything we know about the nature of man . . . no person could have joined the Nazi Party, let alone the S.S., who was not at the very least a *vicious* anti-Semite." *Eichmann in Jerusalem*, he concluded, demonstrated that "intellectual perversity can result from the pursuit of brilliance by a mind infatuated with its own agility and bent on generating dazzle."[4]

Gershom Scholem, a German Jew and distinguished scholar at Hebrew University of Jerusalem, whom Arendt had known in her youth, wrote a letter affirming his "deep respect" but asserting that her version of the Nazi past came between the reader and the actual events because her tone was "heartless," "flippant," "sneering and malicious," replacing balanced judgment with a "demagogic will-to-overstatement." Acknowledging that he could never think of her as anything other than "a daughter of our people," he nevertheless admonished her that in the Jewish tradition there is a concept known as "Ahabath Israel: Love of the Jewish people [and that] in you, dear Hannah, as in so many intellectuals who come from the German Left, I find little trace of this."[5]

Arendt wrote back that she did not come from the German Left, but from the tradition of German philosophy, and that of course she was a daughter of the Jewish people and had never claimed to be anything else: "I have always regarded my Jewishness as one of the indisputable actual data of my life, and I have never had the wish to change or disclaim facts of this kind. There is such a thing as basic gratitude for everything that is as it is." But you are quite right, she told him, in what you say about Ahabath Israel: "I have never in my life 'loved' any people or collective—neither the German people, nor the French, nor the American, nor the working class or anything of that sort. I indeed love 'only' my friends and the only kind of love I know of and believe in is the love of persons."[6]

"I am amazed," Arendt wrote to Jaspers, "and never expected anything like this." Gideon Hausner, she explained, had come to America "for the express purpose of heating things up." She complained that "three or four large organizations, along with whole regiments of 'scholarly' assistants and secretaries" were busying themselves with ferreting out mistakes she might have made as a ruse to delegitimize her criticism of Israel and her characterization of Eichmann as banal. She worried that this was seriously dangerous business. "People are resorting to any means to destroy my reputation. They have spent weeks trying to find something in my past that they can hang on me." Of course, they did not yet know about her youthful affair with the "ex-Nazi," Martin Heidegger; but years later, still incensed over *Eichmann in Jerusalem,* some critics would use this against her, arguing that love for Heidegger distorted Arendt's understanding of German culpability.

In 1965, Jacob Robinson, the deputy prosecutor at the Eichmann trial in Jerusalem published a scathing 400-page denunciation of Hannah's work entitled *And the Crooked Shall Be Made Straight: The Eichmann Trial, The Jewish Catastrophe, and Hannah Arendt's Narrative.* Robinson had the advantage of teams of researchers in New York, London, Paris, and Jerusalem with whose help he scoured *Eichmann in Jerusalem* and found four hundred "factual errors," many of which, as it turned out, were over such minutiae as the correct spelling of a first name, and some of which turned out not to be errors at all (for example, Arendt was correct in saying that the head of the Nazi People's Court was killed in February 1945 and not as Robinson claimed in 1944).[7] Nevertheless, a review in the *New York Review of Books* by Walter Laqueur, an employee of one of Robinson's research institutes, asserted that Arendt lacked the minimum of factual knowledge needed to make a scholarly contribution, and that Robinson, who was characterized as formidable, an eminent authority on international law, an erudite polymath with knowledge of many languages and unrivaled mastery of sources, had been motivated to undertake a full-scale refutation of "Miss Arendt's" flippant display of cleverness by the natural "resentment felt by the professional against the amateur."[8]

Arendt, who had been quiet on the Eichmann matter since publication of the original articles in the *New Yorker,* took this opportunity to respond with an essay in the January 20, 1966, issue of the *New York Review of Books* entitled "The Formidable Mr. Robinson." Mr. Laqueur, she wrote, was so overwhelmed by Mr. Robinson's "eminent authority" that he had failed to acquaint himself with the subject under attack. For a start, he just accepted the assertion in Robinson's subtitle that she had written a narrative about the Jewish catastrophe, when in fact she had criticized the prosecution for having made the Eichmann trial a pretext to put forward exactly such a narrative. It was the prosecutor, not she, who had repeatedly raised the question of why there was not more Jewish resistance; she had merely reported this and dismissed the question as "silly and cruel, since it testified to a fatal ignorance of conditions of the time."

In response to the claim of Mr. Robinson's eminence as a scholar, Arendt pointed out that he was a lawyer not a historian, that he had published practically nothing before this book and that the claim that he was an "eminent authority," never applied to any of his earlier work, had only attached to him after he joined the chorus of critics attacking her. What is formidable about Mr. Robinson, she concluded, is that his words, amplified by the Israeli government with its consulates, embassies, and missions throughout the world, the American and World Jewish Congresses and B'nai B'rith with its powerful Anti-Defamation League, had led to the widespread belief that her book contained hundreds of errors. These organizations had joined in advancing the formidable Mr. Robinson's career and manufacturing his eminence as part of a coordinated effort to characterize her book as an "evil" posthumous defense of Eichmann, and of her as an "evil" person to have written it, and to turn people away from her criticism of Israel and Jewish leaders. In the process they had become increasingly extreme in their rhetoric, with the effect of making the book more important than it could possibly otherwise have been, thus promoting the exact opposite of their goal:

> If they had left well enough alone, this issue, which I had touched upon only marginally, would not have been trumpeted all over the world. In their efforts to prevent people from reading what I had written . . . they blew it up out of all proportion, not only with reference to my book but with reference to what actually happened. They forgot that they were mass organizations, using all the means of mass communication, so that every issue they touched at all, pro or contra, was liable to attract the attention of masses whom they could no longer control. So what happened after a while in these meaningless and mindless debates was that people began to think that all the nonsense image makers had made me say was the actual historical truth.[9]

Although Arendt did have more to say in the years ahead about Adolf Eichmann and the evil with which he is associated, this was her last word on the controversy surrounding the Eichmann book. The tide of history since then has been mostly with her. In politics this is due to the widespread opposition, especially among students and intellectuals to the Vietnam War in the late 1960s and early 1970s. The conduct of American leaders—Lyndon Johnson and Robert McNamara, and then Richard Nixon and Henry Kissinger—brought home the idea of "banal" evil. In social science, landmark studies of obedience to authority by Stanley Milgram[10] at Yale and of prisoners and guards by Philip Zimbardo[11] at Stanford gave shocking evidence of the extent to which ordinary people could be induced to harm others. Among historians, with the notable exception of Daniel Goldhagen's book *Hitler's Willing Executioners: Ordinary Germans and the Holocaust*[12] (which attributes the Holocaust to a tradition of exterminationist anti-Semitism in German culture), recent scholarship on the Third Reich—Ian Kershaw on Hitler,[13] Robert Gellately on the SS,[14] Christopher Browning on the Einsatzgruppen[15]—tends to confirm Arendt's thesis that ordinary people were complicitous with the Nazi regime for reasons best characterized as banal. In international affairs, the collapse of Soviet totalitarianism and recent genocidal catastrophes in Bosnia, Rwanda, and Darfur have reinforced the idea that great evil may arise from the false beliefs and banal motives of ordinary people.

Nevertheless, battle lines are still drawn and the controversy continues. David Cesarani's 2004 book *Becoming Eichmann*, which won the 2006 National Jewish Book Award for History, is illustrative: Cesarani goes to great lengths to separate himself from Arendt, asserting that her depiction of Eichmann was "self-serving, prejudiced and ultimately wrong." Yet his own conclusion is that under the right circumstances normal people can become mass murderers and that "Eichmann appears more and more like a man of our time. Everyman as génocidaire."[16] Perhaps Cesarani felt that he had to tear Arendt down to establish a place in the market for his book outside of the shadow of *Eichmann in Jerusalem*, to which he had very little to add even after half a century. Michael Massing, writing about Iraq in the *New York Times* in October 2004, for example, adopts the conception of banal evil as explanatory for events in Rwanda, Bosnia, and at the Abu Ghraib prison, but rejects it without comment as "simply not credible" in relation to Eichmann.[17]

Richard Wolin's important book about Heidegger and his students[18] published in 2001, asserts that Arendt was "hard-hearted and uncaring" toward the Jewish people, displayed a "lack of empathy," blurred "the lines between perpetrators and victims," and that all of this arose from "her problems with her own Jewish identity, which he associates with her "amorous liaison during the 1920s" with Martin Heidegger. The argument is that Arendt, blinded by love for Heidegger and of German high culture, which he represented, had to excuse his Nazi affiliation as trivial, and did this by blaming the Jews for their own destiny. This is a new twist on the argument that a Jew who criticizes Israel or Jewish leaders must be pathological.

The connection to Heidegger may indeed have some relevance to the ongoing discourse about *Eichmann in Jerusalem*, but it need not be taken as evidence of pathology or self-hatred as Wolin suggests. Rather, Arendt's experience of Heidegger may have prepared her to comprehend, when she saw Adolf Eichmann, that a "terribly and terrifyingly normal" man—or even a man of extraordinary intelligence like Martin Heidegger—might be transformed by the total moral collapse of society into an unthinking cog in the machinery of totalitarianism. The banality of evil had presented itself to Arendt as a shocking epiphany in Jerusalem. Yet it may well have developed intuitively and without clear articulation in relation to Heidegger, who had also been present at the epicenter of evil, and who had been motivated less by racial ideology than by careerist opportunities, combined with thoughtlessness about others. Ultimately, Arendt's observation that Eichmann was a human and not a devil seems a logical corollary of her earlier understanding of totalitarian systems: that they secure the complicity of whole populations—the Eichmanns and the Heideggers—through the use of terror, propaganda, and largesse to undermine any moral compass and to manipulate culture, language, and all the affiliative herd impulses so that average, normal citizens and even truly exceptional people become confused about right and wrong. Heidegger fired Jewish professors and gave his prestige to the Nazis thinking he could achieve something great by salvaging the declining intellectual tradition of the West. Eichmann transported millions of Jews to horrifying deaths believing he was acting in the line of duty.

For most of us, including learned philosophers, even in normal circumstances, the moral compass exists within a field that is influenced by the institutions of church and state, the voices of neighbors, the threat of gossip, the gallows, and the asylum; the Nazis added propaganda (conspicuous in the foreground) and the threat of concentration camps (thinly veiled in the background) while exhorting conformity to violence and crimes against humanity. How then, if the circumstances were similar, could Arendt have reconciled with Heidegger and yet supported, as she did, the execution of Eichmann? The most important distinction, of course, is that Heidegger had not killed anyone; his guilt was moral rather than criminal, and he had separated himself from the Nazis early. Beyond that, however, Hannah also thought that mercy is applicable to the person rather than the deed. Mercy does not forgive murder or betrayal, but pardons the murderer or traitor insofar as he, a person, may be more than anything he ever did. In Anglo-American criminal law this sort of judicial discretion has been called individualized justice, and it was the dominant strategy in sentencing in the postwar years, requiring an individual judgment in every case. There are myriad ways in which a person who has offended may also have demonstrated redemptive virtues, but Arendt did not see this in Eichmann.

The trial in Jerusalem brought into consciousness what Hannah had recognized intuitively about evil in the moment of initial relief in 1950 in the hotel dining room in Freiburg: that Martin Heidegger was not radically different from other human beings, however badly he had behaved; and this prepared the ground from which it was possible to see that even Adolf Eichmann was an ordinary human being. Evil, even great evil, it turns out, does not require radical difference—average human beings are capable enough.

Real justice, in Arendt's view, requires full disclosure, including self-disclosure, not only retribution against an old Nazi, but also an effort to understand how the totalitarian system produced the complicity of perpetrators, bystanders, and even victims. Arendt's critics were outraged by her assertion that the totalitarian regime had sown moral confusion among victims as well as perpetrators and bystanders, and that ordinary people, including Jews as well as Germans, had by-and-large behaved badly when tested. If evil is banal, it can turn up anywhere, even among victims, even among Jews, even in Israel. That a people were victimized, Arendt argued, does not mean that they are absolved from responsibility to examine their own roles or that they do not have to be concerned about the possibility of victimizing others.

Such a perspective makes reconciliation possible, though never a foregone conclusion. The magnitude of Eichmann's crime required retributive judgment. But Hannah was able to reconcile with Martin Heidegger for the same reason that she wanted Israel to reconcile with its Arab neighbors; because she believed in the power of new beginnings, and of the necessity, especially after a disaster, to pick up the pieces and build a better world.

In 2006 a new edition of the Eichmann book was published with an introduction by the Israeli writer and journalist Amos Elon, who observed that no book in living memory aroused the same intensity of passions as *Eichmann in Jerusalem*. Karl Jaspers wrote to Hannah in 1963 that a time would come, which she would not live to see, when Jews would erect a monument to her in Israel as has been done for the freethinking philosopher Baruch Spinoza, formally excommunicated in the year 1656. This has not yet happened, but as Arendt's influence grows among Israelis interested in peaceful coexistence with their neighbors, Elon thinks "we could be getting there."[19]

29

◇◇◇◇
◆

AS THE EICHMANN CONTROVERSY BEGAN TO recede, Jaspers observed that Hannah had suffered greatly but that ultimately the whole critical uproar only added to her prestige, and she confirmed with real pleasure that the students who turned out for her lectures at Yale, Columbia, Chicago, and other universities received her with warmth and enthusiasm, and that these were mostly Jewish students. The old guard, she concluded, had not been able to control the opinions of young people. "The comical thing," she wrote to Jaspers, was that after speaking her mind openly about "the formidable Mr. Robinson," she was once again "flooded with letters from all the Jewish organizations with invitations to speak, to appear at congresses, and so forth—even from those I have attacked."

Nor was it only students or Jewish groups that rallied around Hannah. She was awarded a dozen honorary degrees from American universities including a doctor of laws from Yale, and was inducted into the National Institute of Arts and Letters and the American Academy of Arts and Sciences, which in 1969 awarded her the Emerson-Thoreau Medal for distinguished achievement in literature. Earlier recipients had included Robert Frost, T. S. Eliot, Katherine Anne Porter, and Lewis Mumford.

These years at the end of the 1960s were marked by very substantial intellectual productivity, including important books inspired by the political crises of the period: *On Revolution, Crises of the Republic* (which included essays on lying in politics, civil disobedience, and violence), and numerous other essays, some of which she brought together herself in *Men in Dark Times*, and others of which are still appearing in new collections under such titles as *Responsibility and Judgment*, *The Promise of Politics*, and *The Jewish Writings*. But questions about the nature of evil arising from her insights into Eichmann persisted in Arendt's thinking.

In 1964, when the "furious controversy" not caused but "touched off" by *Eichmann in Jerusalem*, was still raging, she delivered a lecture on "Personal Responsibility Under Dictatorship," telling the audience that her mistake in the Eichmann book had been "to take for granted" that everyone (by which she meant every thinking person) accepted the Socratic proposition that it is "better to suffer than to do wrong." The precondition for moral judgment, Arendt asserted, is not highly developed intelligence or sophistication with moral or legal philosophy, but rather "the disposition to live together . . . with oneself . . . to be engaged in that silent dialogue between me and myself which, since Socrates and Plato, we usually call thinking."[1]

In Jerusalem she had observed that the inability to think—the absence of inner dialogue—seemed to be related to Eichmann's defective moral judgment; in a series of lectures and essays over the next few years, Arendt continued to inquire into the relationship between thinking and judging, the very activities in which her own life had been absorbed. When the Eichmann book came out, there was, she said, "a whole chorus of voices" assuring her that "there sits an Eichmann in every one of us." Others, outraged by her assessment of the Jewish leadership, castigated her with the taunt that the "only true culprits" were people like her who dared to sit in judgment, claiming that "no one can judge who had not been in the same circumstances under which, presumably, one would have behaved like all others."[2] This position, incidentally, was entirely in accord with Eichmann's view of the matter.

Of course, there are good reasons to doubt eyewitness accounts and to mistrust as self-serving the judgments of those, like Eichmann, who participated in an event; but if no one else can judge, then how can either historians or jurists reach decisions? Nor, as Arendt pointed out, does sitting in judgment presuppose arrogance. Even the judge who condemns a man for murder may still say, "There but for the grace of God go I!" Furthermore, refusing to judge individuals, preferring, for example, to accuse all of Germany or all of German history from Luther to Hitler for what transpired between 1933 and 1945, becomes in practice "a highly effective whitewash" of all those who actually did something, "for where all are guilty, no one is."[3]

Far from eschewing the making of judgments, Arendt thought that independent judgment, which derives from independence of mind, is the precondition for right action. There were, after all, individuals who did not go along with the majority. In the Third Reich, moral acts were prohibited, crimes against humanity were legal, the population had become inured to Nazi policies, and slowly through a system of threats and entitlements had adapted to a new and widely accepted moral order. In this way, Hannah argued, the word "moral" had come to lose its common meaning of right conduct and reverted to its ancient root "*mores*," signifying only customary patterns of social conduct without a metaphysical claim of rightness.[4] Under the circumstances of a new legal order based on the Nazi command "Thou shalt kill," the great crimes were committed not by "outlaws, monsters or raving sadists but by the most respected members of respectable society," for whom morality meant obedience to the law of the land, and who had merely exchanged one set of accepted values for another.[5] The moral judgments of the small number of essentially lawless individuals who did not comply, who were, if not active resisters, at least nonparticipants—here we might think of Jaspers—were guided by their own internal dialogues of thought rather than contemporary mores.[6]

30

◇◇◇◇
◆

SHORTLY AFTER THE END OF WORLD War Two, Theodor Adorno wrote that poetry after Auschwitz would be barbaric. He later recanted this statement, but even as he made it, Paul Celan, a German-speaking (and writing) Romanian-Jewish survivor of Nazi labor camps was proving him wrong. *Todesfuge* (Death Fugue) is perhaps Celan's most famous poem, in which victims drink and drink the "Black milk of Daybreak." The poem also hints at the banality of Nazi evil: "death is a master from Germany," who, at day's end writes lovingly to Germany, "your Golden hair Margarete."

On July 24, 1967, Celan read his poetry to an overflow crowd at the University of Freiburg, and Martin Heidegger was in the audience. Afterward, Celan, who admired Heidegger's work but was also familiar with his Nazi past and his postwar silence about it, declined to have a picture taken of the two of them together; but Heidegger gave Celan a copy of *Was heisst Denken* and invited him to visit his *Hütte* at Todtnauberg and walk together in the Black Forest. Celan accepted the invitation and the next day wrote in Heidegger's guest book that he had made the visit in the hope of a "thinker's coming [undelayed] word in the heart";[1] but this hope, so far as we can tell, went unfulfilled.

The day after Celan's visit, Hannah and Martin Heidegger saw each other for the first time since 1952. In October 1966, he had sent a note in honor of Hannah's sixtieth birthday, with a little news about his own travels to Greece and the Aegean, and the wish that "the coming autumn of your existence provide all the support you need for the tasks you have set yourself, as well as for those that, unrecognized, still await you." He enclosed a photograph of the view from his cabin in the Black Forest and a Hölderin poem about quiet autumn days, warmed by mild sun when fields prepare to offer up their yield. At the end, recalling the moment of their first encounter, he wrote: "It seems a long time since the attempt to interpret Plato's *Sophist*. And yet it often seems to me as if what has been converges on a single moment that salvages what can last."

"Your autumn letter," Hannah wrote back, "gave me the greatest joy, really the greatest possible joy," and would accompany her along with the poem and photograph for a long time: "Those whose hearts were brought together and then broken by spring will have their hearts made whole again by autumn."

> Now and then, I hear things about you . . . then my hopes head toward your triangle, Freiburg-Messkirch as the hypotenuse, and above it Todtnauberg. . . . My thoughts also keep returning to the Sophist lecture. What endures, it seems to me [here quoting the same lines from Goethe she had spoken to him at their first reconciliation in Freiburg in 1950] is where one can say—it is at the end the same as it was at the beginning.

This was the moment of their second and more lasting reconciliation; within the year, they had begun to see each other again.

In the summer of 1967, Hannah and Heinrich Blücher went together for a European vacation and to visit the Jasperses in Basel. She made two short trips on her own during this time: one to Israel, the other to Freiburg. In Israel she visited her cousin Ernst Fuerst, his wife (Hannah's childhood friend Kate Lewin Fuerst), and their three children. The Fuersts felt that Hannah was unduly critical of Israel, but this judgment did not intrude on their affection and respect for her. At the same time, however, tensions over the Eichmann book were still so high in Israel that Hannah traveled incognito.[2]

Her other trip alone that summer, to Freiburg, was to deliver a lecture on Walter Benjamin at the invitation of her friend J. Glenn Gray (who under Arendt's supervision had prepared the English translations of much of Heidegger's work). She was motivated to accept, at least in part, by her desire to see Heidegger again. He was in the audience. It was the first time she had seen him even from a distance in fifteen years, and Arendt began her address with a salutation to him: "Dear Martin Heidegger, Ladies and Gentlemen. . . ." They had a few moments together the next afternoon but not enough time for a real talk. Heidegger wrote asking if she could return for a longer visit sometime in August. He complimented her lecture and commented that when she began by addressing him directly, he feared there would be a negative reaction in the room, "and then there was one, too." There was no disruption of the lecture, but there must have been a ripple in the crowd—exchanged glances, perhaps a sense of visceral shock that the distinguished Jewish émigré had addressed herself directly and affectionately to the one-time Nazi *Rektor.*

"The negative reaction," Hannah wrote to Heidegger,

arranging a visit the following week, "I saw it; if I had foreseen it, I would perhaps have taken a somewhat more dramatic approach. But one thing does worry me now: did you find my direct address embarrassing? It seemed the most natural thing in the world to me."

"What a great joy that you will come again," he wrote. "How could I not have been very happy about how you addressed me! I was only concerned that it might produce unpleasantness for you. After the fact, you can gather from the reaction that your addressing me like that was quite brave, seen 'objectively.' "

The autumn of Arendt's life was not long. Seventy-five letters were exchanged between Heidegger's note honoring her sixtieth birthday in October 1966 and her death in December 1975; and each of the years in that period included a visit to Freiburg.

In September 1968, Hannah spent an afternoon and evening with Martin and Elfride in Freiburg, but the primary purpose of her trip was to have time with Karl Jaspers, who was by then eighty-five years old and in failing health after a stroke. She wrote to Blücher that Jaspers could barely walk even with a walker and that he should be in a wheelchair, but that he was lively, talkative, and still enjoying life: "He says: Life *was* beautiful. I say: I know you still think; Life *is* beautiful. He says: You're right [but] sometimes I'm embarrassed, and I feel sorry for the others. How boring for you. But for my part I'm perfectly content. This way is fine."

Hannah saw Heidegger again on a very brief visit to Freiburg early in March 1969; she was dressed in black, having come to Basel at the end of February for Jaspers's funeral. At the memorial service she described Jaspers as an exemplar in actual existence of something the world knows mostly as a concept or ideal: a fusion of freedom, reason, and communication. She reminded the mourners that he was not only among the leading thinkers of his age, but had also been the conscience of Germany during the Nazi period, loyal in love to his Jewish wife, holding firm to conviction when everyone else crumbled, risking everything and living with her in constant fear. Then after the war still the conscience of Germany, a lone voice addressing the problem of collective guilt.

> We don't know what happens when a human being dies. All we know is that he has left us. We cling to the works . . . [which] are what someone who dies leaves behind in the world that was there before he came and will go on when he leaves it. What becomes of them depends on the course the world takes. But the simple fact that these books represented lived life—that fact does not become immediately apparent to the world and can be forgotten. What is at once the most fleeting and at the same time the greatest thing about him—the spoken word and the gesture unique to him—those things die with him, and they put a demand on us to remember him. That remembering takes place in communication with the dead person, and from that arises talk about him, which then resounds in the world again. Communication with the dead—that has to be learned, and we are beginning to learn it now in the communion of our mourning.[3]

Jaspers and Blücher, the most important men in Hannah's life, shared characteristics of virtue, steadiness, and good judgment; which, as she always knew, was not the case with Heidegger, who could never occupy the place in Hannah's life that had been Jaspers's; nor would she have wanted the void to be filled. As Heidegger understood—and the French existentialists after him—the fact of death establishes the meaning of what has been. Nevertheless, Heidegger's renewed presence in her life was a great comfort because he was the only remaining tie to her youth. She had always thought, she wrote to Mary McCarthy, that aging, growing toward one's own death, involved a gradual withdrawal from the world, but increasingly she was becoming aware that as one grows older it is the world that separates from us, leaving us in "a kind of desert," populated by the "strange faces" of people we do not know.

31

◇◇◇◇
◆

AFTER YEARS OF TENSION AND ANIMOSITY, Hannah's relationship with Elfride Heidegger began to improve. A month or so after Hannah's March 1969 visit, Elfride wrote to her that the large two-story house in Freiburg had become unmanageable. She and Martin hoped to build a smaller one-story residence in their backyard; but this was an expensive proposition, and she wanted advice from Hannah about the value of the original manuscript of *Being and Time*, and how it might be offered for sale with the greatest possible discretion. There was a flurry of correspondence between the two women in the next few months, full of practical discussion (the disadvantages of auction houses, likely buyers in Germany and the United States, and advice obtained from experts on how to select a middleman to initiate a discreet approach).

Elzbieta Ettinger, the first person to have access to the Arendt-Heidegger correspondence before it was published, who concluded that Heidegger was predatory and Arendt hopelessly love-struck, read Elfride's letter as anti-Semitic. Of course, Ettinger thought, when Elfride needed information about money, she turned to a Jew.[1] But it is equally plausible that both of the Heideggers recognized that Arendt was far more worldly than they; she had worked for many years in the publishing business and had contacts with publishers, literary archives, and philanthropic organizations on both sides of the ocean. In addition, Ettinger's position is undermined by the warm tone of collaboration in the letters with their friendly exchange of small talk, acknowledgments from Elfride of the "great demands" on Hannah's time, and of gratitude for her help, as well as enthusiastic expressions on both sides of anticipation of Hannah's next visit to Freiburg.

That summer Hannah and Heinrich came to visit Martin and Elfride together. Blücher and Heidegger had a long talk about Nietzsche, which Heidegger told Hannah in a letter after their visit had been a great pleasure: "Such insight and perspective are rare." Elfride and Hannah seem to have grown more at ease with one another after this visit. That winter Hannah sent a note to Elfride and attached a copy of an article that had appeared in a Seattle newspaper about Heidegger's Nazi affiliations. The "whole thing," she thought, was "too stupid" to bother Martin with, but it was best, Hannah thought, for Elfride to be aware. It was as if the two women were now working together to protect the man positioned between them. "I briefly considered responding," Hannah wrote, but as the author "is entirely unknown and the newspaper is also not exactly famous, I am of the opinion that any answer only gives her publicity that she cannot get otherwise. The best thing to do really is just to let it slide."

The next spring Heidegger had a stroke, and Elfride wrote to Hannah to keep her informed about his recovery—within a month no trace of paralysis remained except a slight inhibition of movement in his right hand—and to make arrangements for

Hannah to come visit the two of them. Even though the stroke had been mild and the recovery quick and thorough, Elfride noted that it was now necessary for Heidegger "to take very good care of himself in view of his age."

He was some months past his eightieth birthday, which had been a major event with celebrations in Messkirch, plus major conferences at Heidelberg and Amriswil at which the speakers included Karl Löwith and Hans Jonas (both Jews and both among Heidegger's most famous students). There were many newspaper articles assessing Heidegger's contributions to philosophy and reporting on congratulatory speeches in his honor. Heidegger was interviewed by Richard Wisser, a professor of philosophy at the University of Mainz, on ZDF, the major German public television station. Much of the footage of that interview is in profile, Heidegger and Wisser speaking to each other. Then in the last moments, the talk finished but the program still on air, Heidegger turned and faced the camera full on and smiled with an almost mischievous glint in his eye that reminds the viewer that the old man had also once been a boy; and this, perhaps, as much as anything, shows what it was that drew Hannah to him.

Arendt prepared a speech that was recorded in New York, broadcast by Bavarian radio, and subsequently published under the title "Martin Heidegger Is Eighty Years Old."[2] She began with a reflection of Heidegger's almost unparalleled influence in the twentieth century among abstract thinkers and philosophers, comparing him to Kafka and Picasso. Even before the publication of *Being and Time*, Heidegger had achieved fame as a teacher because he, before anyone else, recognized that philosophy had become formalized, tradition-bound, and boring precisely because it no longer bore any relationship to independence of thought. Among students, who felt that philosophy had become an idle game of erudition, a rumor circulated that Heidegger had broken the thread of tradition, was discovering the past anew and creating an original philosophy for the current age. With Heidegger, students did not simply absorb lessons formulated by philosophers of earlier generations, but learned to interrogate and challenge the great thinkers of the past.

> All this probably sounds quite familiar to you today, because so many now work this way; before Heidegger, no one did. The rumor put it quite simply: thinking is alive again; the cultural treasures . . . which everyone had believed dead, are being made to speak again, (and) it turns out that they are saying quite different things from what one had skeptically assumed. There is a teacher; one can learn, perhaps, to think.

Heidegger, she said, was the "secret king in the empire of thinking." His influence derived less from particular ideas about being, time, or metaphysics developed in his work than from the fact and style of his thinking: probing the depths not to discover something decisive or definitive that could be brought back to the rest of us, but with the purpose of remaining in the depths and setting out pathmarks of thinking so that others might follow. Distinguishing woodland paths from the roads "with their carefully laid out problems," on which most philosophers and social scientists travel, Hannah noted that Heidegger's purpose in blazing trails through deep woods was not to help hikers find the way out, but to offer guidance to those "who love the forest and feel at home in it," showing them where others have been, helping them to find their own way. Perhaps recalling her own experience, Arendt explained that Heidegger's students were introduced to thinking as a pure activity, undertaken for its own sake, rather than a thirst for facts or a desire for results, and that such thinking becomes a passion that "organizes and runs through all other abilities and talents. We are so accustomed to the old oppositions of reason and passion, of mind and life, that the idea of *passionate* thinking, in which thinking and being alive become one, can be a bit startling."

Passionate thinking "which arises from the simple fact of being-born-into-the-world and then contemplates the meaning which reigns in everything that is" is no more purposeful than life itself. "The end of life is death, but man lives not for the sake of death, but because he is a living being; and he thinks not for the sake of some result or other, but because he is a thinking, sensing being." Plato calls astonishment the beginning of philosophy and of thinking, but Heidegger, Arendt said, had adopted this astonishment as his residence;[3] it was for him a place of silence and solitude, requiring fortitude to remain there for extended periods.

If a thinker lives long enough, he will inevitably strive to undo the results of his thinking because he will be drawn to continue thinking, to return to old ground, to revise and sometimes reject what he has done before. The product of thought is less important than the fact of thinking. "The thinking self," Arendt told her audience, "is ageless, and it is the curse and blessing of thinkers . . . that they get old without aging." She quoted Jaspers: "And now, just when one finally wants to get properly started, one is supposed to leave!"

Yet even in honoring him on the occasion of his birthday, Arendt noted that in 1933, Heidegger had succumbed to the temptation to change his residence and intervene in the world of human affairs. This terribly mistaken "escapade" consisted more than anything else in "avoiding the reality of the Gestapo's secret rooms and the torture cells of the concentration camps." But Heidegger, she said (being very generous with him), also recognized his mistake and risked more than most intellectuals and scientists by breaking with the regime. Heidegger, she thought, learned from the shock of the collision, which drove him back to his customary residence. There all that he had experienced took deep hold in his thinking, and this led him to focus on the distinction between thinking and willing (through which humanity imposes itself on the world) and to consider the possibility that one experiences the elusive essence of thinking principally by willing not to will.

Nevertheless, Arendt acknowledged that "both Plato and Heidegger resorted to tyrants and Führers" when they became involved in human affairs. This, she concluded, "must be attributed not simply to the conditions of their times, and even less to innate character, but rather to a *"déformation professionelle,"* which seems to drive many great thinkers to tyrannical tendencies (she offered Kant as the great exception).

Hannah sent a copy of her talk to Heidegger, noting that his birthday was the occasion for his contemporaries to honor "the master, the teacher, and—for some surely—the friend," by acknowledging that the "passionate fulfillment" of his life and work had been to demonstrate what it is to think and to have the courage to venture into unexplored territory: "May those who come after us," she concluded, "when they recall our century and its people and try to keep faith with them, not forget the devastating sandstorms that swept us up, each in his own way, and in which something like this man and his work were still possible."

Heidegger wrote back thanking her, having already thanked

her many times, he said, in his thoughts, and sending several small gifts. "More than anyone," he wrote, "you have touched the inner movement of my thought and of my work as a teacher, which has remained the same since the *Sophist* lecture."

Arendt's biographical essay about Bertolt Brecht published in the *New Yorker* in 1966 extended these ideas,[5] but with a strange new twist: that for artists the punishment for failing to think and judge honestly is loss of talent. She was willing to concede a degree of irresponsibility to poets on the basis that flights of creativity require an escape from the bonds of ordinary reality; but the way to determine the magnitude of a poet's sins was to read the poetry: "the faculty of writing a good line is not entirely at the poet's command but . . . is granted him and . . . he can forfeit it." Brecht's loyalty to communist ideology in the 1920s and 1930s, when it was not yet obvious that Stalin had changed the party into a totalitarian movement, "was no sin but merely an error." His continued loyalty to the party during the Moscow trials, when he knew that innocent men were being victimized, was more serious, as was his silence during the Spanish Civil War, when he knew that the Russians had undermined the Spanish Republic to punish anti-Stalinists. So too was his failure to speak out against the Hitler-Stalin Pact. But Brecht was in exile during these years and did not experience these events firsthand. He was still writing "out of a feeling of solidarity with the downtrodden and oppressed," and it was repulsion to the sight of suffering that explained his loyalty to the Communist Party, which made, or seemed to have made, the cause of the world's unfortunate its own.

It was only after World War Two, when he was living in communist East Berlin, saw directly the suffering and unhappiness of the people, and wrote odes (whether out of fear or political discipline) to Stalin "the useful one" and "the incarnation of hope . . . [for] the oppressed of five continents," that the muse finally abandoned him. The worst thing that can happen to a poet, Arendt wrote, is that he should cease to be a poet, and this is what happened to Brecht when he ceased to make honest, thoughtful judgments about his situation—his writing grew "weak and thin," as if he had become a cheap imitator of his own work.

Arendt's thought about the relationship between thinking and "right" judgments came most sharply together in a lecture before the Society for Phenomenology and Existential Philosophy in New York City on October 30, 1970. When after considerable revision this paper was published the following year under the title "Thinking and Moral Considerations," it was dedicated to her friend the poet, moralist, and thinking man W. H. Auden. The lecture began with a reference to the Eichmann trial and the phenomenon of banal evil, which she described "as no theory or doctrine" but something quite factual: evil deeds on a gigantic scale that did not originate in "base motives" or any special wickedness, pathology, or ideology of the perpetrator, but in his "extraordinary shallowness"—not stupidity so much as an "inability to think." It was this, she explained, that first caused her to wonder about the relationship between thinking and conscience. Might the habit of dialogue with oneself, examining and reflecting upon events, serve the purpose of conditioning men against evildoing?

She began by offering a careful distinction between thinking and knowing: "Our desire to know . . . leaves behind a growing treasure of knowledge . . . [and] is no less a world-building activity than the building of houses. The inclination or the need to think . . . [in contrast] leaves nothing so tangible behind, nor can it be stilled by allegedly definitive insights of 'wise men.' "

There are no dangerous thoughts, Arendt quipped; it is thinking itself that is dangerous because it undermines all established criteria, values, and measurements for good and evil. The Athenians found Socrates to be subversive because the wind of thought that emanated from him promotes disorder by sweeping away social customs that ordinarily form the basis of morals and ethics. These social conventions are such handy guides to mores that they can be used even while asleep. But the thinking to which Socrates hoped to rouse his fellow Athenians has the effect of making people fully awake and alert to the fact that they have only perplexities and problems in hand, and that the most they can do is to share them with each other.

Admittedly, this is a dangerous condition for politics and government, both of which depend upon a degree of social consensus about what is expected of individuals. But not thinking, Arendt pointed out, also carries dangers because it encourages people to hold fast to whatever customs and rules happen to be in effect, avoiding perplexities by never having to make up their own minds about what is beautiful or good. Then, if some element of the body politic rises to power and proposes a new code that abolishes the old system of values and virtues, it will turn out that the men who have held most fast to the old code will be the most eager to embrace the new one: "The ease with which such reversals can take place . . . suggests that everybody is asleep when they occur. . . . How easy it was for the totalitarian rulers to reverse the basic commandment of Western morality—"Thou shalt not kill" in . . . Hitler's Germany, "Thou shalt not bear false testimony against thy neighbor" in . . . Stalin's Russia."

But how in actual practice does the habit of thinking condition men against evildoing? To answer this question, Arendt returned to two fundamental Socratic propositions: first, that it is better to be wronged than to do wrong, and second that *being one*, it is essential not to fall out of harmony with oneself. We may seem to be unitary beings to others, but as soon as we are conscious of ourselves, we have become "two-in-one." This is what Plato means when he refers to thinking as "the soundless dialogue between me and myself." Socrates taught that it is necessary for the "two" who carry on the thinking dialogue to be friends; and it follows from this that it is better to suffer than to do wrong because one can remain the friend of a sufferer, but "who would want to be the friend of—and have to live together with—a murderer? Not even a murderer. What kind of a dialogue could you lead with him?"

It was a matter of great importance to Arendt that thinking is a natural need of human life, not a prerogative of the few but a fundamental capacity of all men; and conversely that it is a mistake to imagine that inability to think is limited to the uneducated or unintelligent. What she called "thoughtlessness" is an ever present possibility for all men, including scientists and scholars, poets and philosophers. Even those, like Martin Heidegger, who have been great thinkers can get caught in the frenzy (and thus fall out of the inner dialogue) when the masses are swept up unthinkingly by what everyone else believes and does. She was also careful to differentiate between the wickedness of great villains who often act out of envy and resentment "with which religion and literature have tried to come to terms," and that of ordinary citizens, including people of exceptional talent and intelligence, who, even without special or malicious motives, are nonetheless "capable of infinite evil."

The importance of thinking, she reiterated, is not that it solves problems, creates things of value, or even that it settles controversies about what is "good," but rather that it dissolves obedience to destructive social conventions in those rare moments of history "when things fall apart [and] the centre cannot hold," such as she had witnessed in Germany. In such dark times only those who enter or sustain the inner dialogue are able to see the implications of the unexamined opinions of others. It is this that frees the most political of all man's abilities, the faculty of judgment. This is the relationship between thinking and moral considerations: judging is the liberating by-product of thinking.

> The manifestation of the wind of thought is not knowledge; it is the ability to tell right from wrong, beautiful from ugly. And this indeed may prevent catastrophes . . . in the rare moments when the chips are down.

32

AFTER DELIVERING HER LECTURE "THINKING AND Moral Considerations," Hannah had dinner at home with Heinrich and friends. Heinrich experienced a little chest pain early in the evening, but it passed quickly and he ate well, drank a little *schnapps*, and participated in discussion with his usual vigor. The next afternoon, while Hannah and he were having lunch together at home, Heinrich felt suddenly ill, made his way to the couch, and there suffered a major heart attack. Hannah called for an ambulance and held his hand. "This is it," he said.

Heinrich Blücher died at Mount Sinai Hospital a few hours later. He was buried on November 4. The ceremony was modest; several friends spoke, including Mary McCarthy, who flew from Paris to be with Hannah. Surprisingly, since Hannah was not religious and Blücher was neither religious nor Jewish, Hannah arranged for the reading of the Mourner's Kaddish. This Hebrew prayer for the dead does not mention death at all, but aims to comfort those who grieve through the magnification and sanctification of the greater Being that transcends the being of individuals, and by offering such solace as can be found in the knowledge that generations are linked through the memory of what has come before and through the repetition of prayer, stories, and poetry.

Hannah was restrained in her mourning, which reminds us of the little girl who spoke bravely of going on at the funerals of her father and grandfather more than half a century before; but in the privacy of her circle of friends, she wondered out loud, "How am I to live now?"[1]

The following week there was a ceremony at Bard College, where Heinrich Blücher was buried in a small cemetery in the campus woods with modest markers scattered here and there. "Very good, very right," she wrote to Mary McCarthy afterward, sitting in Heinrich's room at home and at his typewriter, which, she wrote, gave her something to hold on to. "The weird thing is that at no moment am I actually out of control. Perhaps this is a process of petrifaction. Perhaps not. Don't know." The day after the ceremony at Bard, Hannah had returned to her teaching, and, she told McCarthy, had a very good seminar, but wondered if she should be ashamed of that.

> The truth is that I am completely exhausted if you understand by that no superlative of tiredness. I am not tired, or not much tired, just exhausted. I function all right, but know that the slightest mishap could throw me off balance. I don't think I told you that for ten long years I had been constantly afraid that just such a sudden death would happen. This fear frequently bordered on real panic. Where the fear was and the panic there is now sheer emptiness.

"Yes, I knew for ten years," Mary wrote back, "that you were afraid of that sudden death." She had never spoken of it; perhaps, she thought, a manifestation of "protestant reserve," but on the airplane flying over the ocean on the way to Heinrich's funeral, it had occurred to her that Hannah had lived like that for so long that the actuality of the event must have involved a kind of purging, "leaving you . . . doubly empty . . . to have lost your fear and Heinrich together. . . . I do not know how you will manage this."

Hannah's grief subsided slowly over the next few years, but loneliness was a constant companion. Thirty-seven years earlier, when she fled Germany for exile in Paris, still married—unhappily—to Günther Stern, Hannah had escaped the unpleasantness of her situation through a retreat into work and friends. Now, alone for the first time since she fell in love with Heinrich Blücher in 1936, she escaped again into work and friends. The "tribe" that had been centered around Hannah and Heinrich stayed close. There were frequent dinner invitations and evenings out, and when she was anxious about going out alone into the city at night, there were long telephone calls. Most important, however, were the consolations of philosophy—her immersion in the life of the mind—and, though they were both thousands of miles away, there was a degree of solace in her friendships with Heidegger in Freiburg and Mary McCarthy in Paris. But what is most telling is that Hannah arranged to have a bench placed next to Blücher's grave, and every year on the anniversary of his death, she went to Bard and sat there in loving communion with Blücher, her companion in thought and spirit.

A few weeks after Blücher's death, W. H. Auden came to see Hannah. Auden was a heavy drinker, and it showed in his deeply lined and puffy face, which he himself described as looking like a wedding cake left out in the rain. Great poet and moral thinker that he was, Auden was also what might in those days have been characterized as a dissolute old homosexual, always disheveled, and living in a slovenly tenement in an East Village slum. Hannah once quipped that the problem with Auden was that he had only one suit, which is not such a bad thing, except that if you have only one suit, you can never have it cleaned. The day he came to visit Hannah, who was still fresh in her grief, he looked "so much like a clochard [a drink-sodden tramp or bum]," she wrote to Mary McCarthy, "that the doorman came with him, fearful that he might be God knows what." Auden had come, Hannah told Mary, to say that he loved her and thought they should live together, take care of each other and even marry. She felt that Auden was in great need of someone to help take care of him, but

> I know that I can't do it, in other words [I] have to turn him down. I have a hunch that this [has] happened to him once too often . . . and I am almost beside myself when I think of the whole matter. But I can't change that, it would simply be suicide—worse than suicide as a matter of fact. . . . When he left he was completely drunk, staggering into the elevator. I did not go with him. I hate, am afraid of pity, always have been, and I think I never knew anybody who aroused my pity to this extent.

Hannah admired and respected Auden, but was not drawn to him and did not feel entirely comfortable in his presence. Now, with Jaspers and Blücher both gone, the man in whose presence she felt most happy and comfortable was Martin Heidegger, who was also her only remaining link to the world she had known in youth. In her solitude Hannah became increasingly absorbed by her effort to comprehend the relationship between thinking and moral judgment; and she was never far from her gratitude to Martin Heidegger, the "hidden king of thinking" with whom she had first been introduced to the life of the mind.

Heidegger wrote to Hannah a few days after Blücher's death: "Now this parting, too, is required of you." Her closeness to Heinrich, he wrote, had been transformed into something painful, needing to be borne, but for which we have no name. "Our sympathy comes from a certain closeness too, ever since we had the chance to get to know Heinrich's friendly and clear being when you visited us together." Heidegger enclosed a poem, entitled "Time," that he had written a few months earlier at the death of his friend the poet René Char:

How late?
Only when it stops, the clock
in the pendulum's swing back and forth,
do you hear: it goes
and went and goes
no more.
Late already in the day
the clock
is but a pallid track
to time,
close to what is finite,
From which it comes to light.

Hannah responded that she was grateful for his letter and sympathy, and for the poem, which had been an aid to reflection, and reminded him of a poem he had written for her dying friend Hilde Fränkel in 1950:

Death is, in the world's own rhyme,
Being's mountain chain.
Death will evade what's yours and mine
In the falling weight.
Falling towards silence's gate,
Star of earth, nothing more.

She could not write in any detail, she wrote; perhaps she could speak what she was feeling, but it was not possible to write. "Between two people, sometimes, how rarely, a world grows. It is then one's homeland; in any case, it was the only homeland we were willing to recognize. This tiny microworld where you can always escape from the world, and which disintegrates when the other has gone away." Then, thinking perhaps of Socrates' last words recorded in Plato's *Apology*, which had been the concluding reading at the ceremony for Blücher at Bard: "We must go now, I to die, you to live. Which is better is known to the god alone." She ended: "I go now and am quite calm and think: *away*."

It was four months before Hannah wrote to Heidegger again; and then it was to say that she would be in Europe in April and hoped to visit with him and Elfride. She had a question, as well, which she thought she might not be able to raise in conversation. She was working on a book, a sort of follow-up to *The Human Condition*, about the life of the mind; the talk she had given just before Heinrich's death had been a step in the direction of this book. She was not certain when, if ever, it would be completed: "Perhaps never. But if it does work out—may I dedicate it to you?"

Heidegger responded immediately, apologizing for not having written sooner, explaining that he had to use "the best hours" (of which at eighty-two there were perhaps fewer and fewer) "for work." He looked forward to seeing Hannah in April, and was "pleased" that she had in mind to dedicate to him the book that would follow on her discussion of the *vita activa* in *The Human Condition,* which, he observed, "will be as difficult [to write] as it will be important."

In her loneliness after Blücher's death, Hannah's friendship with Heidegger became increasingly important; and he too, living in a sort of solitude brought on by age and declining health, drew closer to her. There were roughly fifty letters between them in the next few years, Heidegger commenting often that he and Elfride, having moved into a smaller, "quiet" house, were now surrounded by fewer of their things. They led a "very secluded life," hardly ever making their way to town, enjoying only occasional visitors.

In April 1971, Hannah flew to Paris to visit Mary McCarthy. The two of them vacationed together in Sicily, and after that Hannah went to Freiburg for a short visit with Heidegger. They discussed language, the distinctively human capacity that gives rise to thought, and exchanged books and small gifts. Hannah returned home in time to participate in a memorial service for Blücher organized by his former students at Bard. There was a letter waiting for her from Heidegger, who wrote: "We will be there as fellow rememberers." When Hannah wrote back, she noted that the gifts and books he had given her accompanied her everywhere, forming a "kind of constant environment."

Their various projects became regular themes in the correspondence between them in these years. Heidegger often sought Arendt's advice on how to negotiate with publishers, waiting to decide whether to accept or reject offers until he had heard from her, and she took an active role in arranging for the translation of his work into English, selecting translators and supervising their work. The book Arendt proposed to dedicate to Heidegger, *The Life of the Mind*, published posthumously, brought her closer to metaphysics over the last years of life than she had been since her days as a student; and her thoughts about thinking and willing, though she now made them distinctively her own, nevertheless pulled her back to paths blazed and marked by Heidegger's earlier passing there. Thus they drew nearer to one another despite the distance the world had placed between them.

33

◇◇◇◇
◆

IN THE SPRING OF 1972, ARENDT received an invitation to deliver the Gifford Lectures at Aberdeen University in Scotland, which she arranged to do in two sessions, the first series of lectures on "thinking" in spring 1973 and the second on "willing and judging" a year later. Together these would constitute a first draft of the *Life of the Mind*.

She began with thinking, which had been the work of a lifetime, as had been the making of judgments—about what had happened to the Germans, Eichmann, Zionism, the Jewish leadership, pariahs and parvenus, politics, and social movements; even her reconciliation with Heidegger represented a judgment. With "Thinking and Moral Considerations," her essay in honor of W. H. Auden, Arendt had already made a start on the relationship between thought and judgment; and as Mary McCarthy pointed out, Arendt was an intellectual conservationist: "She did not believe in throwing anything away that had once been thought . . . in her own way she was an enthusiastic recycler."[1]

Arendt had been invited to stay for three weeks during the summer of 1972 at Villa Serbelloni, the luxurious Rockefeller

Foundation compound for artists and scholars at Bellagio, Italy; she used this time to make a start on the Gifford Lectures. She also made this the occasion for an extended trip to Europe, including three weeks in Tegna, Switzerland, where she and Blücher had vacationed and to which she had not returned since his death, as well as visits with her family in Israel, with Mary McCarthy in Paris, and, at the beginning and again at the end of her trip, with Heidegger in Freiburg. He showed increasing interest in her project: "I hope to hear something about your own work," he wrote when they were planning her visit, "otherwise I have no more opportunities to learn."

Arendt's thinking about thinking began with an observation by Heidegger, which served as the epigram for *The Life of the Mind:*

Thinking does not bring knowledge as do the sciences.
Thinking does not produce usable practical wisdom.
Thinking does not solve the riddles of the universe.
Thinking does not endow us directly with the power to act.

But why, if thinking does so little, does it seem so significant? For both Heidegger and Arendt, the answer is that thinking is the distinctly human capacity that makes it possible to approach Being and to search for meaning in existence. For Arendt there was also the possibility, which she had already discussed in the lecture in honor of W. H. Auden, that the activity involved in thinking, regardless of specific content or result, could be among the influences that condition men to abstain from evildoing.

She began the Gifford Lectures by explaining that her "preoccupation with mental activities" had its origins in the Eichmann trial, where she first reported on the banality of evil, a concept that she realized ran counter to the tradition of thought about evil, which traditionally focused on Satan and evil men who act out of resentment (Richard III), envy (Cain), weakness (Macbeth), the hatred wickedness feels for good (Iago in *Othello*, or Claggart in *Billy Budd*) or covetousness (as in money is the root of all evil). However, what she had experienced observing Eichmann in Jerusalem was utterly different and yet undeniably factual:

> I was struck by a manifest shallowness in the doer that made it impossible to trace the uncontestable evil of his deeds to any deeper level of roots or motives. The deeds were monstrous, but the doer . . . was quite ordinary, commonplace, and neither demonic nor monstrous. There was no sign in him of firm ideological convictions or specific evil motives, and the only notable characteristic one could detect . . . was something entirely negative: it was not stupidity but thoughtlessness.[2]

By "thoughtless" Arendt did not mean rude or discourteous, nor, she was careful to point out, did it imply anything elitist: thoughtlessness is not coequal with stupidity; indeed it "can be found in highly intelligent people." Since the ability to distinguish between right and wrong is related to the ability to think, it is appropriate to expect moral understanding in every person "no matter how erudite or ignorant, intelligent or stupid." Conversely, as Arendt understood, even the most erudite and intelligent may fall out of the habit of thinking, particularly if, like Heidegger in 1933, they become completely caught up in events in the world of action and politics.

Thinking, as Arendt understood it, following Socrates, Plato,

Aristotle, and Kant, involves withdrawal from the world. Arendt illustrates this with a story told by Xenophon about Socrates' habit of suddenly becoming immobile, breaking off from all company, "deaf to all entreaties," becoming lost in thought; on one occasion in a military camp he suddenly stopped walking and stood unmoving for twenty-four hours "turning his mind to himself." Perhaps this is apocryphal, but Mary McCarthy tells us that Hannah had a similar habit and was the only person she ever watched think: "She lay motionless on a sofa or day bed, arms folded behind her head, eyes shut but occasionally opening to stare upward. This lasted—I don't know—from ten minutes to half an hour. Everyone tiptoed past if we had to come into the room in which she lay oblivious."[3]

Withdrawal into thought is neither a retreat into tranquility nor a descent into loneliness; as Cato observed, a thinking person is "never more active than when he does nothing, never less alone than when he is by himself." For Arendt, still following Socrates, Plato, Aristotle, and Kant, thinking is an expression of the two-in-one mind. "Not man, but men," she wrote, "inhabit this planet. Plurality is the law of the earth." And this law is so deep and encompassing that even the dialogue of thought always involves two: me with myself. "Thinking, existentially speaking, is a solitary but not a lonely business; solitude is that human situation in which I keep myself company. Loneliness comes about when I am alone without being able to split into the two-in-one, without being able to keep myself company, when as Jaspers used to say, 'I am in default of myself.' "

Like Heidegger, Arendt rejected Sartre's assertion that existence precedes essence. The decisions people make may mold them, but when they arrive in the world, it is with a human essence already in place, and this includes both the need and the aptitude to think. Thinking, as Hannah understood it, is not a search for truth, knowledge, or power; it is a search for meaning; and people are drawn to think in the same way they are drawn to making or listening to music or poetry. Thinking, for Arendt and for Heidegger, has more in common with these pursuits than with science or technology.

If thoughtlessness is associated with defects of judgment, it does not necessarily mean that thinking guarantees good judgment. Arendt illustrates this with a story about Tycho Brahe, who proposed to his coachman that they take their bearings from the stars to find the shortest path during a night journey, without any consideration of the danger of not following a road. "My dear sir," the coachman replied, "you may know a great deal about the heavenly bodies; but here on earth you are a fool."

Practical judgment, illustrated by Tycho Brahe's deficiency, is of a substantially different nature than moral or aesthetic judgments. Distinguishing between what is beautiful or ugly, right or wrong, is a type of judgment Arendt considered a "natural gift" unrelated to intellect, but perhaps not wholly unrelated to the inner dialogue of thought, which quiets the clamor of the world by withdrawing from it, and which requires us, each time we are confronted by difficulty in life, to consider our circumstances and make up our minds anew.

Approaching the end of her argument—that thinking advances moral judgment—Arendt turned again to Socrates, who at the conclusion of a dialogue tells Hippias, a thick-headed fellow who prefers not to think, that he is more fortunate than Socrates. For when Socrates departs the public arena and is alone at home, he is confronted in internal dialogue by "an obnoxious fellow" who challenges him about everything that he has done during the day. Yet it is this confrontation, Arendt asserts, that gives rise to the faculty of making judgments. "The manifestation of the wind of thought is not knowledge; it is the ability to tell right from wrong, beautiful from ugly." And this, she thought, may be—in those "rare moments when the stakes are on the table"—the force of mind that makes it possible to save oneself from falling into moral catastrophe.

Arendt did not mention Heidegger in this context, but we cannot help but think that he and many other "decent" Germans had prior experience of the inner dialogue, and yet (in the moment of testing, when the stakes were high) the second voice fell silent or was not heard. A man who persists in telling lies, as Heidegger sometimes did, must have experience of avoiding the inner voice that challenges everything one has done and been.

34

THE WEEK AFTER HER LECTURES IN Aberdeen, Hannah visited Heidegger in Freiburg; after that she traveled for two weeks with her friend and sometime colleague at the University of Chicago, the political scientist Hans Morganthau, and then spent the rest of the summer at Tegna, Switzerland. Responding to an inquiry from Mary McCarthy, Hannah noted that she was not "writing furiously," but was reading, taking notes, and revising her thinking about "willing," the element of the life of the mind which, unlike thinking, does not withdraw from the world, but aims instead to leave a mark upon it. Writing about willing, she explained to McCarthy, was much more problematic for her than writing about thinking, a context in which she always felt that she could trust her own instincts and experience." Perhaps, too, thinking and writing about willing presented a special challenge for Arendt because while the relationship between thinking and the great catastrophe of the twentieth century was entirely negative (she related the absence of thought to bad judgment), what had been done, as even Heidegger in his "turn" recognized, was a product of the will.

Hannah hoped to see Heidegger again in August, but he and Elfride were traveling, so plans were made to put off another visit until the next series of Gifford Lectures, scheduled for the following spring. Hannah returned home at the end of the first week in September. W. H. Auden, whose poetry and thought Hannah always had in mind as she worked through the relationship between thinking and moral considerations, died three weeks later. She was hard-struck by grief, in part because she saw Auden, despite his many virtues and accomplishments, as having been unhappy and unfulfilled in life, suffering too often with unrequited love, and she could not forget, she wrote to Mary McCarthy, that she had refused to take care of him when he came and asked for shelter. "Homer said that the gods spin ruin to men that there might be song and remembrance . . . [but Auden] was both the singer and the tale [and] God knows, the price is too high and no one in his right mind could be willing to pay it knowingly." At the memorial service for Auden at the Cathedral of St. John the Divine in New York, Hannah scrawled a couplet from Auden's requiem "In Memory of W. B. Yeats" on her copy of the program:

Sing of human unsuccess
In a rapture of distress.[1]

Heidegger wrote to Hannah in the fall, saying how sorry he was not to have been able to see her in August. Their correspondence in the next few months suggests a growing darkness of his mood: The world, he wrote, scarcely recognizes the destructive "power inherent in the essence of technology. The individual can no longer do anything to oppose the arrogance of the 'mass media and the institutions;' " nevertheless, from "the seclusion of our quiet retirement home . . . we are looking forward to a visit from you."

When Hannah did see Heidegger, in the summer of 1974, it was later than they had anticipated and under different circumstances. She flew to London on April 28 and began her second series of lectures at Aberdeen—this time on the subject of the human will—a few days later. During the night of May 5, Hannah felt ill, and asked her friend the publisher William Jovanovich, who was in Aberdeen to attend the lectures, to come to her room. He recognized the symptoms of a heart attack and called for an ambulance. Mary McCarthy came from Paris the next day, and stayed with Hannah while she was in the hospital. Then Lotte Kohler, a member of "the tribe" in New York (and subsequently an executor of Arendt's estate and the editor of her correspondence with Karl Jaspers and Heinrich Blücher) came from New York to stay with her in a hotel in Aberdeen until May 27, when the doctors allowed that Hannah was well enough to travel to London and then on to Switzerland.

A letter from Mary McCarthy written when she was back in Paris indicates that Hannah, her talks on the will having been disrupted, was nonetheless a willful patient, resisting the control of nurses, insisting that she would not slow down, go on a special diet, stop smoking, or live for her health. Mary implored her: "Please, now, my dear, obey the doctor and direct your *will* to recuperation rather than to resistance . . . enjoy . . . the rest, enforced though it is . . . [and remember] no doctor would prescribe an agitated life, two packs of cigarettes a day, and running while carrying heavy objects."

Hannah corresponded with Heidegger from Tegna, and they arranged a visit in Freiburg in mid-July. The news that she had to break off the lectures in Aberdeen had not surprised him, he wrote from his own "quiet seclusion," because the tone of her letters in the preceding months suggested that she was tired and listless; moods, he acknowledged, that he understood all too well: "A poor mood is even more tiresome than the excess of the effort you have undertaken with your quite difficult topic. . . . Being old and getting old make . . . demands on us. The world reveals a different face, and equanimity is necessary."

Writing again a few days later, noting that their letters had crossed in the mail, Heidegger observed that "you are clearly getting better again, which is a great relief to me. Nonetheless, I would like to advise you to return to work slowly and calmly." Then thanking her, apparently for an invitation to go to dinner in a restaurant when she came to visit, he wrote that it would be better "to stick with the tradition [of dinners at home] . . . for we no longer go out in the evening—neither to lectures nor social gatherings. I have not made it into the city in months, and Elfride does so quite rarely, too."

Hannah did not follow Heidegger's advice to slow down. She returned to New York on August 15, then spent much of the rest of the month visiting Mary McCarthy in Maine. At summer's end she continued to work on preparing "Thinking" for publication and on revising the lecture on willing in advance of the next series of lectures at Aberdeen, but took time off to visit with Mary in New York in November, and then flew to Paris to be with Mary at Christmas and to celebrate the New Year, 1975.

Back in New York, she received a letter from the rector of the University of Copenhagen informing her that the government of Denmark had selected her to receive the Sonning Prize and an award of $35,000 (in 2008 the value of the award, 1 million

Danish kroner, was approximately $200,000) in recognition of her meritorious contributions to European civilization. She was the first woman and the first United States citizen to receive this honor. Earlier recipients had included Winston Churchill, Albert Schweitzer, Niels Bohr, Lawrence Olivier, Karl Barth, Arthur Koestler, and Karl Popper. Mary McCarthy, busy making her own plans to attend the ceremony, prevailed on Hannah to buy a new dress for the occasion, which she did. Hannah reported happily that William Jovanovich was going to travel to Copenhagen with her for what was essentially a long weekend trip in mid-April; but "Mary," she wrote, "believe me the whole thing is a nuisance."

Hannah had kind words for her hosts in Copenhagen, telling them that as a Jew she shared in the special admiration that all Jews feel for the way the Danish people and their government responded to the "highly explosive problems posed by the Nazi conquest of Europe," rescuing not only their own Jewish citizens, but also refugees and asylum seekers, which no other country attempted, and achieving this moral feat through a highly instructive example of the great power of nonviolent resistance. Only in Denmark were Nazi masters confronted by a conquered people who dared to speak out in opposition; and in the face of public censure, "overpowered by mere words, spoken freely and publicly," Nazi officials in Denmark became "unreliable" and looked away when a flotilla of small fishing boats carried thousands of condemned persons across the Oresund Strait to shelter and safety in neutral Sweden. Not only had the Danes shown courage and independence in thinking and judging, they had demonstrated that even the unthinking conformity of Nazi functionaries melted away when confronted by moral conviction.[2]

Then, perhaps for the only time in her life, Arendt, who had little sympathy for psychology as a discipline and who was so intensely private that she generally avoided television interviews because she wanted not to be recognized on the street, talked about herself and her feelings, particularly her discomfort in having to come forward to accept the recognition inherent in the Sonning Prize. It was not "the delicate question of merit" that concerned her, despite her doubts that she deserved so great an honor, for she understood that no one is in a position to judge himself, and that no one appears to himself as he appears to others; but by temperament she was not comfortable in the public realm, preferring the contemplative life of the thinker's "soundless dialogue between me and myself."[3]

The preparation and travel necessitated by the Sonning Prize were not the only disruption of Arendt's intended withdrawal into the *vita contemplativa* during the first months of 1975. The Watergate Scandal intruded too, calling Arendt back to the *vita activa* of the citizen and public figure (to which, Mary McCarthy noted, Arendt was a constant recruit though only seldom a volunteer).[4]

Both Arendt and Mary McCarthy had disliked and distrusted Richard Nixon intensely, thinking him sleazy and dishonest since the 1950s when as a young congressman from California he was a leading anticommunist ally of Senator Joseph McCarthy and a member of the House Un-American Activities Committee. Their opposition to Nixon hardened after 1968 when as president he ordered the intensification of bombing in the Vietnam War.

McCarthy was by then a leading figure in the antiwar movement, having traveled to Saigon and Hanoi the year before for the express purpose, she wrote in the *New York Review of Books*, of "looking for material damaging to the American interest"—and finding it. (She was handed a pithy example when a representative of the Agency for International Development said of refugees forcibly herded into camps after their villages had been burned to the ground: "We're teaching them free enterprise."[5]) Still, Mary's dispatches from North Vietnam were thought by many, even in the antiwar movement and even by Arendt[6] to be a little over the top in her adulation of the North Vietnamese leadership, whose simple but cultured lifestyle she admired, despite her own penchant for luxury.[7]

Arendt had also been opposed to the war in Vietnam, though with less intensity than Mary. She signed petitions and made contributions to antiwar groups. But it was President Nixon's plotting and covering-up the break-in at the national headquarters of the Democratic Party in the Watergate Hotel during the presidential election of 1972—and subsequent revelations of enemies lists, spying on citizens, and malicious, politically inspired tax audits—that caused her most intense feelings of disquiet.

Hannah and Mary both derived a degree of satisfaction from Nixon's humiliation but were concerned at the extent to which democratic institutions had been undermined. McCarthy took on Watergate as the central focus of her work, traveling to Washington to attend the Senate hearings and writing a series of articles for the *Observer* of London and the *New York Review of Books*.[8] Arendt tried to maintain her focus on "Willing," the next section of *The Life of the Mind*, but events in Washington, she wrote to Mary, were cutting "rather deeply and sharply into [her] time and attention." Despite the fact that she was enjoying Nixon's disgrace, Arendt feared that uncontrolled executive power sustained by the same type of banal evil she had seen before (observing, for example, that Watergate coconspirator E. Howard Hunt looked and acted pretty much like Eichmann)[9] constituted a threat to the continued well-being of the Republic.

In the spring of 1975 an invitation from the mayor of Boston to speak at an early celebration of the bicentennial of American independence became the occasion for Arendt to reflect on the manifold crises of the Republic, not only the Vietnam War, Watergate, and Ford's pardon of Nixon, but more generally the stunning and unprecedented decline in the political power of the United States. The deterioration of the nation's institutions of liberty, she asserted, had begun with Senator Joe McCarthy's attack on the nation's devoted and reliable civil service; and if after the Nixon presidency the country remained cheerful, it was because the cataclysm of events "cascading like a Niagara Falls of history" left everyone in its path numbed and paralyzed.[10] Disaster and ignominy in the war had been simultaneous with the ruin of American foreign policy, the loss of allies, debacles in the Middle East, trouble in NATO, uncertainties of détente, proliferation of nuclear arms, as well as inflation, urban decay, and rising unemployment and crime at home. She was afraid that even if there were periods of remission, these forces would eventually undo the political order the Founding Fathers had established two hundred years earlier: "The dividing lines between eras may hardly be visible when they are crossed; only after people stumble over them do the lines grow into walls which irretrievably shut off the past."[11] The greatest threat, she thought, sounding an alarm, came from the emergence of lying as a way of life in politics. This had been the central strategy of totalitarian regimes in the twentieth century, and that experience had made clear that lying as a matter of public policy is most effective only when it is accompanied by terror, "the invasion of the political processes by sheer criminality."[12]

She did not think that Nixon could be compared to Hitler or Stalin, nor even that Nixon was the first American leader in recent years to lie to Congress and the American people (pointing here to Lyndon Johnson's claim that North Vietnam had attacked the United States Navy at the Gulf of Tonkin); but Watergate, "third-rate" burglaries, cover-ups of illegal behavior, harassment of citizens, and the attempt to organize a Secret Service that worked just for the president and not for the government, were emblematic of the intrusion of criminality into the political process and the undermining of the Constitution. "In other words," she concluded, "it is as though a bunch of con men, rather untalented Mafiosi, had succeeded in appropriating to themselves the government of 'the mightiest power on earth.' "[13]

The speech, entitled "Home to Roost," was broadcast five days later on National Public Radio, praised in Tom Wicker's column in the *New York Times*, published in the *New York Review of Books*, and quoted at year's end in the *New York Times* "Abstract for the Year." Hannah wrote to Mary McCarthy that she had never received so many fan letters, referring to one in particular from a young man who had written that he heard she was getting on in years and wanted her to know his opinions before she passed away.

35

THE EXECUTOR OF AN ESTATE IS charged with implementing the last will of one who is deceased. With writers, artists, and other public figures there are special intangible complications arising from one's reputation and the interest of succeeding generations. Is the privacy of the deceased to be protected? Should potentially embarrassing information (about a youthful romance, for example) be destroyed or preserved? What is to be done with unfinished work or pieces left behind with which the author was not satisfied? Judgments of this type require a special sensitivity in response to which the role of literary executor has emerged. The literary executor, combining the functions of an editor and agent, has potential to magnify (or perhaps diminish) a writer's legacy; and the literary executor is not legally bound to honor instructions of the deceased. If Max Brod, for example, had fulfilled Kafka's wish that his papers be destroyed, practically none of Kafka's stories would exist.

Writers know all this, in consequence of which they take the appointment and responsibilities of literary executors very seriously. Hannah and Mary McCarthy each asked the other to take on the role, depending on who died first. Karl Jaspers, who died in 1969, assigned this role jointly to his assistant, Hans Saner and to Hannah, both of whom approached it as a solemn obligation. In the spring of 1975, already distracted by Watergate and her speech in Boston, Arendt made arrangements to postpone the second series of Gifford Lectures on "Willing" to spring 1976 in order to honor a request from the German Literature Archive in Marbach to deposit her correspondence with Karl Jaspers and organize his letters for eventual publication.

Mary McCarthy visited in Marbach in mid-June. At the end of the month Hannah visited Heidegger in Freiburg, where they celebrated what he characterized as "the great Prize you received in Denmark." From there she went on to Tegna, ostensibly to prepare for the Gifford lectures, but when Mary wrote inquiring how the work was going, Hannah wrote back that she was being "extremely lazy" and was a little concerned about not having accomplished very much during the months of July and August; on the other hand, she reported, something "really funny" had happened: James Kirkpatrick, the "very powerful" executive secretary of the American Political Science Association, with whom she had "a terrific row" some years earlier over the Pentagon Papers, had written to inform her that the association, which "had ignored [her] for twenty years," selected *The Human Condition* to receive the first Lippincott Award as the best work of political theory in the past fifteen years. Even during lazy moments of quiet retreat, the world was still beating a path to Arendt's door.

Toward the end of August, Hannah took another trip to Freiburg to visit Heidegger, after which she wrote to Mary McCarthy from Tegna that she had come back feeling depressed: "Heidegger is now suddenly really very old, very changed from last year, very deaf and remote, unapproachable as I never saw him before." As things turned out, this was the last time they were to see each other. She stayed on in Switzerland until the end of September and then stopped in Paris on her way home to participate as a respondent in a conference ominously titled "Terror in the Year 2000."

Arendt continued working on "Willing," by late November completing the first draft of a manuscript, which while still needing revision and editing before publication, was nevertheless ready to be presented at Aberdeen in the spring. On December 4, 1975, Salo Baron and his wife Jeanette, were guests at Hannah's apartment. After dinner they retired to the living room for coffee and conversation in comfortable chairs. Then, after a sudden brief spell of coughing, Hannah fell into unconsciousness; her doctor was summoned and came immediately, but Hannah, who was sixty-nine years old, died of a heart attack without regaining consciousness.

Mary McCarthy, Arendt's literary executor, in deep mourning, stopped her own work for two years in order to prepare "Willing" for publication. While the writing is beautiful, there is something missing in the text: no central theme emerges; Arendt's scholarship outshines her thinking. Of the three functions of the mind, thinking, willing, and judging, Arendt was on the least familiar ground with willing;[1] if she had lived long enough to make revisions, perhaps she would have found her own footing. Mary McCarthy did an excellent job of editing and refining the text that Arendt left behind, but no other person could bring Arendt's own creativity and perspective to a revised draft. The book on thinking, for all its complexity, is organized around a central question: the relationship of thoughtlessness to evil. There is nothing comparable in the text on willing, so all that we are left with is a striking example of Arendt's erudition, ranging across the history of thought about volition and free will from Greek and Roman antiquity through the early Christian period from St. Paul to Augustine, the Middle Ages, Aquinas, Meister Eckhardt, and Duns Scotus, and concluding in modernity with Kant, Hegel, Nietzsche, and Heidegger, who is in this volume the most frequently cited thinker and the subject of the penultimate chapter. *Willing* was in many ways for Hannah a last visit with old friends.

The will seeks influence over events even from the grave; that is the meaning of "a last will and testament." Arendt asserts (following Heidegger) that, striving for control, the will comes to hate the past because events in the past are beyond control. All that is possible in the future is to shape the memory of the past, or to forget, or to destroy the past the way Nazi willing had destroyed so much of Europe and its traditions.

Even if we attempt to restrain our will, willing and thinking are central features of the life of the mind, and they are oppositional. Thinking is the organ of the past because every thought is an afterthought, a reflection on experience; willing is the organ of the future, engaging us with the ways in which we want events to unfold.[2] Thinking pulls us out of the world into a reflective posture sometimes accompanied by nostalgia, joy, regret, grief, or sorrow, but never by anxiety, since there is nothing we can do about the past. Willing, the seat of volition and ambition, is of the world, and looks forward rather than backward, seeking to influence the unfolding of experience; but since it is by no means certain that the goals of the willing mind will be accomplished, the activity of willing generates "a mixture of fear and hope," especially when we come to grips with the fact that we may not be able to actualize our plans. There is no great art or science without the will to achieve it; but not everyone who wills himself to become an artist or scientist has the capacity or good fortune to arrive at the hoped-for destination. Thinking causes a sort of paralysis drawing us away from the world into internal dialogue; willing is the motor that drives us toward action. The tonal mood of thinking is serenity; the predominant mood of the will is disquiet. The relationship between the thinking ego and the willing ego is conflict: one aiming to withdraw into contemplation of what is or has been, the other striving to shape what lies ahead.

What we know, and even what we wonder, about the will—how it operates, the extent to which it is free (and if it is not free, can it be anything other than an illusion?), the extent to which it may be influenced by reason—all these questions have been brought to our attention by men who were thinkers, who, unlike men of action, were not really comfortable with the will. Arendt's contemplation of the will inevitably involved withdrawal into the realm of thought and into contact with other thinkers. In the last weeks of work on this project, which turned out also to be the last weeks of life, she was thinking principally about Martin Heidegger and especially his "turn," in the Nietzsche lectures while the Nazis were still in power, which he announced later in the "Letter on humanism," his turn in the direction of willing-not-to-will: "What the reversal originally turns against is primarily the will-to-power. In Heidegger's understanding, the will to rule and to dominate is a kind of original sin, of which he found himself guilty when he tried to come to terms with his brief past in the Nazi movement."

Arendt saw in Heidegger's "turn" an expression of regret (perhaps inscrutable to the uninitiated) for the harm done by the Nazi will to power, and his part in it. Now, approaching the end, she reflected on Heidegger's subsequent assertion of the identity of thinking and thanking *(denken und danken)* and its corollary that human conscience has its origins in the debt of gratitude owed for the naked fact of existence, the "That" given to all. Heidegger's idea, late in life, that "the attitude of man, confronted with Being, should be thanking," Arendt characterized as a variant of Plato's *thaumazein*, the admiring wonder that is the beginning principle of thinking. She supported this with references to Nietzsche's praise of "yes-sayers," Osip Mandelstam's assertion that "earth for us has been worth a thousand heavens," the declaration in Rilke's Ninth Elegy that a single spring on earth "is already more than my blood can endure," and Auden's observation of the singular command that has to be obeyed: *"Bless what there is for being."*

The night Arendt died, there was in her typewriter the title page of the third section of *The Life of the Mind*, with the word "Judging" near the top and just below a quote from Cato: "The gods love those who are victorious, but Cato loves the vanquished."

The gods bestow immortality on the victorious who get to write history and celebratory poems, but Cato, recognizing that the vanquished may have been every bit as brave and heroic as those who defeated them, and that their cause may have been as good or better, loves them, because he is human and his heart goes out to them in response to all they have lost. Making his own judgments, Cato is not intimidated by the preferences of the gods. Nor was Arendt, who like Cato made her own judgments, independently, without concern for the opinions of the powerful, and also without prejudice: this is why she could make critical judgments not only about the society from which she had been forced to flee into exile, but also about the society in which she found refuge; it is why she could criticize the Jewish people of whom she was a daughter, and also their enemies. It is also why she could forgive Martin Heidegger, whom she loved and admired despite his serious shortcomings.

Mary McCarthy spoke at Hannah's funeral before hundreds of mourners, describing Hannah as alluring, seductive, and feminine: "Above all, her eyes, so brilliant and sparkling, starry when she was happy or excited, but also deep, dark, remote, pools of inwardness. There was something unfathomable in Hannah that seemed to lie in the reflective depths of those eyes." Arendt, she explained, was not ambitious in the traditional way of striving for personal success; what she did strive for in her work was to achieve a summit from which she could see, like an explorer finishing the last stages of an ascent alone, the world below:

> What would be spread out before her were the dark times she had borne witness to, as a Jewess, and a displaced person, the long drawn-out miscarriage of a socialist revolution, the present perils of the American Republic, where she had found a new home in which to hang, with increasing despondency, the ideas of freedom she had carried with her. From her summit she would also look out at the vast surveyor's map of concepts and insights, some inherited from a long philosophical tradition and some her own discoveries, which, regarded from a high point, could at least show us where we were.[3]

Arendt, Mary said, "had heard such a voice as spoke to the prophets," and the presence with which she relayed what she had heard to public audiences was that of a "magnificent stage diva . . .

enacting a drama of mind," projecting herself as the one who acts and the one who suffers in the arena of consciousness and reflection, "where there are always two, the one who says and the one who replies or questions."

William Jovanovich also spoke at the funeral, noting that Arendt believed passionately in both justice and mercy, that she followed serious inquiry wherever it might take her, never with fear, and never with the intention of making enemies, although she knew that could happen. In the end, he said, his voice breaking with emotion, "As for me, I loved her fiercely."[4]

Martin Heidegger, informed of Hannah's death by telegram, sent back a message to Hans Jonas: DEEPLY MOURNING WITH THE CIRCLE OF FRIENDS.[5] In response to a letter from Jonas a few weeks later, Heidegger wrote, acknowledging his own obtuse inability to see what had always been before him, that he now understood "for the first time, how much, and how constantly, Hannah was the center of a large, diverse circle." Noting the inadequacy of words, he noted that "only grief and remembrance are left for us."[6] Martin Heidegger died less than half a year later, on May 26, 1976, four months before his eighty-seventh birthday. He is buried where he was born, in the small town of Messkirch in the Black Forest.

The night before Hannah's funeral, family and friends debated whether Jewish prayers should be read, as they were at Heinrich Blücher's funeral; for reasons that are obscure it was decided not to recite the Mourner's Kaddish.[7] Since there are so many admirers who keep her in memory, it is possible that since then others have recited the Kaddish, as is the custom, on the anniversary of her death. Hannah was buried at Bard College next to Heinrich Blücher. There is still a simple rough-hewn graveside bench inviting visitors to pause and think.

36

◇◇◇◇
◆

MARTIN HEIDEGGER, HOPING PERHAPS TO HAVE the last word on his own past, granted an interview to the editors of *Der Spiegel* on September 26, 1966, on the condition that they not publish it during his lifetime. He died on May 26, 1976, and the interview appeared five days later under the title "Only a God Can Save Us." In it Heidegger reiterated the same revisionist lies and half-truths that he had told without success to the denazification commission thirty years earlier: he was apolitical, was never an enthusiastic Nazi, took up the rectorship only to protect the university, resisted the firing of Jewish professors, did not break with Husserl and Jaspers, and did not wish to align the university with National Socialism.

A decade later Victor Farias's book, undermined in some ways by extravagant claims of anti-Semitism, including allegations of a deep psychological connection between Heidegger and the seventeenth-century monk Abraham a Sancta Clara (for whom Jews were "an archetype of evil"),[1] nevertheless went a long way to set straight the record of Heidegger's embrace of the

Nazi revolution. Since then Richard Wolin has gone even further, in more measured tones, to preserve a record of Heidegger's misdeeds and postwar dissembling,[2] and a recent book by Emmanuel Faye offers a few additional details combined with a great deal of highly abstract argument about the relationship between Heidegger's thought and Nazi ideology.[3] As a consequence, more details are available to us about Heidegger's politics and character than were ever available to Hannah Arendt. Would it have made a difference if she had known all that we now know?

Presumably her detractors think not. In their view Arendt was a self-hating, German-loving, anti-Semitic Jew, and this alone explains her criticism of the Jewish leadership for its role in the Holocaust, her disapproval of Israel's exclusionary and militaristic identity, and her characterization of Nazi evil as banal. Only a Jew who did not love Jews, it is still said in some quarters, could think such things; such a Jew would have to forgive Heidegger and go on loving him in order to preserve and protect her own identity as a German.

It is true that Arendt was a product of German culture and tradition. Even her claim that she was a *Mädchen aus der Fremde* was a reference to Schiller, and what could be more German? But why is there anything wrong or pathological about this? German culture produced not only Heidegger, but also Blücher and Jaspers, Kant, Beethoven, Bach, Mozart, Lessing, Schiller, Goethe, Hesse, Mann, and Planck, not to mention such German Jews as Heine, Einstein, Freud, and Arendt's greatly admired friend, the Zionist leader Kurt Blumenfeld. It is no more a sign of self-hatred for Arendt to have had regard for the culture in which she was raised than for African Americans in the twenty-first century to have patriotic sentiments despite awareness of the nation's history of slavery and racism. And it is far from clear that the Nazis represented a logical extension of the German tradition rather than its radical perversion.

This hostile (dare we say sexist) view of Arendt does not dominate the discourse about her work. Nevertheless, it is obstinately present at least as innuendo, seeking to blunt her human rights criticisms of Israel and trivialize her advocacy of reconciliation between Germans and Jews, and between Jews and Arabs, by characterizing her ideas as the distorted conclusions of one whose judgment and self-image were so impaired that she could not even see through her deceitful Nazi lover.

It is more appropriate to understand Arendt's reconciliation with Heidegger as a reflection of the place of honor occupied by love in Arendt's life and thought, not only the love of friends—Heinrich Blücher, Karl Jaspers, and Mary McCarthy among many others—but also love of the world itself—*amor mundi*—thankfulness for the mere fact of existence even in the face of evil and suffering. If, as Arendt wrote to Gershom Scholem, she did not love whole peoples—the Jews, the Germans, or the working class—but only individuals, neither did she make categorical judgments or condemn whole cultures—criticizing not the Germans, but only the Nazis, not the Jews or the Arabs, but the leadership of both groups. Gratitude and respect for Being in all its diversity gave form and vitality to her convictions about the pursuit of peace, and as we have seen, the possibility of forgiveness was central to Arendt's philosophical commitment to natality, regeneration, and new beginnings.

Equally central to Arendt's philosophy and to her way of living was the importance of self-reflective inner dialogue (what she called thinking) and the willingness to make independent judgments. Even if the work of biographers and historians has added detail to the record of Heidegger's life and prevarication, Arendt already knew enough to understand the weakness of his character. Even without imputing pathological motives it does not seem likely that a reading of Farias or Wolin would have altered Arendt's judgment about Heidegger.

After Arendt's death, Mary McCarthy commented to Carol Brightman, who edited *Between Friends: The Correspondence of Hannah Arendt and Mary McCarthy*, that Heidegger had been the great love affair in Hannah's life.[4] But a love affair and love are not identical, and there were other and greater loves for Hannah. In understanding her reconciliation with Martin Heidegger, one cannot underestimate the depth of Arendt's love for Heinrich Blücher, with whom she felt secure, as within her "own four walls," no matter what disasters world history threw their way. In light of the richness of Arendt's life, it seems too convenient, too facile a trope, for her critics to suggest that she reconciled with Heidegger because she pined for his love, could not see him clearly, or had no other source of happiness in life.

The friendship between Hannah Arendt and Martin Heidegger survived and transcended the crises of their own lives and the storms of world. If the first response of perpetrators (and victims) was, like Heidegger's, to hide behind a barrier of silence and denial, subsequent events have opened the wound to daylight and memory to the power of honest thinking. Arendt, "stranger from abroad" though she felt herself to be, played an important role in advancing this *cura posterior. Origins of Totalitarianism*, *Eichmann in Jerusalem*, and *The Life of the Mind*, along with a host of essays, interviews, and speeches, and also her efforts to promote the international visibility of others, including Jaspers and Heidegger (who fared so differently when put to the test), all contributed to the restoration of the intellectual and ethical traditions of the cultures in which she made her first appearance. Chastened, the Germans have built more memorials to the victims of their aggression, greed, and delusions than any other nation in history; it is significant that the most solemn of these, the Memorial to the Murdered Jews of Europe, in the very heart of the nation's capital, next to the Brandenburg Gate, is bordered by the newly constructed Hannah-Arendt-Strasse.

Even if we reject politically inspired, ad hominem attacks on Arendt's psyche and recognize the importance of her contribution to the literature on totalitarianism and on crimes against humanity, it does not mean that we have to accept Arendt's conclusions about Heidegger. Since we too participate in the life of the mind—thinking and judging for ourselves—it is necessary to consider whether she may have fundamentally misjudged him. It is this question—whether Heidegger was so deeply associated with the Nazis as to be among the Germans with whom reconciliation was inappropriate, or whether Arendt was correct to judge him as a flawed human being with redeeming virtues—more than any other that has made it necessary to disturb the peace of long-dead lovers.

Remembering that Heidegger was alienated from the Nazis early on and was never part of the killing machine, we may nonetheless feel unsympathetic, seeing him as dishonest, manipulative, unfaithful, provincial. Arendt also saw all that—but it is in the nature of reconciliation that there is something which has to be overcome, and no doubt there was quite a bit that had to be overcome in Heidegger's character and record. Arendt did not believe in an obligation to forgive, but only that forgiveness is a perpetual possibility—so long as one can see the betrayer as a person who is something more than the act of betrayal.

What more was Heidegger than a man of flawed character

and a betrayer? The answer of course is that he was a brilliant philosopher whose thinking and language was richly poetic. Does this mean that Arendt thought only people with special gifts deserve to be forgiven? In her essay on Brecht (who like Heidegger was opportunistic and self-serving, perhaps especially in relationships with women), she accepted that creativity and genius may thrive only outside the restrictions of conventionality. But when Germans tried to apologize for the Nazi past by commenting on how egregious the expulsion of Jewish intellectuals and artists had been, Arendt upbraided them with a reminder that it was a bigger crime to have killed the little boy next door, "even though he was no genius." If she thought creativity and talent deserved or even required indulgence, this does not mean that she thought women and children or anyone else should be thrown overboard to save philosophers and poets.

Ordinary people were never excluded from Hannah's sympathy, but forgiveness for her was always personal, not, as she told W. H. Auden, a matter of turning the other cheek toward any and all who offend, but of mending something broken and starting anew with a friend. With Martin Heidegger there was for Hannah both the memory of love and a debt of gratitude for a lifetime of thinking with and against him. In the process, she focused on his issues—Being, language, and thinking—as well as others that were distinctly her own: justice and politics as the way human beings live together in the world.

In the end, perhaps Arendt's readiness to forgive Heidegger was an affair of the heart—forgiveness of neither the act nor the idea of betrayal, only this man whom she had loved, whose mind and magnetism she admired more than his character, and with whom there was wordplay and the shared occupation of working with ideas. From our own circumstances and the distance of the current moment, Heidegger may seem undeserving, but for one who knew him, understood his thinking, felt happy in his company, and recognized both the temptations and banality of evil, forgiveness in the name of friendship cannot be dismissed as evidence of self-hatred or personal pathology.

For us, who have come after, there are personal as well as political lessons to be learned from Hannah Arendt's reconciliation with Martin Heidegger. At the end of life, thinking about thinking, willing, and judging, Arendt was close to Heidegger's thought and method while still engaged with her own questions. He continued to be for her a companion and close presence on the pathways of thought, where each of us are surrounded in our singularity by the ideas of others. The principal benefit of reconciliation, as Arendt understood, is that it brings peace, understanding, and human warmth into a world too often hostile, confused, and cold. The promise of reconciliation, which is neither forgetfulness nor an averted glance, but a full-bodied recognition of the human condition, is that it preserves the possibility of love—in the case of Hannah Arendt and Martin Heidegger, an easy commerce between old friends—and friendship, as Hannah understood, is the foundation of all humanity.

Notes

CHAPTER ONE

1. Unless otherwise noted, this and all subsequent references to correspondence and conversations between Hannah Arendt and Martin Heidegger and also to correspondence between Hannah Arendt and Elfride Heidegger are drawn from Hannah Arendt and Martin Heidegger, *Briefe, 1925–1975*, ed. Ursula Ludz (Frankurt am Main: Vittorio Klostermann, 1998), or the English translation, *Letters, 1925–1975*, ed. Ursula Ludz; trans. Andrew Shields (Orlando, Fla.: Harcourt, 2004).
2. Hannah Arendt, *The Origins of Totalitarianism*, with a new introduction by Samantha Powers (New York: Schocken Books, 2004), p. 616.
3. Hannah Arendt, "What Remains? The Language Remains: A Conversation with Günter Gaus," in Hannah Arendt, *Essays in Understanding, 1930–1954*, ed. Jerome Kohn (New York: Harcourt Brace, 1994), pp. 1–23, 13.
4. Unless otherwise noted, characterizations of the conditions of Jewish life in Germany during the Enlightenment are drawn from Amos Elon's comprehensive and poignant history *The Pity of It All: A History of Jews in Germany, 1743–1933* (New York: Metropolitan Books, 2002).
5. Unless otherwise noted, factual statements about Arendt's life, family,

and friends are drawn from Elisabeth Young-Bruehl's comprehensive study *Hannah Arendt: For Love of the World*, 2d ed. (New Haven, Conn.: Yale University Press, 2004).

6. Stefan Zweig, *The World of Yesterday: An Autobiography* (New York: Viking, 1943).
7. Arendt, "What Remains?" p. 7.
8. Victor Klemperer, *I Will Bear Witness, 1942–1945: A Diary of the Nazi Years* (New York: Modern Library, 2001), p. 63.
9. Arendt, "What Remains?" p. 8.

CHAPTER TWO

1. Elzbieta Ettinger, *Hannah Arendt/Martin Heidegger* (New Haven, Conn.: Yale University Press, 1984), p. 11.
2. Martin Heidegger, *Plato's Sophist*, trans. Ricard Rojcewicz and André Schuwer (Bloomington: Indiana University Press, 1997).
3. Eric Havelock, *Preface to Plato* (New York: Grosset & Dunlap, 1967).
4. Hannah Arendt, "Martin Heidegger at Eighty," trans. Albert Hofstadter, *New York Review of Books*, October 21, 1971.
5. This characterization is attributed to Mary McCarthy by Carol Brightman, in the "Introduction" to Hannah Arendt and Mary McCarthy, *Between Friends: The Correspondence of Hannah Arendt and Mary McCarthy, 1949–1975*, ed. Carol Brightman (New York: Harcourt Brace, 1995), p. xii.

CHAPTER THREE

1. Hannah Arendt and Heinrich Blücher, *Within Four Walls: The Correspondence Between Hannah Arendt and Heinrich Blücher, 1936–1968* ed. Lotte Kohler; trans. Peter Constantine (New York: Harcourt, 2000), p. 128.
2. Unless otherwise noted, factual statements about Elfride Heidegger and the marital relationship and correspondence between Martin and Elfride Heidegger are drawn from Martin Heidegger and Elfride Heidegger, *"Mein liebes Seelchen!": Briefe Martin Heideggers an seine Frau*

Elfride, 1915–1970, ed. Gertrud Heidegger (Munich: Deutsche Verlags-Anstalt, 2005).

3. Hugo Ott, *Martin Heidegger: A Political Life*, trans. Allan Blunden (New York: Basic Books, 1993), pp. 137–138.
4. Young-Bruehl, *Hannah Arendt*, p. 61.
5. Victor Farias, *Heidegger and Nazism*, ed. Joseph Margolis and Tom Rockmore; trans. Paul Burrell, Dominic Di Bernardi, and Gabriel Ricci (Philadelphia: Temple University Press, 1989).
6. Ibid., pp. 19–48.
7. Unless otherwise noted, factual statements about Martin Heidegger, characterizations of him by others, and his correspondence with persons other than Elfride Heidegger, Karl Jaspers, and Hannah Arendt are drawn from Hugo Ott, *Martin Heidegger: A Political Life*, trans. Allan Blunden (New York: HarperCollins, 1993).
8. Hans-Georg Gadamer, *Heidegger's Ways*, trans. John W. Stanley (Albany, N.Y.: State University of New York Press, 1994), p. 170.
9. Ibid., pp. 167–180.
10. Arendt and McCarthy, *Between Friends*, p. 49.

CHAPTER FOUR

1. Arendt and Heidegger, *Letters*, p. 35.
2. Ettinger, *Hannah Arendt/Martin Heidegger*, p. 28.
3. Arendt, and Blücher, *Within Four Walls*, p. 128.
4. Karl Jaspers, *Notizen zu Heidegger*, ed. Hans Saner (Munich: Piper Verlag, 1978), p. 34.
5. Hannah Arendt, *Love and Saint Augustine*, eds. Joanna Vecchiarelli Scott and Judith Chelius Stark (Chicago: University of Chicago Press, 1998).

CHAPTER FIVE

1. Harold Marcuse, "Günther Anders Biography," http://www.history.ucsb.edu/faculty/marcuse/anders.htm#biog.
2. Arendt and Heidegger, *Letters*, pp. 37–38.
3. Young-Bruehl, *Hannah Arendt*, pp. 79–80, 109.

4. Arendt, and Blücher, *Within Four Walls*, p. 10.
5. Unless otherwise noted, references to Rahel Varnhagen are drawn from Hannah Arendt, *Rahel Varnhagen: The Life of a Jewess*, ed. Liliane Weissberg, trans. Richard Winston and Clara Winston (Baltimore: Johns Hopkins University Press, 1997).
6. Howard M. Sachar, *The Course of Modern Jewish History* (New York: World Publishing, 1958), pp. 25–52.
7. Seyla Benhabib, *The Reluctant Modernism of Hannah Arendt* (Lanham, Md.: Rowman & Littlefield, 2003), pp. 1–34. See also Deborah Hertz, *Jewish High Society in Old Regime Berlin* (New Haven, Conn.: Yale University Press, 1988).

CHAPTER SIX

1. Richard Wolin, *Heidegger's Children: Hannah Arendt, Karl Löwith, Hans Jonas, and Herbert Marcuse* (Princeton, N.J.: Princeton University Press, 2001), p. 22.
2. See, for example, "An Exchange of Letters Between Gershom Scholem and Hannah Arendt," in Hannah Arendt, *The Jew as Pariah: Jewish Identity and Politics in the Modern Age*, ed. Ron H. Feldman (New York: Grove Press, 1978), pp. 240–251, 246.
3. Ian Kershaw, *Hitler: 1889–1936 Hubris* (New York: W. W. Norton, 2000), pp. 257–258.
4. Arendt, "What Remains?" p. 4.
5. Ibid., p. 12.
6. Arendt, *Rahel Varnhagen*, p. 82.
7. Hannah Arendt, "From the Dreyfus Affair to France Today," *Jewish Social Studies* 4, no. 3 (July 1942): pp. 235–240; excerpted in Arendt, *The Jew as Pariah*, pp. 125–130.
8. Arendt, *Rahel Varnhagen*, pp. 179, 258–259. See also Elon, *The Pity of it All*, pp. 8, 82.
9. Arendt, *Rahel Varnhagen*, p. 251.
10. Ibid., p.256.
11. Hannah Arendt and Karl Jaspers, *Correspondence, 1926–1969*, ed. Lotte Kohler and Hans Saner; trans. Robert Kimber and Rita Kimber (New

York: Harcourt Brace Javanovich, 1992), pp. 98–99. See also Arendt, *The Origins of Totalitarianism*, p. 155.

12. The author attributes this insight to a conversation with Professor Jerome Kohn, the current literary executor of the Hannah Arendt estate.

CHAPTER SEVEN

1. From a letter written by Husserl to Ernst Jaensch, located in the Hesse State Archives, cited in Ott, *Martin Heidegger*, p. 127.
2. Unless otherwise noted, references to correspondence and other contacts between Martin Heidegger and Karl Jaspers are drawn from Martin Heidegger and Karl Jaspers, *Martin Heidegger/Karl Jaspers Briefwechsel: 1920—1963*, ed. Walter Biemel and Hans Saner (Frankfurt am Main: Verlag Vittorio Klosterman, 1990), or the English translation, *The Heidegger-Jaspers Correspondence: 1920–1963*, ed. Walter Biemel and Hans Saner; trans. Gary E. Aylesworth (Amherst, N.Y.: Humanity Books, 2003).
3. Hannah Arendt, "Martin Heidegger at Eighty," trans. Albert Hofstadter *New York Review of Books*, October 21, 1971.
4. Arendt discusses this point in Hannah Arendt, "What Is Existential Philosophy," *Partisan Review* 18, no. 1 (1946). A German translation appears in Hannah Arendt, *Sechs Essays*, and a translation of this back into English by Robert and Rita Kimber appears in Hannah Arendt, *Essays in Understanding, 1930–1954*, ed. Jerome Kohn (New York: Harcourt Brace, 1994), pp. 163–187, 168–169. For an interesting presentation of this idea, see Mark Twain, *The Mysterious Stranger* (New York: Harper & Brothers, 1916), pp. 148–151.
5. Kant, Immanuel, *Prologemena to Any Future Metaphysics: With Selections from the Critique of Pure Reason*, ed. Gary Hatfield (Cambridge: Cambridge University Press, 1997), p. 10.
6. Karl Jaspers, *Kant*, ed. Hannah Arendt; trans. Ralph Manheim (New York: Harcourt Brace, 1962), p. 151.
7. Ibid., p. 152.
8. Ibid.

9. Arendt, "What Is Existential Philosophy," in *Essays in Understanding*, pp. 164–165.
10. See, for example, Modris Eksteins, *The Rites of Spring: The Great War and the Birth of the Modern Age* (New York: Houghton Mifflin, 1989).
11. See Heidegger and Heidegger, *"Mein liebes Seelchen!"* and Rüdiger Safranski, *Martin Heidegger: Between Good and Evil*, trans. Ewald Osers, (Cambridge, Mass.: Harvard University Press, 1998), p. 180.
12. Arendt, "Martin Heidegger at Eighty," reprinted in Arendt and Heidegger, *Briefe, 1925–1975*. See also Arendt and Heidegger, *Letters, 1925–1975*, pp. 148–162.
13. Martin Heidegger and Elizabeth Blochmann, *Briefwechsel, 1918–1969* ed. Joachim Storck (Marbach, Ger.: Deutsches Literatur-Archiv, 1989), p. 30, cited in Safranski, *Martin Heidegger*, pp. 185–186.
14. Toni Cassirer, *Mein Leben mit Ernst Cassirer* (Hildesheim: Gerstenberg, 1981), p. 165.
15. Carl H. Hamburg, "A Cassirer-Heidegger Seminar," *Philosophy and Phenomenological Research* 25, no.2 (December 1964): pp. 208–222.
16. Emmanuel Faye, *Heidegger: The Introduction of Nazism into Philosophy*, trans. Michael B. Smith (New Haven: Yale University Press, 2009).

CHAPTER EIGHT

1. Arendt, "What Remains?" p. 5.
2. Ibid., pp. 5–6.
3. Unless otherwise noted, all references to correspondence and conversations between Hannah Arendt and Heinrich Blücher are drawn from Arendt and Blücher, *Within Four Walls*, in this instance p. 21.
4. Jeffrey H. Jackson, *Making Jazz French: Music and Modern Life in Interwar Paris* (Durham, N.C.: Duke University Press, 2003).
5. Alexander Koyré, *From the Closed World to the Infinite Universe* (New York: Harper & Row, 1958).
6. Raymond Aron, *The Opium of the Intellectuals*, trans. Terence Kilmartin (New York: Doubleday, 1957).
7. Hannah Arendt, "Walter Benjamin, 1892–1940," in Hannah Arendt, *Men in Dark Times* (New York: Harcourt, Brace & World, 1968), pp. 153–206, 159. This essay, was written in Germany and translated by Harry

Zohn; it appeared originally in *The New Yorker,* October 19, 1968, and as Arendt's introduction to a collection of essays by Benjamin entitled *Illuminations* (New York: Harcourt, Brace & World, 1968).

8. Walter Benjamin, "Theses on the Philosophy of History," in Benjamin, *Illuminations*, pp. 253–264.
9. Heather Marcelle Crickenberger, *The Arcades Project Project: The Rhetoric of Hypertext,* http://www.thelemming.com/lemming/dissertation-web/home/arcades.html. See also Walter Benjamin, *The Arcades Project*, ed. Roy Tiedemann; trans. Howard Eiland and Kevin McLaughlin (Cambridge, Mass.: Harvard University Press, 2002).
10. Arendt, *Men in Dark Times*, pp. 153–206, 154.
11. Hannah Arendt, "We Refugees," in Arendt, *The Jew as Pariah*, pp. 62–63.
12. Young-Bruehl, *Hannah Arendt*, pp. 120–121.
13. Arendt, "What Remains?" p. 10.
14. Harold Marcuse, "Günther Anders Biography," http://www.history.ucsb.edu/faculty/marcuse/anders.htm#biog.
15. Arendt, "What Remains?" p. 11.

CHAPTER NINE

1. Ott, *Martin Heidegger*, p. 146. See also, Safranski, *Martin Heidegger*, pp. 238–241.
2. Quoted in Safranski, *Martin Heidegger*, pp. 256.
3. This letter was found and published by Ulrich Sieg in *Die Zeit,* December 22, 1989. See Safranski, *Martin Heidegger*, p. 255. See also Ott, *Martin Heidegger*, pp.378–379.
4. Heidegger and Jaspers. *The Heidegger-Jaspers Correspondence*, p. 209.
5. Safranski, *Martin Heidegger*, pp. 254.
6. Ibid., pp. 234–235.
7. Heidegger's rectoral address, "The Self-Assertion of the German University," and the text of other political speeches that he delivered in 1933 and 1934 are translated and reprinted in Richard Wolin, *The Heidegger Controversy: A Critical Reader* (Cambridge, Mass.: MIT Press, 1998), pp. 29–60.
8. Farias, *Heidegger and Nazism*, pp. 119–121.

9. Karl Jaspers, *Philosophische Autobiographie* (Munich: Piper Verlag, 1984), p. 101.
10. German Propaganda Archive, www.bytwerk.com/gpa/images/hoff1/hitler5.jpg.
11. Nathan Stoltzfus, *Resistance of the Heart: Intermarriage and the Rosenstrasse Protest in Nazi Germany* (New York: W. W. Norton, 1996).
12. Karl Jaspers, *Notizen zu Heidegger*, ed. Hans Saner (Munich: Piper Verlag, 1978), p. 34. See also, Ettinger, *Hannah Arendt/Martin Heidegger*, p. 44; Arendt and Jaspers, *Correspondence, 1926–1969*, pp 629–630.
13. Eberhard Bethge, *Dietrich Bonhoeffer: A Biography*, trans. Eric Mosbacher (Minneapolis: Augsburg Fortress, 2000), p. 775.
14. Leni Yahil, *The Holocaust: The Fate of European Jewry, 1932–1945* (New York: Oxford University Press, 1991), p. 41.
15. Kershaw, *Hitler: 1889–1936 Hubris*.
16. Martin Heidegger, "Why Do I Stay in the Provinces?" in Martin Heidegger, *Philosophical and Political Writings*, ed. Manfred Stassen (New York: Continuum International Publishing Group, 2003), pp. 16–19.
17. Theodor Adorno, *Jargon der Eigentlichkeit: Zur deutschen Ideologie* (Frankfurt: Suhrkamp Verlag, 1964); Theodor Adorno, *The Jargon of Authenticity*, trans. Knut Tarnowski and Frederic Will (London: Routledge, 1973), p. 45.
18. Ott, *Martin Heidegger*, pp. 246–243. See also Safranski, *Martin Heidegger*, p.271.
19. Arendt, *Origins of Totalitarianism*, p.449.
20. Martin Heidegger, "Letter to the Rector of Freiburg University, November 4, 1945," in Wolin, *The Heidegger Controversy*, pp. 61–66.
21. Karl Löwith, "My Last Meeting with Heidegger in Rome, 1936," in Wolin, *The Heidegger Controversy*, pp 140–143.
22. Safranski, *Martin Heidegger*, pp. 280–281.
23. Kershaw, *Hitler: 1889–1936 Hubris*. pp. 512–522.
24. Karl Jaspers, *The Question of German Guilt*, trans. E. B. Ashton (New York: Dial Press, 1947), pp. 68–69.

CHAPTER TEN

1. Arendt, *Men in Dark Times*, pp. 153–206, 167.
2. Young-Bruehl, *Hannah Arendt*, pp. 122–130.
3. See, for example, Arendt's characterization of Blücher as a military historian in Arendt, "What Remains?" p.13
4. Arendt, "We Refugees," p. 56.
5. Hannah Arendt, letter to the editor, *Midstream*, Summer 1962, p. 87, in response to an article by Bruno Bettelheim.
6. Ibid.

CHAPTER ELEVEN

1. Heidegger, "Letter to the Rector of Freiburg University," in Wolin, *The Heidegger Controversy*, pp. 60–66. For a more detailed and objective assessment, see Ott, *Martin Heidegger*, pp. 263–269, 284–292.
2. Heidegger, Martin, "Letter on Humanism," in Martin Heidegger, *Basic Writings*, ed. David Farrell Krell; trans. Frank A. Capuzzi and J. Glenn Gray (New York: HarperCollins, 1993), pp. 217–265.
3. Heidegger, "Letter to the Rector of Freiburg University," pp. 60–66, 65. See also Gadamer, *Heidegger's Ways*, p. 132.
4. Hannah Arendt, *The Life of the Mind: Willing* (New York: Harcourt Brace Jovanovich, 1978), pp. 172–194; on Heidegger's turn and the Nietzsche lectures, see especially pp. 172–173.
5. See Martin Heidegger, "The Origin of the Work of Art," in Martin Heidegger, *Basic Writings*, ed. David Farrell Krell; trans. Albert Hofstadter (New York: HarperCollins, 1993), pp. 143–206 .
6. Heidegger, "Letter on Humanism," pp. 217–265.
7. Hans-Georg Gadamer, *Heidegger's Ways*, trans. John W. Stanley (Albany: State University of New York Press, 1994), pp. 167–180.
8. Hannah Arendt, "The Aftermath of Nazi Rule: Report from Germany," *Commentary* 10, no. 10 (1950), reprinted in Hannah Arendt, *Essays in Understanding, 1930–1954*, ed. Jerome Kohn (New York: Harcourt Brace, 1994), pp. 248–269, 249.

CHAPTER TWELVE

1. Arendt and Blücher, *Within Four Walls*, pp.58–76.
2. Hannah Arendt, "The Jewish Army—The Beginning of a Jewish Politics?" *Aufbau*, November 14, 1941; reprinted in Hannah Arendt, *The Jewish Writings*, ed. Jerome Kohn and Ron H. Feldman; trans. John E. Woods (New York: Schocken Books, 2007), pp. 136–139.
3. Hannah Arendt, "Paper and Reality?" *Aufbau*, November 14, 1941; reprinted in Arendt, *The Jewish Writings*, pp. 152–154, 153. The translation of this phrase used here, however, is from Young-Bruehl, *Hannah Arendt*, p. 173.
4. Hannah Arendt, "From the Dreyfus Affair to France Today," *Jewish Social Studies* 4, no. 3 (July 1942): pp. 235–240.
5. Lord Robert Vansittart, *The Black Record: Germans Past and Present* (London: John Trotter Books, 1941).
6. Hannah Arendt, "Organized Guilt and Universal Responsibility," *Jewish Frontier*, no. 12 (January 1945): pp. 19–23, reprinted in Arendt, *Essays in Understanding*, pp. 121–132, 124.
7. Arendt, "What Remains?" pp.1–23, 13–14.
8. Hannah Arendt, "Approaches to the German Problem," *Partisan Review* 12, no. 1, (Winter 1945), reprinted in Arendt, *Essays in Understanding*, pp.106–120.
9. Arendt, "Organized Guilt and Universal Responsibility," pp. 121–132.

CHAPTER THIRTEEN

1. Hannah Arendt and Karl Jaspers, *Correspondence, 1926–1969*, ed. Lotte Kohler and Hans Saner; trans. Robert Kimber and Rita Kimber (New York: Harcourt Brace Jovanovich, 1992), pp. 132, 168.
2. Unless otherwise noted, all reference to correspondence or meetings between Hannah Arendt and Karl or Gertrud Jaspers, or between Heinrich Blücher and Karl Jaspers are drawn from Arendt and Jaspers, *Correspondence, 1926–1969*, pp. 23–24.
3. Karl Jaspers, *The Question of German Guilt*, trans. E. B. Ashton (New York: Dial Press, 1947).

4. Ibid., p. 71.
5. Karl Jaspers, *General Psychopathology*, trans. J. Hoenig and Marian W. Hamilton; (Baltimore: Johns Hopkins University Press, 1997).
6. Birgit Maier-Katkin, *Silence and Acts of Memory: A Postwar Discourse on Literature, History, Anna Seghers, and Women in the Third Reich* (Lewisburg, Pa.: Bucknell University Press, 2007), pp. 49–60.
7. Hans Saner, "Karl Jaspers," Encyclopedia Britannica Online. http://search.eb.com.proxy.lib.fsu.edu/eb/article-3676.

CHAPTER FOURTEEN

1. All references in quotations in this chapter about Zionism and the creation and early years of the State of Israel are drawn from the following essays, which have been collected and republished in Hannah Arendt, *The Jewish Writings*, ed. Jerome Kohn and Ron H. Feldman (New York: Schocken Books, 2007); most of these essays also appear in Hannah Arendt, *The Jew as Pariah: Jewish Identity and Politics in the Modern Age*, ed. Ron H. Feldman (New York: Grove Press, 1978): Hannah Arendt, "From the Dreyfus Affair to France Today," *Jewish Social Studies* 4, no.3 (July 1942): pp. 235–240; Hannah Arendt, "Zionism Reconsidered," *Menorah Journal*, October 1944, pp. 162–196; Hannah Arendt, "The Jew as Pariah: A Hidden Tradition," *Jewish Social Studies* 4, no. 2 (April 1944): pp. 99–122; Hannah Arendt, "The Jewish State: Fifty Years After, Where Have Herzl's Politics Led?" *Commentary* 1 (May 1945–1946): p. 1; Hannah Arendt, "Peace or Armistice in the Near East?" *Review of Politics* 12, no. 1 (January 1950): pp. 56–82; Hannah Arendt, "To Save the Jewish Homeland," *Commentary* 5 (May 1948): p. 398; Hannah Arendt, "About Collaboration," *Jewish Frontier* (October 1948) pp. 55–56; Hannah Arendt and others, "An Open Letter," *New York Times*, December 4, 1948; Hannah Arendt, "Magnes, the Conscience of the Jewish People," *Jewish Newsletter* 8, no. 24 (November 24, 1952).
2. Arendt, "The Jew as Pariah: A Hidden Tradition," reprinted in Arendt, *The Jew as Pariah*, pp. 67–90, and also in Arendt, *The Jewish Writings*, pp. 275–297, 280.
3. Hannah Arendt, "Zionism Reconsidered," *Menorah Journal*, October

1944, pp. 162–196, reprinted in Arendt, *The Jew as Pariah*, pp. 131–163, and also in Arendt, *The Jewish Writings*, pp. 343–374, 343.

4. Benny Morris, *The Birth of the Palestinian Refugee Problem, 1947–1949* (Cambridge, UK: Cambridge University Press, 1989). See also, Benny Morris, *1948: A History of the First Arab-Israeli War* (New Haven Conn.: Yale University Press, 2009); Ilan Pappé, *The Ethnic Cleansing of Palestine* (Oxford: Oneworld Publications, 2007).

CHAPTER FIFTEEN

1. Unless otherwise noted, all references and quotations in this chapter are drawn from Hannah Arendt, *The Origins of Totalitarianism* (New York: Harcourt Brace, 1951; New York: Schocken Books [with a new introduction by Samantha Power], 2004).
2. Stanley G. Payne, *Fascism: Comparison and Definition* (Madison: University of Wisconsin Press, 1980), p.73.
3. Arendt, *The Origins of Totalitarianism*, p. xxvii.
4. Samantha Power, "Introduction," in Arendt, *The Origins of Totalitarianism*, pp. xi–xii.
5. Arendt, *The Origins of Totalitarianism*, pp. 307–312.

CHAPTER SIXTEEN

1. Robert G. Waite, "Returning Jewish Cultural Property: The Handling of Books Looted by the Nazis in the American Zone of Occupation, 1945 to 1952," *Libraries & Culture* 37, no. 3 (2002): pp. 213–228.
2. Jewish Cultural Reconstruction, Inc., "Records (microfilm)" Wiener Library Institute of Contemporary History, London, http://www.aim25.ac.uk/cgi-bin/search2?coll_id=7869&inst_id=104.
3. Hannah Arendt, "The Aftermath of Nazi Rule: Report from Germany," *Commentary* 10, no. 4 (October 1950), reprinted in Hannah Arendt, *Essays in Understanding, 1930–1954*, ed. Jerome Kohn (New York: Harcourt Brace, 1994), pp. 248–269, 249.
4. Ibid., p. 254.
5. See, for example, "Swiss Banks and the Status of Assets of Holocaust Survivors or Heirs," Hearing Before the U.S. Senate Committee on

Banking, Housing, and Urban Affairs, 104th Cong. 2d Sess. April 23, 1966.

6. Arendt and Blücher, *Within Four Walls,* p. 111.
7. Jaspers's note to Blücher was typed by Arendt and attached to one of her letters to him while she was visiting Jaspers in Basel. The letter and note, both dated December 28, 1949, appear in two sources with slightly different translations. The translation used here is from Arendt and Blücher, *Within Four Walls,* p. 113. See also Arendt and Jaspers, *Correspondence, 1926–1969,* pp. 143–144.
8. Unless otherwise noted, all references in this chapter to existential philosophy and existential philosophers, including Heidegger, Jaspers, Kierkegaard, and Nietzsche, are drawn from Hannah Arendt, "What Is Existential Philosophy?" *Partisan Review* 18, no. 1 (1946). A German translation appears in Hannah Arendt, *Sechs Essays,* and a translation of this back into English by Robert and Rita Kimber appears in Arendt, *Essays in Understanding, 1930–1954,* pp. 163–187.
9. Hannah Arendt, "The Image of Hell," originally published as a review of *The Black Book: The Nazi Crimes Against the Jewish People,* and Max Weinreich, "Hitler's Professors," *Commentary* 2, no. 3 (September 1946): p. 291; reprinted in Arendt, *Essays in Understanding, 1930–1954,* pp. 197–205, 198.
10. Ibid., p. 201.
11. Karl Jaspers, "Letter to the Freiburg University Denazification Committee (December 22, 1945)," translated and reprinted in Richard Wolin, *The Heidegger Controversy: A Critical Reader* (Cambridge, Mass.: MIT Press, 1998), pp. 147–151.

CHAPTER SEVENTEEN

1. Hugo Ott, *Martin Heidegger: A Political Life,* trans. Allan Blunden (New York: HarperCollins, 1993), pp. 312–313. See also Rüdiger Safranski, *Martin Heidegger: Between Good and Evil,* trans. Ewald Osers (Cambridge, Mass.: Harvard University Press, 1998), pp. 334–335.
2. Safranski, *Martin Heidegger,* pp. 335–336.
3. Martin Heidegger, "Letter to the Rector of Freiburg University, November 4, 1945," in Wolin, *The Heidegger Controversy,* pp. 61–66.

4. On the moral confusion of the denazification process, see Hannah Arendt, "The Aftermath of Nazi Rule: Report from Germany," *Commentary* 10, no. 4 (October 1950), reprinted in Arendt, *Essays in Understanding, 1930–1954*, pp. 248–269, 256–264.
5. Jaspers, "Letter to the Freiburg University Denazification Committee (December 22, 1945)," p. 149.
6. Safranski, *Martin Heidegger*, p. 352.
7. Arendt and Blücher, *Within Four Walls*, p. 112.
8. Herbert Marcuse and Martin Heidegger, "An Exchange of Letters," in Wolin, *The Heidegger Controversy*, pp. 152–164, 160–161.
9. See, however, Herbert Marcuse, *Soviet Marxism: A Critical Analysis*, reprinted with a new introduction by David Kellner (New York: Columbia University Press, 1985).
10. Marcuse and Heidegger, "An Exchange of Letters," pp. 162–163.
11. Ott, *Martin Heidegger*, pp. 363–365.

CHAPTER EIGHTEEN

1. Arendt and Blücher, *Within Four Walls*, pp. 115–127.
2. Hannah Arendt, "Letter to Hilde Fränkel, January 1950, Arendt Archive, Library of Congress.
3. Hannah Arendt and Martin Heidegger, *Briefe, 1925–1975*, ed. *Ursula Ludz* (Frankurt am Main: Vittorio Klostermann, 1998). See also, *Letters 1925–1975*, ed. Ursula Ludz; trans. Andrew Shields (Orlando, Fla.: Harcourt, 2004), pp. 61–62.
4. Hannah Arendt, *Denktagebuch*, ed. Ursula Ludz and Ingeborg Nordmann (Munich: Piper, 2002), pp. 3–7.

CHAPTER NINETEEN

1. Arendt, *The Origins of Totalitarianism*, p. 383.
2. Mary Jarrell, ed., *Randall Jarrell's Letters: An Autobiographical and Literary Selection* (Boston: Houghton Mifflin, 1985), p. 275. All references to the correspondence of Randall Jarrell with Arendt and others are drawn from this source.
3. This characterization—"they were a Dual Monarchy"—is used to

describe a fictional couple, Gottfried and Irene Rosenbaum, in Randall Jarrell, *Pictures from an Institution* (New York: Knopf, 1954), p. 141; but Jarrell wrote to Arendt that these characters and their relationship were based on Arendt and Blücher; see Mary Jarrell, ed., *Randall Jarrell's Letters*, pp. 392–393.

4. Unless otherwise noted, Arendt's characterizations of Jarrell and of the friendship between the two are drawn from Hannah Arendt, "Randall Jarrell, 1914–1965," in *Men in Dark Times*.
5. Randall Jarrell, "Deutsch Durch Freud," in Randall Jarrell, *The Complete Poems* (New York: Farrar, Straus & Giroux), p. 266. See also Arendt, "Randall Jarrell, 1914–1965," in *Men in Dark Times*, p. 264.
6. Randall Jarrell, *Pictures from an Institution*, p. 13.
7. Ibid., p. 134.
8. Mary Jarrell, ed., *Randall Jarrell's Letters*, p. 520.
9. All references to the "prehistory" of the Arendt-McCarthy friendship are drawn from Carol Brightman, "Introduction," in Arendt, and McCarthy, *Between Friends*.
10. Ibid., p. xxix. All references to the correspondence between Arendt and McCarthy are drawn from Arendt and McCarthy, *Between Friends*.
11. Mary McCarthy, *Memories of a Catholic Girlhood* (New York: Harcourt Brace Jovanovich, 1957).
12. Carol Brightman, *Writing Dangerously: Mary McCarthy and Her World* (New York: Harcourt Brace, 1992), pp. 173–267, 265.
13. Ibid., p. xiii.
14. Mary McCarthy, "Editor's Postface," in Hannah Arendt, *The Life of the Mind: Willing* (New York: Harcourt Brace Jovanovich, 1978), pp. 243–244.
15. Ibid., pp. 244–245.

CHAPTER TWENTY

1. Arendt and Blücher, *Within Four Walls*, p. 138.
2. For a brief overview of the neighborhood and its art clubs, see the Web site of the Grey Art Gallery of New York University, http://www.nyu.edu/greyart/information/Greenwich_Village/body_greenwich_village.html.

3. Neil Jumonville, *Critical Crossings: The New York Intellectuals in Postwar America* (Berkeley: University of California Press, 1991).
4. Hannah Arendt, "The Ex-Communists," *Commonweal,* March 20, 1953, p. 596.
5. *Trop v. Dulles,* 356 U.S. 86, 102 (1958).
6. Arendt and Blücher, *Within Four Walls,* p. 172.
7. For the full text transcript of the *See It Now* program on March 9, 1954, see the University of California at Berkeley Library Web site: http://www.lib.berkeley.edu/MRC/murrowmccarthy.html.
8. For the video record of this transaction, see http://www.americanrhetoric.com/speeches/welch-mccarthy.html.

CHAPTER TWENTY-ONE

1. Martin Heidegger, *Was Heisst Denken?* (Tübingen: Max Niemeyer Verlag, 1954); Martin Heidegger, *What Is Called Thinking?* trans. J. Glenn Gray and F. Wieck (New York: Harper & Row, 1968).
2. Heidegger, *Was Heisst Denken?*; Heidegger, *What Is Called Thinking?* p. 145.
3. Arendt, *Denktagebuch,* pp. 403–404.

CHAPTER TWENTY-TWO

1. Arendt and Blücher, *Within Four Walls,* pp. 295–296.
2. Hannah Arendt, "Karl Jaspers: A Laudatio," in *Men in Dark Times,* pp. 71–80, 76.
3. Bertolt Brecht, "To Posterity," http://www.poemhunter.com/poem/to-posterity/.
4. Arendt, *Men in Dark Times,* pp. vii–x, ix–x.

CHAPTER TWENTY-THREE

1. Martin Heidegger and Elfride Heidegger, *Mein liebes Seelchen: Briefe Martin Heideggers an seine Frau Elfride, 1915–1970,* ed. Gertrud Heidegger (Munich: Deutsche Verlags-Anstalt, 2005).

2. Arendt and Heidegger, *Briefe, 1925–1975*; see also *Letters, 1925–1975*, pp. 115–122.
3. Hannah Arendt, *The Human Condition*, 2d ed., with an introduction by Margaret Canovan (Chicago: University of Chicago Press, 1998), pp. 1–3.
4. Ibid., p. 247. See also Susannah Young-ah Gottlieb, *Regions of Sorrow: Anxiety and Messianism in Hannah Arendt and W. H. Auden* (Stanford, Calif.: Stanford University Press, 2003), p. 137 (n. 50), who observes that the "glad tidings" to which Arendt refers do not appear precisely as she states in the Gospels: "A child has been born unto us" is drawn from the opening messianic passages of Isaiah; the closest language in the New Testament is the words of the angel Gabriel to the Shepard: "Fear not: for, behold, I bring you good tidings of great joy, which shall be to all people. For unto you is born this day in the city of David a Savior, which is Christ the Lord" (Luke 2:11).
5. All references to Arendt's thinking about forgiveness in the chapter are drawn from Arendt, *The Human Condition*, pp. 236–243.
6. Ibid., p. 241.
7. Arendt, *Denktagebuch*, p. 701.
8. Elisabeth Young-Bruehl, *Hannah Arendt: For Love of the World* 2d ed. (New Haven, Conn.: Yale University Press, 2004), p. 371.
9. W. H. Auden, "The Prince's Dog," in *The Dyer's Hand* (New York: Random House, 1962; Vintage ed., 1989), pp. 182–208, 202.
10. Hannah Arendt, "Letter to W. H. Auden," February 12, 1960. Arendt Archive, Library of Congress, http://memory.loc.gov/cgi-bin/query/P?mharendt:3:./temp/~ammem_LgNf::.
11. Hannah Arendt, "On Humanity in Dark Times: Thoughts About Lessing," in Arendt, *Men in Dark Times*, pp. 3–31, 14.
12. Ibid., p.26.

CHAPTER TWENTY-FOUR

1. Safranski, *Martin Heidegger*, pp. 348–349.
2. Ibid., pp. 342–343.
3. Ibid., p. 343. James Miller, however, maintains that Aron recalled the conversation as having occurred over a glass of beer, and that Simone

de Beauvoir recalls that the drink involved was an apricot cocktail. So much for history! See James Miller, *The Passions of Michel Foucault* (New York: Simon & Schuster, 1993), pp. 64, 404.

4. Jean-Paul Sartre, *The Transcendence of the Ego: An Existentialist Theory of Consciousness*, trans. Forrest Williams and Robert Kirkpatrick (New York: Farrar, Straus & Giroux, 1960; 2000), p. 105.
5. Ronald Aronson, *Camus and Sartre: The Story of a Friendship and the Quarrel That Ended It* (Chicago: University of Chicago Press, 2004), p. 29. See also Safranski, *Martin Heidegger*, p. 346.
6. Jean-Paul Sartre, *Nausea* trans. Lloyd Alexander (New York: New Directions, 1964), p. 131.
7. Jean-Paul Sartre, *War Diaries: Notebooks from a Phony War*, trans. Quintin Hoare (New York: Verso, 1999). See also Miller, *The Passions of Michel Foucault*, p. 47.
8. Edward W. Said, "Labyrinth of Incarnations: The Essays of Maurice Merleau-Ponty," *Kenyon Review* 29, no. 1 (January 1967), pp. 54–68.
9. Safranski, *Martin Heidegger*, p. 356.
10. Ibid.
11. Jean-Paul Sartre, *Existentialism Is a Humanism*, trans. Carol Macomber (New Haven, Conn.: Yale University Press, 2007), pp. 22–23.
12. Victor Farías, *Heidegger and Nazism*, ed. Joseph Margolis and Tom Rockmore; trans. Paul Burrell, Dominic Di Bernardi, and Gabriel Ricci (Philadelphia: Temple University Press, 1989), p. 287.
13. Safranski, *Martin Heidegger*, p. 356.
14. Martin Heidegger, "Letter on Humanism," trans. Frank A. Capuzzi and J. Glenn Gray, in Martin Heidegger, *Basic Writings*, ed. David Farrell Krell (New York: HarperCollins, 1993), pp. 217–265, 233–234.
15. This lecture at the Bremen Club, entitled "The Frame," was never published; see Herman Philipse, *Heidegger's Philosophy of Being: A Critical Interpretation* (Princeton, N.J.: Princeton University Press, 1998), pp. 309, 518. For a modified version of this lecture, from which this language was eliminated, see, Martin Heidegger, "The Question Concerning Technology," trans. William Lovitt, in Heidegger, *Basic Writings*, pp. 311–341, where there is still a reference to mechanized agriculture and atomic energy, p. 320.

16. Heidegger, "The Question Concerning Technology," p. 341. See also Safranski, *Martin Heidegger*, p.394.

CHAPTER TWENTY-FIVE

1. Elie Wiesel, *Night* (New York: Hill & Wang, 1960).
2. Primo Levi, *Survival in Auschwitz*, trans. Guilio Einaudi (New York: Touchstone Books, 1996).
3. Birgit Maier-Katkin, *Silence and Acts of Memory: A Postwar Discourse on Literature, History, Anna Seghers, and Women in the Third Reich* (Lewisburg, Pa.: Bucknell University Press, 2007), pp. 49–57.
4. Hannah Arendt, *On Revolution* (New York: Viking Press, 1963).
5. Elisabeth Young-Bruehl, *Hannah Arendt: For Love of the World* (New Haven, Conn.: Yale University Press, 1982), p. 329.
6. Amos Elon, "Introduction: The Excommunication of Hannah Arendt," in Hannah Arendt, *Eichmann in Jerusalem: A Report on the Banality of Evil*, 4th ed. (New York: Penguin Books, 2006), pp. vii–xxiii.
7. Arendt and Jaspers, *Correspondence, 1926–1969*, pp. 434–436; Arendt and Blücher, *Within Four Walls*, pp. 354–358.
8. Arendt and McCarthy, *Between Friends*, pp. 126–127.
9. Unless otherwise noted, all reference to the trial of Adolph Eichmann and quotations from Arendt's account of the trial are drawn from Arendt, *Eichmann in Jerusalem*.
10. Despite her approving comments about Hilberg's work, Arendt had some years earlier advised Princeton University Press against publishing it, which Hilberg felt had impacted his career negatively and for which he never forgave her. She seems to have thought that although the book was an excellent compendium of facts, it was insufficiently analytic. In a letter to Karl Jaspers written on April 20, 1964, Arendt says that Hilberg's book "is really excellent, but only because he just reports facts in it. His introductory chapter that deals with general and historical matters wouldn't pass muster in a pigpen."
11. Robert Pendorf, *Mörder und Ermordete: Eichmann und die Judenpolitik des Dritten Reiches* (Hamburg: Rütten & Loenig, 1961).
12. Raul Hilberg, *The Destruction of the European Jews* (Chicago: Quad-

rangle Books, 1961; also 3d. ed. (New Haven, Conn.: Yale University Press, 2003).

13. H. G. Adler, *Theresienstadt, 1941–1945* (Tübingen: J. C. B. Mohr, 1955).
14. Arendt, *Eichmann in Jerusalem*, p. 30.

CHAPTER TWENTY-SIX

1. Arendt, *Eichmann in Jerusalem*, p. 25.
2. Ibid., pp. 22–25.
3. Ibid., p. 279. See also Arendt and McCarthy, *Between Friends*, p. 136.
4. "Adolf Eichmann Tells His Own Damning Story," *Life* (Part I) November 28, 1960; (Part II) December 5, 1960.
5. Arendt, *Eichmann in Jerusalem*, p. 24.
6. Ibid., p. 113.

CHAPTER TWENTY-SEVEN

1. Henry Schwartzchild, letter to Arendt, March 6, 1963, Arendt Archive, Library of Congress.
2. Siegfried Moses, letter to Arendt, March 7, 1963, Arendt Archive, Library of Congress.
3. Young-Bruehl, *Hannah Arendt*, pp. 348–349.
4. William Shawn, telegram to Arendt, March 8, 1963, Arendt Archive, Library of Congress.
5. Hans J. Morganthau, "Review of Eichmann in Jerusalem," *Chicago Tribune*, May 26, 1963.
6. Young-Bruehl, *Hannah Arendt*, p. 349.
7. Ibid., p. 348.
8. See, for example, Herbert Strauss, "The Thesis of Hannah Arendt," *Aufbau* 29, no. 20, (May 17, 1963), p. 13.
9. Irving Howe, "The New York Intellectual: A Chronicle and a Critique," *Commentary* 46, no. 4 (October 1968), pp. 29–51.
10. Arendt, and McCarthy, *Between Friends*, p. 149.
11. Alfred Kazan, *New York Jew* (New York: Knopf, 1978), p. 196.
12. Leo Mindlin, "During the Week . . ." *Jewish Floridian*, March 15, 1963.

13. Trude Weiss-Rosmarin, "Self-Hating Jewess Writes Pro-Eichmann Series for New Yorker Magazine," *Jewish News*, April 19, 1963.
14. Joachim Prinz, *Arendt Nonsense: A Reply to Hannah Arendt's 'Eichmann in Jerusalem'* (New York: American Jewish Congress, 1963).
15. Young-Bruehl, *Hannah Arendt*, pp. 352–353.
16. Arendt, *Eichmann in Jerusalem*, p. 210.
17. Micheal A. Musmanno, "Man with an Unspotted Conscience," *New York Times*, May 19, 1963.
18. Letters to the Editor: "Eichmann in Jerusalem," *New York Times*, June 23, 1963.
19. Irving Spiegel, "Hausner Criticizes Book on Eichmann," *New York Times*, May 20, 1963.
20. Unsigned letter to Arendt, Arendt Archive, Library of Congress.
21. Lionel Abel, "The Aesthetics of Evil," *Partisan Review* 30, no. 2 (Summer 1963), pp. 210–230.
22. References to Mary McCarthy's review of *Eichmann in Jerusalem* are drawn from Mary McCarthy, "The Hue and the Cry," *Partisan Review* 31, no.1 (Winter 1964), pp. 82–94; reprinted in Mary McCarthy, *The Writing on the Wall and Other Literary Essays* (New York: Harcourt, Brace & World, 1970), pp. 55–71.

CHAPTER TWENTY-EIGHT

1. Bruno Bettelheim, "Eichmann; the System; the Victims," *New Republic*, June 15, 1963, pp. 23–33.
2. "More on Eichmann," *Partisan Review* 31, no. 2 (Spring 1964), pp. 253–283.
3. Hugh Trevor-Roper, "How Innocent Was Eichmann?" *Sunday Times* (London), October 13, 1963; reprinted in *Jewish Affairs* 19 (January 1964), pp. 4–9.
4. Norman Podhoretz, "Hannah Arendt on Eichmann: A Study in the Perversity of Brilliance," *Commentary* 36, no. 3 (September 1963), pp. 201–208.
5. Hannah Arendt and Gershom Scholem, "Eichmann in Jerusalem: An Exchange of Letters Between Gershom Scholem and Hannah Arendt,"

Encounter 22 (January 1964), pp. 51–54; reprinted in Hannah Arendt, *The Jew as Pariah: Jewish Identity and Politics in the Modern Age*, ed. Ron. H. Feldman (New York: Grove Press, 1978), pp. 240–251, 241.

6. Arendt and Scholem, "Eichmann in Jerusalem, pp. 51–54; reprinted in Arendt, *The Jew as Pariah*, pp. 240–251, 245–246; also reprinted in Hannah Arendt, *The Jewish Writings*, ed. Jerome Kohn and Ron H. Feldman (New York: Schocken Books, 2007), pp. 465–471, 465–467.
7. Jacob Robinson, *And the Crooked Shall Be Made Straight: The Eichmann Trials, the Jewish Catastrophe, and Hannah Arendt's Narrative* (New York: Macmillan, 1965).
8. Walter Z. Laquer, "Footnotes to the Holocaust," *New York Review of Books*, November 11, 1965, pp. 20–22; reprinted in Arendt *The Jew as Pariah*, pp. 252–259, 253.
9. Hannah Arendt, "The Formidable Mr. Robinson: A Reply," *New York Review of Books*, January 20, 1966, p. 20; reprinted in Arendt, *The Jew as Pariah*, pp. 260–276, 276; also reprinted in Arendt, *The Jewish Writings*, pp. 496–511, 510–511.
10. Stanley Milgram, *Obedience to Authority* (New York: Harper & Row, 1975).
11. Philip Zimbardo, *The Lucifer Effect: Understanding How Good People Turn Evil* (New York: Random House, 2007).
12. Daniel Jonah Goldhagen, *Hitler's Willing Executioners: Ordinary Germans and the Holocaust* (New York: Knopf, 1996).
13. Ian Kershaw, *Hitler, vol. 1, 1889–1936 Hubris; vol. 2, 1936–1945 Nemesis* (New York: W. W. Norton, 2000), pp. 257–258.
14. Robert Gellately, *The Gestapo and German Society: Enforcing Racial Policy, 1933–1945* (New York: Oxford University Press, 1990).
15. Christopher Browning, *Reserve Police Battalion 101 and the Final Solution in Poland* (New York: HarperCollins, 1992).
16. David Cesarani, *Becoming Eichmann: Rethinking the Life, Crimes, and Trial of a "Desk Murderer"* (New York: Da Capo Press, 2006), p. 368.
17. Michael Massing, "Trial and Error," *New York Times* (Sunday Book Review), October 17, 2004.
18. Richard Wolin, *Heidegger's Children: Hannah Arendt, Karl Löwith, Hans Jonas, and Herbert Marcuse* (Princeton, N.J.: Princeton University Press, 2001); see especially pp. 52–62.

19. Amos Elon, "Introduction: The Excommunication of Hannah Arendt," in Arendt, *Eichmann in Jerusalem*, pp. vii–xxiii, xxii.

CHAPTER TWENTY-NINE

1. Hannah Arendt, "Personal Responsibility Under Dictatorship," in Hannah Arendt, *Responsibility and Judgment*, ed. Jerome Kohn (New York: Schocken Books 2003), pp. 17–48.
2. Hannah Arendt, "Some Questions of Moral Philosophy," in Hannah Arendt, *Responsibility and Judgment*, pp. 49–146, 59.
3. Arendt, "Personal Responsibility Under Dictatorship," p. 21.
4. Arendt, "Some Questions of Moral Philosophy," pp. 50, 54.
5. Arendt, "Personal Responsibility Under Dictatorship," 42–43.
6. Arendt, "Some Questions of Moral Philosophy," p. 78.

CHAPTER THIRTY

1. Paul Celan, "Todtnauberg," in *Selected Poems and Prose of Paul Celan*, trans. John Felstiner (New York: W. W. Norton, 2001), p. 315. See also Wolin, *Heidegger's Children*, pp. 1–3.
2. Edna Brock, "Afterward: 'Big Hannah'—My Aunt," in Arendt, *The Jewish Writings*, pp. 512–521.
3. Arendt, and Jaspers, *Correspondence, 1926–1969*, pp. 684–686.

CHAPTER THIRTY-ONE

1. Elzbieta Ettinger, *Hannah Arendt/Martin Heidegger* (New Haven, Conn.: Yale University Press, 1984), p. 126.
2. All references to Arendt's speech in honor of Heidegger's eightieth birthday are drawn from Hannah Arendt, "Martin Heidegger at Eighty," trans. Albert Hofstadter *New York Review of Books*, October 21, 1971, reprinted in Arendt, and Heidegger, *Briefe, 1925–1975*. See also *Letters 1925–1975*, pp. 148–162.
3. Arendt and Heidegger, *Briefe, 1925–1975*. See also *Letters 1925–1975*, p. 156.
4. All references to thinking and moral considerations in this chapter

are drawn from Arendt, "Thinking and Moral Considerations," *Social Research* 38 (1971): pp. 417–446; reprinted in Arendt, *Responsibility and Judgment*, pp. 159–189.

5. All references to Bertolt Brecht and quotations from Arendt's writing about Brecht in this chapter are drawn from Hannah Arendt, "Bertolt Brecht 1898–1956," in Arendt, *Men in Dark Times*, pp. 207–250. A somewhat shorter version of this essay appeared originally as Hannah Arendt, "Profiles: What is Permitted to Jove," *The New Yorker*, November 5, 1966.

CHAPTER THIRTY-TWO

1. Arendt, and McCarthy, *Between Friends*, p. 266.

CHAPTER THIRTY-THREE

1. Mary McCarthy, "Saying Good-bye to Hannah, *New York Review of Books*, January 22, 1976; reprinted in Mary McCarthy, *Occasional Prose* (New York: Harcourt Brace Jovanovich, 1985), p. 37.
2. All references in this chapter to the content of the Gifford Lectures are drawn from Hannah Arendt, *The Life of the Mind: Thinking* (New York: Harcourt Brace Jovanovich, 1978), pp. 3–4.
3. McCarthy, "Saying Good-bye to Hannah," reprinted in McCarthy, *Occasional Prose*, p. 41.

CHAPTER THIRTY-FOUR

1. Arendt, and McCarthy, *Between Friends*, pp. 343–344.
2. Hannah Arendt, "Sonning Prize Speech," Hannah Arendt Archive, Library of Congress, Essays and Lectures—Sonning Prize speech, Copenhagen, Denmark—1975 (Series: Speeches and Writings File, 1923–1975), pp. 4–5, http://memory.loc.gov/ammem/arendthtml/arendthome.html.
3. Ibid., pp. 5–8.
4. Mary McCarthy, "Editor's Postface," in Hannah Arendt, *The Life of the Mind: Thinking.* (New York: Harcourt Brace Jovanovich, 1978), p. 217.

5. Carol Brightman, *Writing Dangerously: Mary McCarthy and Her World* (New York: Harcourt Brace, 1992), p 535.
6. Arendt and McCarthy, *Between Friends*, pp. 218–219.
7. Brightman, *Writing Dangerously*, pp. 541, 544.
8. Mary McCarthy, "Watergate Notes," *New York Review of Books,* July 19, 1973; Mary McCarthy, "Lies," *New York Review of Books,* August 9, 1973; Mary McCarthy, "Watergate," *New York Review of Books,* April 4, 1974; Mary McCarthy, "Postscript to Nixon," *New York Review of Books,* October 17, 1974.
9. Arendt, and McCarthy, *Between Friends*, p. 344.
10. Hannah Arendt, "Home to Roost," in Hannah Arendt, *Responsibility and Judgment*, ed. Jerome Kohn (New York: Schocken Books, 2003), pp. 257–275, 257–258.
11. Ibid., p. 259.
12. Ibid., pp. 264–265.
13. Ibid., pp. 267.

CHAPTER THIRTY-FIVE

1. Mary McCarthy, "Saying Good-bye to Hannah," *New York Review of Books*, January 22, 1976; reprinted in McCarthy, *Occasional Prose,* p. 35.
2. All references and quotations related to "Willing" and other aspects of the life of the mind in this chapter are drawn from Hannah Arendt, *The Life of the Mind: Willing* (New York: Harcourt Brace Jovanovich, 1978).
3. All references and quotations from Mary McCarthy's eulogy for Hannah Arendt are drawn from McCarthy, "Saying Good-bye to Hannah."
4. Young-Bruehl, *Hannah Arendt*, p. 468.
5. Arendt, and Heidegger, *Briefe, 1925–1975*. See also, *Letters, 1925–1975*, p. 217.
6. Ibid., p. 218.
7. Young-Bruehl, *Hannah Arendt*, p. 469.

CHAPTER THIRTY-SIX

1. Farias, *Heidegger and Nazism*, pp. 24–27, 288–300.
2. Wolin, *The Heidegger Controversy.*
3. Faye, *Heidegger: The Introduction of Nazism into Philosophy.*
4. Carol Brightman, introduction to Arendt and McCarthy, *Between Friends*, p. xii.

CREDITS

Essays in Understanding, 1930–1954 by Hannah Arendt. Copyright © 1994, 1954, 1953, 1950, 1946, 1945, 1944 by The Literary Trust of Hannah Arendt Bluecher. Reprinted by permission of Georges Borchardt, Inc., on behalf of The Literary Trust of Hannah Arendt Bluecher.

"The Common Life," copyright © 1963 by W. H. Auden, from *Collected Poems* by W. H. Auden. Used by permission of Random House, Inc.

INDEX